Superintensive
Foreign Journal Reading

三味外刊精华

孙三五　徐志坚　吴则磊　编著

中国人民大学出版社
·北京·

推荐序

英语学习，输入是输出的基础。只有当"听"和"读"达到一定数量之后，才能具备"说"和"写"的能力。在选择输入材料的时候，外刊学习是非常重要的环节。通过外刊学英语的优点是：

1. 规范

英语没有普通话，所以，选择被主流媒体所广泛接受的表述方式，有助于提高自己语言表达的规范性。

2. 时尚

外刊的题材，聚焦时事热点，读者可以学习到流行事件的表达方式，感受现代流行语中的活跃元素。

3. 有趣

很多刊物，为了强化品牌特点，会选择一些容易吸引眼球的素材。这使得英语学习不那么枯燥。

在选择外刊作为学习资料的时候，有几点需要特别注意：

1. 分类学习

分类学习的好处在于可以强化字、词、句以及写作技巧的积累。比如同样是进行人物描写。有的文章强化人物整体介绍，纵横一生，而有的文章则侧重细节描写，突出某方面的贡献。同样是介绍一个人的成绩，有的突出产品对世界的影响，有的则突出风格和特色。但是有一些词汇和表达，却是反复出现的。这样的复现效果，也符合英语学习的规律。这种分类学习，不仅仅对英语学习有帮助，对拓展中文的写作思路也有帮助。

2. 积累词汇和表达

这是阅读的重要功能。所有的单词和短语，只有放到鲜活的语境中才有意义。通过阅读记单词，可以参透单词和短语的弦外之音。但是也不必每个单词都查找，这样会降低阅读的乐趣。所以在选择单词的时候，以高频词、核心词为首选。本书特别聘请具有长期高校教学经验和海外考试培训经验的老师联合编写，确保选词的时尚和时效。

3. 长难句翻译

长难句是阅读过程中较难逾越的一关。很多意思需要"品"，强化中英文的对比，既不影响阅读的流畅性，又不放弃教学指导方法。

4. 模仿与学习

语言的魅力建立在表达技巧之上。同样的意思，用不同的表达方式，会有不同的效果。分析优秀的句型、句式，一方面是提高自己的阅读准确性，另一方面也是巩固读者自身的语法知识。通过对亮点句式的分析，提高自己的输出能力，这也是外刊阅读的目的所在。

5. 理论与实践相结合

纯粹的阅读，即使很有趣，也是在被动接受知识。要想让大脑变得积极起来，适量的练习就显得非常重要。针对新掌握的单词，练习不宜太难，以免让人望而生畏，削弱继续学习的勇气。因此，本书设置了简单的抠空练习。调动大脑，提高复现，同时不影响趣味性。

全书包括人物、环境、健康、经济、科普、社会、教育、文艺、语言等 9 个领域，53 篇文章，涵盖了雅思、托福、SAT、考研、四级、六级以及高考的常见话题。英语高手，可以直接阅读文章，学习句子和翻译。基础较为薄弱的同学则可以先背单词，然后再进入阅读状态。本书配有音频，通过扫描二维码可以直接获得。当然，如果喜欢进一步探究阅读的乐趣，可以直接联系独课教育，更多的小伙伴在等着你。

吕蕾微信公众号：lvlei1973

吕蕾微博：http://weibo.com/lvlei1973

吕蕾一直播ID：76304044

前　言

最新出版的《普通高中英语课程标准 (2017 年版)》(人民教育出版社),将英语报刊阅读纳入了普通高中英语课程中,作为选修类课程。此举意味着英语报刊阅读在高中英语学习阶段势必占有一席之地,其重要性也可窥一斑。四六级英语考试等大学英语考试,还有托福、雅思、SAT 等考试,有相当一部分的素材,特别是阅读素材都是选自原汁原味的外刊。

但是外刊上的文章五花八门,切实符合各种考试的选材要求的少之又少,比如雅思考试和高考中出现的文章,层次分明,一目了然,内容的积极性和科学性要求较高。在难度上,比如高考阅读,逐年增加些许难度,2017 年江苏高考阅读材料直接选用 *The Economist* 上的文章。

针对上述情况,我们从最近一年的英美国家主流报刊中精选了一批题材多样、体裁各异的文章,并邀请具有丰富命题经验的大学和高中一线英语教师,参照各种中高级英语命题风格进行解读和习题设置。本书旨在将原汁原味的外媒文章带给读者,帮着读者熟悉外媒文章的文风,提高外媒文章的阅读理解能力,从而自如地应对考试。

本书的策划和编写围绕以下五个维度展开:

1. 语篇来源

本书共计 53 篇文章,分别选自三十余种世界知名刊物近一年期间发布的文章。入选的文章文风迥异,内容鲜活,涉及面广,紧密对接大学和高中新课标英语课程内容。

2. 语篇内容

入选语篇涉及了人与自我、人与社会、人与自然三大主题语境,涵盖记叙文、说明文、议论文和应用文四大语篇类型。

3. 语篇难度

参考高考较难的语篇难度,兼顾大学英语考试平均难度,我们对入选语篇进行了仔细的解读。即使读者英语水平很一般,有了我们的解读,基本上都能畅读下来。

4. 语篇解读

众所周知,现在各种高级考试都对语篇结构的把握提出了很高的要求,因此我们特地设计了"话题概要"栏目,这个部分能让读者以最快速度检验自己是不是把握了文章。

5. 语篇练习

学习外刊文章,除了研习英语语篇思维外,语言的学习必不可少。书中设置的练习基本上围绕词块进行,提醒读者进行佳句模仿。

致谢

在本书的编写过程中，贺冰、陈志强、东雪珍、严晔骁、靳书聪、张春开、黎楚明、李娜、张霞、马志芬、马连振、桑建超、陆萍、史婕、孙海玲、缪林晓、刘斌河、郑玮、孙风华、杨雅琦、汤平、崔秋等也参与了资料搜集与部分编写工作，在此一并致谢。

徐志坚

目　录

Chapter 1

人物 / People

01 Harlan Ellison[M]

科幻大师哈兰·埃里森

1   The great AM, the supercomputer/tormentor/god at the centre of Harlan Ellison's story "I Have No Mouth and I Must Scream" (1967), **outdid** its creator in bile（憎恨）and anger. But not by all that much. [①]Celebrated as a pyrotechnic（出色的）writer of short fiction, screenplays, comic books and criticism, Mr Ellison was as prodigious（巨大的）a source of anecdote, **vendetta** and **litigation.** The **dust jacket** of one book called him "possibly the most contentious（有争议的）person on Earth."

2   Mr Ellison would **unleash** his **indignant** and **ingenious** fury on anyone who offended him, **relishing** every opportunity to rage at reactionaries（保守分子）and Republicans. But he saved his fiercest and most litigious ire（怒火）for people who had snubbed（冷落）, perverted（侵害）, stolen or paid too little for his work. He was **expelled** from Ohio State University for hitting a professor who once belittled his writing ability. Over the next 20 years he sent the professor a copy of every story he published. **In the midst of** a dispute over a contract, he mailed 213 bricks to a publisher, postage to be paid by the recipient. He accused a studio executive of having the intellectual capacity of an artichoke（洋蓟）. A YouTube rant（怒吼）about Warner Bros wanting to use an interview with him without paying has become justly famous. [②]"I've only been an asshole to assholes," he would say; he seemed to come across enough of them to remain almost permanently in their ranks.

3   Mr Ellison was small and Jewish, both of which got him bullied a lot growing up in Cleveland in the 1930s and 1940s. On leaving home he claimed to have become a crop-picker, tuna（金枪鱼）fisherman, gun for hire（合约杀手）, nitroglycerine（硝化甘油）truck driver, lithographer（石印工）, short-order cook, door-to-door salesman both of books and brushes (not at the same time) and a customer-services representative in a department store. He wrote his first novel, "Web of the City", while undergoing basic training for the army at Fort Benning, Georgia. Previously peripatetic（流动工作的）, in 1962 he moved to California and stayed there. It was not exactly a settling down. By the 1980s Mr Ellison had had five wives. He **credited** the last, Susan Toth, whom he wed in 1986, **with** saving him.

4   Novels, although he wrote three between 1958 and 1961, **turned out** not to be his thing. ③"Mr Ellison's stories", his friend, the writer Neil Gaiman, says, "**sparkle** and glitter (闪光) and shine and wound and **howl**…you can see Harlan experimenting, trying new things, new techniques, new voices." To maintain such intensity and **inventiveness** for hundreds of pages would have been exhausting to all concerned.

5   The stories repeatedly **garnered** him science fiction's top prizes; he won eight of the Hugo awards voted on by fans at science fiction's world conventions, or WorldCons. One of those Hugos was for writing "The City on the Edge of Forever", perhaps the most popular episode of "Star Trek (星际迷航)" (and the occasion of an epic **feud** with the show's creator, Gene Roddenberry). ④Another was for editing "Dangerous Visions" (1967), an **anthology** that served as a **rallying-point** for the "New Wave" of science fiction.

6   His television work **was feted**, too; the Writers Guild of America honoured three more of his teleplays, as well as the one for "Star Trek". One of his **lawsuits** (诉讼) accused the producers of "The Terminator (终结者)" (1984) of **ripping off** his script for "Soldier" (1964), an episode of "The Outer Limits" about a remorselessly (无情地) efficient soldier thrown back in time who ends up saving a family. ⑤He also sued the producers of "In Time" (2011) for its similarities to another of his Hugo winners,"**Repent**, Harlequin!' Said the Ticktockman" (1965), which explores **repression** in a world where time can be conserved, like energy, to be recycled and used later; on that occasion, though, he dropped the suit.

◆ 课文小助手

一、生词和词块释义

outdo /ˌaʊtˈduː/ *v.* 超过

vendetta /venˈdetə/ *n.* 宿怨

litigation /ˌlɪtɪˈgeɪʃn/ *n.* 诉讼

unleash /ʌnˈliːʃ/ *v.* 释放

indignant /ɪnˈdɪgnənt/ *adj.* 愤慨的

ingenious /ɪnˈdʒiːnjəs/ *adj.* 巧妙的

relish /ˈrelɪʃ/ *v.* 享受

expel /ɪkˈspel/ *v.* 开除，驱逐

sparkle /ˈspɑːkl/ *v.* 闪耀

howl /haʊl/ *v.* （狼、狗）嚎叫

inventiveness /ɪnˈventɪvnɪs/ *n.* 创造性

garner /ˈgɑːnə/ *v.* 积累，收获

feud /fjuːd/ *n.* 长期斗争，世仇

anthology /ænˈθɒlədʒɪ/ *n.* 精选集

rallying-point /ˈrælɪɪŋ-pɔɪnt/ *n.* 聚集点

lawsuit /ˈlɒsjuːt/ *n.* 诉讼

repent /rɪˈpent/ *v.* 忏悔，后悔

repression /rɪˈpreʃn/ *n.* 压抑，抑制

dust jacket 书皮，包书纸

in the midst of 在……之中

credit with 把……归功于

turn out 结果是

be feted 受欢迎

rip off 偷窃

二、话题概要

大意： 科幻大师哈兰·埃里森于 2018 年 6 月 27 日逝世，享年 84 岁。这位才华横溢、脾气暴躁的作家生前著有多篇科幻大作。

Para. 1–2： 哈兰·埃里森创作了许多科幻作品、剧本、漫画和评论文章，同时他也是许多轶事、宿怨和官司的主角。他被认为是最具争议性的作家。他对任何冒犯他的人都毫不吝啬地释放怒火，对那些看不起或者侵害他作品的人更是毫不留情，因而他与其他人的争执和官司也总是源源不断。大学的时候他打了轻视他的写作能力的一位教授，并在其后的 20 多年间，每出版一部作品，就给这位教授寄上一份。

Para. 3–4： 埃里森是一个小个子犹太人，从小被霸凌。他宣称他做过各种各样的工作。在参加军队训练的时候，他写下了他的第一部小说。1958 年到 1961 年间他写了三部小说，但都还没有形成他的风格，而据他的朋友说，埃里森不断尝试新的事物和技巧、不断地创新。

Para. 5–6： 他之后的作品则不断地为他赢得了众多的重量级奖项。他获得了八次雨果奖，为电影《星际迷航》系列写的《永恒边界之城》也为他赢得了雨果奖。而他的电视作品也很受欢迎，美国编剧协会为他的三部作品授予了荣誉。同时，与他相关的诉讼和官司也并未停止，例如，他曾起诉电影《终结者》的制片人抄袭了他的作品。

◆ 同步练习

一、长难句翻译（见文章划线处）

二、词块填空

1. His forecast _____ to be quite wrong.

2. She _____ her teacher _____ the discovery.

3. He could see nobody _____ the desert.

4. They went so far as to_____ banks in broad daylight.

5. If someone _____, they are welcomed, or admired by the public.

三、佳句模仿

原文佳句	you can see Harlan experimenting, trying new things, new techniques, new voices.
亮点评析	voice 在这里是指文学作品或作者的独特风格或腔调。
写作应用	She tried different literary voice, but didn't find her thing. 她尝试了不同的文学风格，但并没有找到她的那一个。

◆ 答案

一、长难句翻译

1. 埃里森先生是一名出色的作家，以写短篇小说、电影剧本、漫画书、评论文章著名，而他也是众多轶事、争执、官司的源头。

2. "我只是在混蛋面前表现得像一个混蛋。"他这样说。然而他似乎遇到了太多的混蛋以至于他永久地留在了他们这一行列。

3. 他的朋友，作家 Neil Gaiman 说，"埃里森的故事是闪烁的、发光的，这些故事会让人伤感，也会让人想要长啸，你可以发现哈兰不断地在实验，不断尝试新的事物、新的技巧，新的文学风格。"

4. 另一个则是编辑《危险影像》，这是一本科幻小说选集，它被认为是科幻小说"新浪潮"运动的汇合点。

5. 他还起诉了电影《时间规划局》的制片人，因为这部电影和他的另一部获得雨果奖的小说《"忏悔吧，小丑！"嘀嗒人说》很像，该小说主要展现了一个时间可以像能量一样存储、循环利用、延后使用的世界，探索了人类在这个世界中的压抑感。但在这一次，埃里森最后撤销了诉讼。

二、词块填空

1. turns out/ turned out

2. credits with/credited with

3. in the midst of

4. rip off

5. is feted

02 Overlooked No More: Bette Nesmith Graham, Who Invented Liquid Paper[M]

贝蒂·奈史密斯·格莱姆，修正液的发明者

1 Bette Nesmith Graham didn't tell anyone about the first few bottles of her whitish concoction (灰白色的调制品). ①She had mixed it in her kitchen blender (搅拌机) and poured it into nail polish (指甲油) containers, then hid it in her desk, **furtively** applying it only when needed to avoid the **scrutiny** of a disapproving boss.

2 The substance was Liquid Paper, the correction fluid that relieved secretaries and writers **of all stripes** from the pressure of perfection.

3 ②Graham later brought it to market and was soon leading an international business, based in Dallas, that produced 25 million bottles of Liquid Paper a year at its peak, with factories in Toronto and Brussels. She would sell the company for $47.5 million in 1980 and donate millions to charity—six months before she died at 56.

4 ③But in 1954, Graham was a divorced single mother supporting herself and her son **from paycheck to paycheck**, earning $300 a month (about $2,800 in today's money) as a secretary for a Texas bank. She was a bad typist **to boot**. And then she was forced to use a new typewriter model which had sensitive key triggers and a carbon ribbon instead of one made of fabric. The typos (打字错误) **piled up**, and when she tried to use an eraser, carbon ink would **smear** all over the page.

5 So she **sneaked** some fast-drying white tempera (蛋彩画法) paint into work and **concealed** her typos with a watercolor brush. This was much faster and cleaner than an eraser, and barely noticeable on the page.

6 Bette Clair McMurray was born in Dallas on March 23, 1924. Her mother, Christine Duval, was an artist and a businesswoman who opened her own knitting store and taught Bette oil painting.

7 Bette **was passionate about** painting and sculpting, if not particularly skilled. She left school at 17 to become a secretary and married her high school sweetheart, Warren Nesmith, two years later. Then Nesmith **went off** to fight in World War II. The marriage ended in divorce shortly after he returned, in 1946.

8　④Graham—the name she took after a <u>subsequent</u> marriage—struggled to <u>make ends meet</u>, <u>taking on</u> side jobs (兼职) like painting lettering on bank windows, designing letterheads.

9　Graham's invention of correction fluid <u>gave her a glimpse of</u> a potential way out of her troubles, and she tried to form a business, calling it The Mistake Out Company, but could not afford the $400 patent fee. ⑤<u>She moved forward anyway, poring over books in the public library to study formulas for tempera paint, and working with a chemistry teacher to improve the consistency (黏稠度) of her product.</u>

10　Every evening she returned home from work to tinker with the formula, write letters to potential buyers and send samples. She <u>solicited</u> wholesalers (批发商) and traveled from Dallas to San Antonio and Houston on weekends to market her product.

11　Graham became so devoted to her venture (企业) that she accidentally signed a letter at her job with the notation (记号) "The Mistake Out Company." She was <u>promptly</u> fired, giving her a chance to become a full-time small business owner in 1958. That year she applied for a patent and changed the name to the Liquid Paper Company.

12　Graham's product began to <u>catch on</u>. She was written about in an office supply magazine, had a meeting with I.B.M. and received a large order from General Electric.

13　Bette Graham was now wealthy. She established two foundations (基金会), which gave grants (补助金) and financial support to promote women in the arts and business.

14　But her wealth and influence came with <u>setbacks</u>. In 1962, Graham married a frozen-food salesman, Robert Graham, who took an increasingly active role in the company, including a seat on the board. In 1975 they went through an acrimonious divorce.

15　The bitterness remained, and Robert Graham <u>maneuvered</u> to have the company <u>bar</u> her <u>from</u> making any corporate decisions. <u>Amid</u> the power struggle, and despite declining health, Graham managed to <u>wrest</u> back <u>control of</u> the company. She died on May 12, 1980, of complications (并发症) of a stroke. She left her fortune to her son, who took over her foundations and continued to <u>dole out</u> money to striving women.

◆ 课文小助手

一、生词和词块释义

furtively /ˈfɜːtɪvli/ *adv.* （人）偷偷摸摸地	**to boot** 除此以外
scrutiny /ˈskruːtɪni/ *n.* 仔细审查	**pile (sth.) up** （不好的事物）堆积起来
smear /smɪər/ *v.* 涂抹	**be passionate about** 酷爱
sneak /sniːk/ *v.* 偷带	**go off** 离开
conceal /kənˈsiːl/ *v.* 隐藏	**make ends meet** 使收支刚好能相抵
subsequent /ˈsʌbsɪkwənt/ *adj.* 随后的	**take on** 接受（工作）
glimpse /ɡlɪmps/ *v.* 瞥见	**give sb. a glimpse of** 短暂的感受（或体验、领会）
solicit /səˈlɪsɪt/ *v.* 招揽（生意）	
promptly /ˈprɒmptli/ *adv.* 迅速地	**pore over sth.** 研读（通常指书）
setback /ˈsetbæk/ *n.* 挫折	**catch on** 变得受欢迎
manoeuvre /məˈnuːvər/ *v.* 操纵	**bar sb. from doing sth.** 阻止某人做某事
amid /əˈmɪd/ *prep.* 在……当中	**wrest control of** 夺取……控制权
of all stripes 各式各样的	**dole sth. out** 分发（钱等）
from paycheck to paycheck （工资）入不敷出	

二、话题概要

大意：Graham 无意中发明了修正液，后成立公司，将修正液推向市场，取得巨大成功。Graham 的一生，不管是生活还是事业，都不是一帆风顺的。

Para. 1–3: Graham 与修正液。Graham 发明了修正液，平时上班时候她偷偷带着备用，这种修正液对于秘书和作家来说，简直就是一种福音。后来将其推向市场，取得巨大成功，并向慈善机构捐款数百万美元。后来 Graham 去世，享年 56 岁。

Para. 4–5: 修正液的发明。Graham 是一个糟糕的打字员。打字错误后，当她试图使用橡皮擦时，碳墨会在整个页面上涂抹。因此，她将一些快干的白色蛋彩画涂料带去上班，可以掩盖之前的错别字，效果很好。

Para. 6–8: Graham 早年的生活。Graham 从小就对绘画和雕刻充满热情，17 岁离开学校成为一名秘书，并与她的高中恋人 Nesmith 结婚，之后 Nesmith 参加第二次世界大战，后二人离婚。为维持生计，Graham 不得不做些兼职。

Para. 9–13: Graham 的奋斗史。 Graham 对修正液的发明让她看到了摆脱困境的潜在方法，她成立了一家公司。她仔细阅读书籍、研究配方，以提高她的产品的黏稠度；给潜在买家写信并寄样品；寻找批发商，推销产品。由于过于投入，以至于上班时出现差池遭到解雇，但这反而让她更有时间专注自己的小公司。慢慢地，Graham 的产品开始流行起来，大订单纷纷而至。富裕后的 Graham 创建了两个基金会，为女性在艺术和商业方面的发展提供支持。

Para. 14–15: Graham 事业受挫与遗志的继承。 Graham 的财富和影响伴随着挫折。Graham 在 1962 年与 Robert Graham 结婚，1975 年，他们离婚。然而 Robert Graham 操纵公司将她架空。在权力斗争中，尽管健康状况不佳，Graham 最终还是成功夺回了公司的控制权，后于 1980 年因病去世。她把自己的财产留给了她的儿子，让其接管她的基金会，并继续造福女性。

◆ **同步练习**

一、长难句翻译（见文章划线处）

二、词块填空

1. I've always _____ about football.

2. She spends her evenings _____ textbooks.

3. When Mike lost his job, we could barely _____.

4. She was a great sportswoman, and beautiful _____.

5. I wonder if the game will ever _____ with young people?

6. They seized his passport and _____ leaving the country.

7. The programme gives us a rare _____ a great artist at work.

8. Don't _____ too much work—the extra cash isn't worth it.

9. Unpaid bills began to _____ alarmingly, and they soon went bankrupt.

10. The shareholders are planning to _____ the company from the current directors.

三、佳句模仿

原文佳句	The bitterness remained, and Robert Graham maneuvered to have the company bar her from making any corporate decisions.

亮点评析	bar 作名词时，有"长杆，棒，铁栅栏"之意。作动词时，自然也会联想到有"阻挡，阻挠；防止，禁止"之意，如：I tried to push past her but she barred my way/path (= stood in front of me and prevented me from getting past). 我试图从她旁边挤过去，但她还是挡住了我的去路。原文中的 bar sb. from (doing) sth. 指的就是"阻止某人做某事"，被动形式是 sb. be barred from (doing) sth.
写作应用	According to the regulation, the players are barred from drinking alcohol the night before a match. However, he wouldn't listen. Finally, the incident led to him being barred from playing for England. 根据规定，运动员在参赛前夜不得喝酒。但他就是不听，最终这次事件导致他无法再为英国队效力。

◆ 答案

一、长难句翻译

1. 她在厨房的搅拌机里混合它，把它倒进指甲油容器里，然后把它藏在桌子里，偷偷地在需要的时候才用它，以免遭到持反对意见的老板的审查。

2. 格莱姆后来将其推向市场，并很快领导了总部位于达拉斯的一家国际公司，该公司在高峰期时年产 2500 万瓶修正液，生产的工厂分别在多伦多和布鲁塞尔。

3. 但在 1954 年，格莱姆是一个离异的单身母亲，她在德克萨斯一家银行做秘书，每月挣 300 美元（相当于今天的 2800 美元），又要照顾儿子，每月入不敷出。

4. 格莱姆——这是她婚后的名字。为了维持生计，她也做些兼职，比如在银行的窗户上绘字，设计信笺。

5. 不管怎样，她还是继续前行，在公共图书馆里仔细阅读书籍，研究蛋彩画颜料的配方，并与一位化学老师合作，以提高她的产品的黏稠度。

二、词块填空

1. been passionate

2. poring over

3. make ends meet

4. to boot

5. catch on

6. barred him from

7. glimpse of

8. take on

9. pile up

10. wrest control of

03 Willing Hearts Founder Tony Tay[E]
"愿之心"创始人托尼·泰

1　Just before Tony Tay's mother passed away in 2003, she gave him her **well-worn** commercial kitchen（指饭店、餐馆等饮食业的厨房；商用厨房）and cooking utensils（炊具）. "You never know when you will need them," she told him. <u>①The **assorted** pots, pans and ladles（长柄勺）were as familiar to Tony as were her special dishes—she used them countless times when cooking for family occasions and large gatherings.</u> What am I going to do with all this? he thought.

2　Not long afterwards, while at his mother's funeral, a nun attending the ceremony asked Tony for help with collecting bread from a bakery and delivering it to the church's orphanage. <u>②He didn't hesitate—here was a chance to give back for the charity shown to him over 55 years earlier.</u> Tony was only five when, in 1947, his mother was forced to place him in a Catholic children's home（儿童福利院）for five years after his father abandoned the family. At the time, Singapore was struggling to recover from the Asia-Pacific War. With four children to feed, no education and jobs hard to find, his mother fought to **make ends meet**. With a low-paying job as a housekeeper with the British army, she had to work at several jobs to **keep food on the table**. In the children's home, she knew, Tony wouldn't go hungry. By age ten, Tony often accompanied his mother as she walked from church to church, and temple to temple, kneeling and praying for food. Dinners **comprised of** whatever food there was—cauliflower stems（花椰菜茎）, bacon offcuts（培根碎肉）, and whatever leftovers she could get from her employers. "We had the hardest life," recalls Tony. As he got older, Tony found a job working for the then British-owned grocery store Cold Storage. "In those days, you either **slogged** or joined the gangsters." He eventually found success in the insurance and printing business, married and raised a family. He was looking forward to spending more time with his family and grandchildren when he eventually retired.

3　"Distributing the bread reminded me of the times when I had to queue for food and nobody asked why," he says. "The temple just gave the food to us." Soon after, another nun asked Tony to distribute unsold vegetables from a wholesaler（批发商）to the poor. While distributing the vegetables with his wife, an elderly man in a rented government flat approached them and asked for food. He was living by himself and could not cook. The couple began making and delivering a home-cooked meal to the man every day.

4 Over time, the number of meals Tony was cooking in his kitchen at home grew and two friends decided to **pitch in** and help. But as the number of meals grew, so did the rubbish and complaints from his neighbours. "A policeman, a Land Transport Agency officer, and the National Environment Agency were even called," says his daughter Anne. "The house was filling up with volunteers to help cook, prepare and deliver the food. We were like strangers in our own home." Then one day, they ran out of rice needed to make the 1000 meals needed for the next day. "We'll pray about it," Tony remembers saying to his worried family. It worked—before day's end, a rice merchant had given them an excess shipment he needed to offload (卸货). Soon after, the family's entire house—the living room, kitchen and bedrooms—was filled with sacks (麻袋) of rice.

5 Within two years the high number of meals Tony and his small team cooked each day forced them to move operations to a larger kitchen. After briefly occupying church premises and an industrial complex, the meal centre moved to a government-managed community hub (中心) in Eunos, east of Singapore. *Willing Hearts*, a non-profit organisation, was born. Today, *Willing Hearts* serves around 7000 meals a day, has ten full-time staff, and is dependent on donors and volunteers for rent, electricity, food and labour. ③Every day Tony faces the challenge of getting enough volunteers to help with food preparation, cooking and delivering—often without knowing what ingredients will be donated for the meals. "We once had so much peanut butter that we did not know what to do," he recalls. "I thought for a moment, then cooked the Malay dish of Mee Siam (thin rice noodles with **gravy**)." Tony arrives at the *Willing Hearts* kitchen at 3am to cook and **co-ordinate**. ④About 200 volunteers gather round rectangle tables to cut, peel and wash vegetables and other ingredients, while another group of volunteers deliver the cooked lunches to 40 collection points (集中派发点), all with in walking distance of **beneficiaries**. The day ends in the evening after collecting donated ingredients and vegetables for preparation the following day. Like the elderly man who asked him for the first meal, Tony never asks why people are taking his food. "We do not judge," he says. At 71, Tony has no plans to stop. Instead, he intends to increase the number of meal deliveries to feed more people. "More people are coming in asking for help, especially stroke patients and the disabled and we have to move forward," he says.

6 What keeps him going? "The smile on people's faces when they see the food," Tony says. "Food in the stomach is the most basic thing. ⑤I can't take care of all their problems but at least when there is food in the stomach, thoughts of other things can change; it binds people and communities. In Singapore, we call it the kampong spirit (Malay-village community spirit)."

◆ 课文小助手

一、生词和词块释义

well-worn /ˌwelˈwɔːn/ *adj.* 用了很久的

assorted /əˈsɔːrtəd/ *adj.* 各式各样的

slog /slɑːg/ *vi.* 苦干

gravy /ˈgreɪvi/ *n.* 肉汁

co-ordinate /kouˈɔːrdɪneɪt/ *vi.* 协调

beneficiary /ˌbenɪˈfɪʃieri/ *n.* 受惠人

make ends meet 收支平衡

keep food on the table 糊口

comprise of 包括

pitch in 加入

二、话题概要

大意： 本文讲述新加坡慈善家托尼·泰 (Tony Tay) 为贫穷或有需要的人提供膳食并最终创立非盈利慈善机构"愿之心"的事迹。

Para. 1: 面对母亲遗留下来的使用多年的商用厨房以及各式炊具，托尼·泰 (Tony Tay) 该怎样处置呢？

Para. 2: 一位参加母亲葬礼仪式的修女请求托尼·泰帮忙从面包店收集些面包送给教堂孤儿院。托尼·泰一口答应。55 年前他同样受惠于这样的慈善行为。1947 年，5 岁的托尼·泰寄居在儿童福利院。母亲没有文化，努力用微薄的收入养育 4 个孩子。10 岁时，他随母亲去教堂、寺庙乞食。他用苦干精神度过了最艰难的岁月，并最终在保险业和印刷业中取得成功。现已退休，希冀含饴弄孙。

Para. 3: 在另一位修女的请求下，托尼·泰和妻子帮忙分发蔬菜给穷人。在此过程中，一位不能做饭的独居老人向托尼·泰他们要吃的，从此，托尼·泰夫妇每天做好饭送给这位老人。

Para. 4: 逐渐地，托尼·泰做饭的份数越来越多。因此产生了大量垃圾还受到邻居的投诉。不过，志愿者也越来越多。有一次，大米用完了，但第二天还有 1000 份膳食要准备。所幸，一位米商解了燃眉之急。

Para. 5: 两年来，托尼和他的小队每天做饭的量都在增加，这迫使他们不断更换厨房。最终，厨房搬到新加坡东部友诺士 (Eunos) 的一个由政府管理的社区中心内。至此，"愿之心"诞生。每天，做好的饭被送往 40 个集中点统一派发。托尼他们从不评判前来领饭的人。他们打算增加送饭的次数以帮助更多的人，特别是中风患者和残疾人。

Para. 6: 填满饥饿的胃，打造社区精神。这就是托尼·泰做慈善的不竭动力源泉。

◆ 同步练习

一、长难句翻译（见文章划线处）

二、词块填空

1. Men and women , old and young , all _____ to make Willing Hearts better and better in

the beginning.

2. The committee is _____ representatives from both the public and private sectors.

3. In some developing countries, many in their 60s, 70s and beyond, desperate to find work so they can _____ and a roof over their heads.

4. Being out of work and having two young children, they found it impossible to _____.

三、佳句模仿

原文佳句	Dinners comprised of whatever food there was—cauliflower stems, bacon offcuts, and whatever leftovers she could get from her employers.
亮点评析	本句中 2 个 whatever 均引导宾语从句，做 comprised of 的宾语。
写作应用	Be thrifty and hardworking in whatever undertaking you are to start on. 办任何事都要勤俭。

原文佳句	"Distributing the bread reminded me of the times when I had to queue for food and nobody asked why," he says.
亮点评析	本句中 Distributing the bread 为动名词做主语；when 引导定语从句。
写作应用	1. Going to a British high school for one year was a very enjoyable and exciting experience for me. 在英国上了一年的高中对我来说是一段非常令人愉快和兴奋的经历。 2. There are times when we procrastinate simply because it is difficult for us to concentrate on a project, the benefits of which will not be realized until some time in the future. 我们多次拖延只是因为一旦做一件工作要很久以后才能有现实的好处，这样就很难集中精神到这件工作上。

◆ **答案**

一、长难句翻译

1. 托尼就像熟悉母亲的特别菜肴一样熟悉这些锅碗瓢盆勺——在家庭聚餐和大型聚会时，母亲无数次使用过这些炊具。

2. 他没有迟疑——这是可以回馈 55 年他被给予的慈善行为的一个机会。

3. 托尼每天都面临这样的挑战：找到足够多的志愿者帮忙备餐、烹饪、送餐——经常不知道将要捐赠来的食材是什么。

4. 大约 200 名志愿者围着数个长方形餐桌切菜、削皮、清洗蔬菜和其他食材，而另一组志愿者则将做好的午餐送到 40 个集中点统一派发。所有集中派发点离受惠人不过步行几步的距离。

5. 我不能解决他们所有的问题，但是至少当他们不再挨饿时，才会改变对其他事物的看法。它把人们和社区紧紧联系起来。

二、词块填空

1. pitched in

2. comprised of

3. keep food on the table

4. make ends meet

04 Paul Mecurio[E]

保罗·梅库里奥

A Wall Streeter who turned to comedy

1   [1]When PAUL MECURIO was working as a Wall Street lawyer in his twenties, he never imagined he'd one day star in his own off-Broadway comedy show. "I was always the funniest lawyer in my law firm, which is kind of like being the sexiest I.T. guy," he says. Mr. Mecurio, now 58, spent nearly six years leading a double life, working on Wall Street by day and performing at dive bars (廉价酒吧) at night. Trying to keep his comedy gigs (现场戏剧表演) a secret from his Wall Street colleagues proved **tricky**: He once had to do a set (曲目) with his back to the audience after seeing two of the firm's partners' wives in the crowd.

2   Today, he has left his Wall Street days long behind. [2]Now a veteran of the comedy business, he has a host of marquee credits on his résumé. He's written for "The Colbert Report" and "The Daily Show", for which he won an Emmy Award, and is currently the warm-up comedian (暖场喜剧演员) for "The Late Show with Stephen Colbert", getting the audience **revved up** before Mr. Colbert **takes the stage**. Later this month, Mr. Mecurio will open a one-man off-Broadway show. Called "Permission to Speak with Paul Mecurio", the improve (即兴的) show is set to run through Aug. 15. Mr. Mecurio says that he'll base his performances on his conversations with audiences each night, coming up with jokes and **banter** as he goes along.

3   [3]It's an unlikely journey for someone whose parents thought he might someday take over his father's floor covering business in Providence, R.I.. As a child, Mr. Mecurio watched comedians such as Steve Martin, Rodney Dangerfield and George Carlin on television but didn't imagine that he could actually pursue a career in comedy. After graduating from Providence College in 1982, he went on to Georgetown University Law Center. Right after law school, he made a few short comedy films as a side project (业余项目) and submitted them to film festivals, but he never saw film as a future career. Instead, he got a job as a Wall Street mergers and acquisitions lawyer (华

尔街并购律师）at Willkie, Farr & Gallagher in New York City. "The plan was, you work for 25 years, you have 2.2 kids and a white picket（尖木桩）fence and then you retire," he says.

4　He kept writing jokes as a hobby. One day in 1988 he noticed that Jay Leno **was slated to** perform at a work function（社交聚会）he was attending. Mr. Mecurio printed out some of his jokes and gave them to Mr. Leno at the end of the night. To his surprise, two days later, Mr. Leno called him. Mr. Mecurio thought it was his friend **pranking** him and told Mr. Leno, "You do a **lousy** Leno impression." But it wasn't a **hoax**: Mr. Leno offered to pay $50 if he used one of Mr. Mecurio's jokes. A week later, Mr. Leno told one of Mr. Mecurio's jokes on television. The joke got laughs, and Mr. Mecurio "became obsessed" with comedy, he says.

5　④As he moved around in his career, jumping to what is now Credit Suisse and later to Bear Stearns, he started bringing two notebooks to all of his meetings—one for deal notes and another for joke notes—and he soon realized that his work notebook was empty. He started booking his own comedy gigs on the side（作为兼职）. He wrestled for the next few years with whether to make comedy his career. Finally, in 1994, he quit Wall Street for good（永远）. Two years later, he landed a job as one of The Daily Show's original writers through a producer who had seen him perform. There he met Mr. Colbert, who hired him to write and perform on "The Colbert Report" and later, "The Late Show."

6　⑤These days, he fills his days writing material for his act, testing the jokes in clubs, talking with people about new shows and interviewing celebrity guests for his weekly podcast（播客）, The Paul Mecurio Show. He also tours the country doing standup. His jokes often **revolve around** life with his wife and teenage son. He **pokes fun at** his wife's insistence on hiding the pickles（泡菜）in the fridge and **bemoans** the constant demands of parenting. "I love my son, but some days I wish he'd walk into the woods and never come back," he jokes. He makes fun of relationships and self-help, saying that when people ask what's more important, sex or communication, he insists, "Sex! Because no one fantasizes about communication!" He gets into politics as well, making fun of both the left and the right. Last year, he posted a YouTube video about the presidential inauguration that **skewered** Donald Trump but also needled Hillary Clinton. Someday, he says, he hopes to have his own late night show. What would he do after that? "I would actually go back and start writing and reading prospectuses（募股章程）" as a lawyer, he jokes.

◆ 课文小助手

一、生词和词块释义

tricky /'trɪki/ *adj.* 棘手的	**skewer** /'skjuːər/ *vt.* 讽刺
banter /'bæntər/ *vi.* 开玩笑	**rev up** 更活跃起来
prank /præŋk/ *vt.* 恶作剧	**take the stage** 登台演出
lousy /'laʊzi/ *adj.* 蹩脚的	**be slated to** 打算
hoax /hoʊks/ *n.* 恶作剧	**revolve around** 围绕
bemoan /bɪ'moʊn/ *vt.* 哀怨	**poke fun at** 嘲笑

二、话题概要

大意：本文讲述保罗·梅库里奥 (Paul Mecurio) 怎样从华尔街的并购律师转变成喜剧演员的故事。

Para. 1: 年轻时，梅库里奥曾是一名华尔街律师，但他热爱喜剧表演。曾经历过 6 年的双重生活：白天上班做律师工作，晚上在酒吧表演喜剧。

Para. 2: 现在，梅库里奥是一名暖场喜剧演员。在喜剧界也取得不少成就。8 月 15 号，他将开播自己的独角秀。

Para. 3: 成为喜剧演员并非梅库里奥的人生规划。法学院毕业后，虽然也制作了一些喜剧，但是他绝没想过将表演喜剧作为自己的职业；相反，他在华尔街获得一份并购律师的工作，计划着工作 25 后便退休颐养天年。

Para. 4: 梅库里奥一直把创作段子作为自己的业余爱好。一次，他的段子被杰·雷诺 (Jay Leno) 使用，很有"笑果"。从此梅库里奥便迷上喜剧。

Para. 5: 逐渐地，梅库里奥开始兼职表演喜剧。最终在 1994 年，他辞去华尔街的工作，成为栏目的一名原创写手。

Para. 6: 现在，梅库里奥每天忙于为自己的表演创作、测试素材，并在全国巡演自己的单口喜剧。他有时也调侃政客；他希望能拥有自己的一档晚间秀节目。

◆ 同步练习

一、长难句翻译（见文章划线处）

二、词块填空

1. And this year, people with musical ability from around the world _____ to try to realize their dreams, big or small.

2. It's his job to _____ the audience before the show starts.

3. The 2018 FIFA World Cup kicks off on Friday, with Germany _____ play South Korea this weekend.

4. The world does not _____ you until your wedding day.

5. In America, he says, it's funny to _____ yourself. But in China, there's no humor in misfortune.

三、佳句模仿

原文佳句	It's an unlikely journey for someone whose parents thought he might someday take over his father's floor covering business in Providence, R.I..
亮点评析	cover 在这里意思为"处理"。
写作应用	So, the problem is not my job or the amount of work, but rather how I cover it. 所以，问题不在我的工作或者工作的数量，而在于我是如何处理的。

原文佳句	These days, he fills his days writing material for his act, testing the jokes in clubs, talking with people about new shows and interviewing celebrity guests for his weekly podcast, The Paul Mecurio Show.
亮点评析	fill 在这里意思为"耗去，打发，消磨"。
写作应用	If she wants a routine to fill her day, let her do community work. 如果她想做些日常的事务来打发白天的时间，就让她去做社区工作吧。

◆ 答案

一、长难句翻译

1. 二十几岁时，保罗·梅库里奥是一名华尔街律师，当时他绝不会想到自己有一天会表演自己创作的喜剧秀。

2. 现在，他已是喜剧界老兵。他的履历上记录着许多辉煌的成就。

3. 这是不可能的人生选项，因为父母原以为有朝一日他会接管他父亲的工作，处理罗德岛普罗维登斯上的业务。

4. 先供职于现在的"瑞士信贷集团"，后来跳槽到"贝尔斯登投资公司"，当他在职业生涯中辗转时，他开始在开会时带上 2 本笔记本——一本记录交易信息，另一本记录笑话——很快他意识到记录交易信息的工作笔记本空空如也。

5. 目前，他每天都在为自己的表演写素材，在俱乐部中尝试写好的段子，与人们谈论新节目，并为自己的每周播客《保罗·梅库里奥秀》采访名人嘉宾。

二、词块填空

1. take the stage

2. rev up

3. slated to

4. revolve around

5. poke fun at

05 The Life of Bryan Cranston[M]

布莱恩·克兰斯顿的生活

1 We meet in the rather fancy Hotel de Rome in Berlin, with Bryan dressed casually in a **crisp** white shirt and dark slacks (休闲裤). Clean-shaven, his hair neatly combed, he comes equipped with a booming voice (洪亮的声音) and a broad smile. His looks, he says, are the reason he's managed to avoid stereotyping since *Breaking Bad* (《绝命毒师》) finished; ①he received an Oscar nod (奥斯卡奖提名) for his portrayal of a blacklisted (被列入黑名单的) screenwriter in *Trumbo* (《特朗勃》) and has appeared on the London stage—he's currently **treading the boards** in *Network*.

2 "I don't have a distinctive shape," he says. "I'm not short and bald. I'm not exceedingly tall. I'm average height, average weight…." Before you roll your eyes, know this is no "woe is me (我真惨啊)" **tirade** from a prima donna (爱慕虚荣的) performer. "For an actor—what I want to do—it's perfect," he beams (微笑着说). "I don't want to be a personality actor (本色演员). I want to hide in a character. I love it when people say to me, 'I didn't even know that that was you.' " That's more than likely to happen with his latest project, animated Wes Anderson flick (电影) *Isle of Dogs*. Bryan voices Chief, a **stray** dog who—along with all Japan's other mutts (杂种狗)—has been shipped out to an island off the coast after all canines (犬) are **outlawed**. An inveterate (根深蒂固的；骨灰级的) dog lover, he's even been on TV to campaign for rescue pups. "Dogs are the best," he grins. "They're loyal. All they want is love and to play and to be walked, and they're so faithful." With the likes of Bill Murray, Jeff Goldblum and Scarlett Johansson also voicing some of the characters, the story isn't just for kids; it **smuggles in** some heavyweight issues (重大问题) like "xenophobia (仇外), greed, fear-mongering (散布恐慌), immigration, segregation", he says. Voicing the emotionally **turbulent** Chief was the ideal gig. "I have a habit of playing damaged characters (情感受伤的角色). I'm very attracted to damaged characters. I relate to damaged characters."

3 How so? "Because I am one," he replies, **without missing a beat**. "I came from a busted-up (闹翻的，破裂的) home that was filled with alcoholism and physical abuse," he admits. "It turned me into an introvert, very shy, very unsure of myself, very insecure about what to do." The second of three children, Bryan was raised in Los Angeles in dire (可怕的) circumstances.

His mother, Peggy, a radio actress, became an alcoholic, while his father Joe went from job to job before he left when Bryan was just 11. "My dad was gone. I didn't see him for ten years and even when I did see him again there was a lot of damage. So I had anger issues and resentment and insecurities and things like that. ②So part of the reason I love to act so much is that it creates an opportunity for me to live through that vicariously (间接感受到地) and have a cathartic (起宣泄作用的) and therapeutic (治疗的) experience in my work." It also explains why he wrote the candid autobiography, *A Life In Parts*, in 2016.

4　Even when he reunited with his father—after he and his brother tracked him down—it remained a strained relationship. "I knew we were never going to have a truly open relationship. ③And yet on his death bed, we found a scribbled note in shaky handwriting that said the greatest day in his life was when his children forgave him. Wow! He never told us that. That was his life, that was the way he chose to live. I don't want to be that way. I don't want to have to write a note to my daughter. I want to tell her now how much I love her. That's what I've learned." Fatherhood is clearly a top priority now. Bryan has been married to his second wife Robin since 1989, after they met on the TV show *Airwolf* (《飞狼》), and their daughter Taylor, 25, is now a blossoming actress **in her own right**. He positively glows when talking about her and the wisdom they share. Like dealing with life's **ups and downs**. ④"If you're an adventurous person—and I teach my daughter this—when something that appears negative at the time happens, remember it. That's going to be a good story."

5　Open and honest, Bryan is the sort of raconteur (健谈者) you could spend hours with. He has an infectious enthusiasm for his work but comes armed with **forthright** beliefs. "I think it's good to be able to voice your opinion. If it stirs the pot (引起麻烦), it stirs the pot. There's a lot to be stirred right now in America." He's a regular on Twitter. The day we meet, he's just tweeted about the horrifying school shooting in Florida. "These events are no longer a tragedy, they're commonplace," he wrote. "The tragedy is the **impotence** and cowardice (懦弱) of Congress."

6　⑤Recently, he's been dividing his time between Los Angeles and London, where he's been performing at the National Theatre for the past three months as the iconic TV **anchorman** Howard Beale in a stage adaptation of the Oscar-winning movie *Network*. It's been an exciting run that's required him to "guard" his reserves of energy. "I love doing it," he says. "I don't realise I'm tired until hours afterwards." With this much effervescence (活力), it's difficult to imagine Bryan ever **winding down**.

◆ 课文小助手

一、生词和词块释义

crisp /krɪsp/ adj. 洁净的，挺括的

tirade /'taɪreɪd/ n. 激烈的长篇演说

stray /streɪ/ adj. 流浪的

outlaw /'aʊtlɔ:/ vt. 取缔

turbulent /'tɜ:rbjələnt/ adj. 狂暴的

forthright /'fɔ:rθraɪt/ adj. 直率的

impotence /'ɪmpətənt/ n. 无能

anchorman /'æŋkərmən/ n.（尤指新闻节目的）电（视）台节目主持人

tread the boards 演戏

smuggle in 偷运，暗含

without missing a beat 一点没有迟疑

in her own right 依靠自己的能力

ups and downs 沉浮，坎坷

wind down 休息

二、话题概要

大意：本文介绍影视演员布莱恩·克兰斯顿的从影经历、家庭情况、育子心得以及性格特点等。

Para. 1：初遇布莱恩，他给我们留下的印象是"休闲、干净、干练"。布莱恩这身装扮旨在摆脱在电视剧《绝命毒师》中塑造的那个刻板形象。现在，他正在伦敦舞台表演《人脉》(Network)。

Para. 2：布莱恩觉得自己自身条件一般，但他并不抱怨。他喜欢演一些情感受伤的角色，这一点体现在他最新电影《犬之岛》(Isle of Dogs) 中。

Para. 3：由于儿时家庭的不幸，使布莱恩在情感上受到极大伤害。因此，他通过饰演情感受到伤害的角色可以间接感受当时的情感并起到宣泄和治疗作用。

Para. 4：多年后，父子重聚，但布莱恩感觉父子关系中仍有疙瘩。布莱恩从父亲弥留之际留下的短信中体会到爱子女就要告诉子女。现在，做好父亲是布莱恩最重要的事。他与女儿分享生活智慧，教育女儿要积极面对挫折。25 岁的女儿现在凭自己的能力成为一名出色的演员。

Para. 5：布莱尔直率、坦诚、健谈，喜欢发推特，针砭时弊。

Para. 6：目前，布莱恩往返于洛杉矶和伦敦。在伦敦，他正参演由奥斯卡获奖电影改编的舞台剧。他活力满满，很难想象他会隐退息影。

◆ 同步练习

一、长难句翻译（见文章划线处）

二、词块填空

1. She's a rich woman _____ rather than by inheritance.

2. "That's what I thought," replied Olivia, _____.

3. The customs officer said that now your gang was paid to _____ a package into the U.S.

4. Like most married couples we've had our _____, but life's like that.

5. If you _____, you relax after doing something that has made you feel tired or tense.

三、佳句模仿

原文佳句	We meet in the rather fancy Hotel de Rome in Berlin, with Bryan dressed casually in a crisp white shirt and dark slacks.
亮点评析	fancy 在这里意思为"昂贵的，奢华的"。
写作应用	Make lunch time fun by pretending you're at a fancy restaurant. 为了让你的午餐时段鲜活有趣，你可以假装你是在一家豪华饭店就餐。

原文佳句	I love it when people say to me, "I didn't even know that that was you.'"
亮点评析	I love it when 是个固定句型，it 是形式宾语，when 从句是真正的宾语。意思为"我喜欢什么时候"。
写作应用	I love it when I catch you looking at me then you smile and look away. 我喜欢这样的时刻：我抓住你正在看我，然后你羞涩地别过头去。

◆ 答案

一、长难句翻译

1. 布莱恩因饰演电影《特朗勃》(Trumbo) 中那个被列入黑名单的编剧而获得奥斯卡奖提名。他现在出现在伦敦舞台上，参演舞台剧《人脉》(Network)。

2. 因此，我这么喜欢表演部分原因是表演为我创造出一个间接感受那种情感的机会，并在工作的同时获得情感宣泄和治疗的体验。

3. 然而在父亲去世的床榻之上，我们发现一张字迹潦草的便条上歪歪斜斜地写着孩子们原谅他的那一天是他最开心的一天。

4. "如果你是个喜欢冒险的人——我会教给女儿这个——当发生了当时看上去并不乐观的事的时候，记住这一点。那将会变成一件好事。"

5. 最近，他在洛杉矶和伦敦之间来回奔波。在伦敦，三个月来，他一直在国家大剧院表演改编自奥斯卡获奖影片《人脉》(Network) 中偶像电视节目主持人霍华德·比尔 (Howard Beale) 这个角色。

二、词块填空

1. in her own right

2. without missing a beat

3. smuggle in

4. ups and downs

5. wind down

06 Rescue in the River[E]

东河营救

> When they see a man struggling in the water, three strangers take the plunge.

1   It was 7:15 A.M. on June 1, 2016, and Gary Messina, now 58, was on his morning run along New York City's East River. ①Suddenly something <u>caught his eye</u>—a large 60-year-old man balancing on the four-foot-high railing that guarded the path from the water. As Messina, a New York City Police Department captain (now a deputy inspector), got closer to the scene, the man took a step forward and plunged into the dark, **choppy** river below.

2   When Messina reached the railing, the man was **bobbing** in the water, clearly unable to swim. If he had intended to kill himself that morning, he had now changed his mind. He screamed **frantically** for help as the current pulled him away from the seawall（防波堤）. Other joggers also heard the man's **pleas**. David Blauzvern, now 25, and John Green, now 31, dropped their phones and keys on land, along with Green's sneakers, and jumped in. "People had called the police, but it was unclear when they'd get there," says Green, a commercial insurance broker. "We just reacted." Messina joined them in the river.

3   Just as the jumper was **losing strength**, Blauzvern, an investment banking analyst at CSG Partners, **grabbed hold of** him. The pair were about 30 yards from the seawall when Messina and Green caught up to them. They **stabilized** the man, with Blauzvern supporting his back and Messina and Green holding him up from either side. He was **unresponsive** but not unconscious and no longer **thrashing about**. ②<u>As the men made their way toward the concrete seawall that stretched for blocks in each direction, Blauzvern had an awful realization: With the water flowing a good eight feet below the lip of the wall and no ladder or dock in sight, there was no way out of the river.</u>

4   By now, a crowd had gathered on land. "A rescue boat is on its way," someone yelled to them. Treading water (踩水) was getting tougher by the minute. The jumper, who was six foot two and weighed around 260 pounds, was **deadweight** in his rescuers' arms, which meant they could use only their legs to **maneuver** themselves. After ten minutes, they managed to get to the river's edge. ③Green tried **wedging** a hand and a foot into a tiny crack in the wall, cutting himself in the process. But he couldn't hold on for long. ④Fighting the current and holding the man above the water quickly became exhausting, so they **gave in to** drifting while staying as close to the wall as they could. "I've never been so out of breath," says Blauzvern.

5   Fifteen minutes after the men had jumped into the river, the two-man rescue boat appeared. But because it couldn't risk getting too close to the seawall, the men had to swim out to it. As they approached the boat, they encountered a new threat: The undertow (回头浪) created by the current was sucking them under the boat. ⑤Blauzvern remembers being pulled down just as someone in the boat grabbed onto the man, allowing Blauzvern to let go. "I was completely out of energy at this point," he says. Somehow, he grasped a pole attached to the boat deck and **hauled** himself aboard. The men in the water pushed the jumper while the men in the boat pulled him up and, finally, to safety. Messina and Green then got themselves aboard, and within ten minutes, the group was back on land. The man they had saved was taken to the hospital for evaluation. Details on his condition have not been released.

6   As for the rescuers, each of them was at work by 10:30 a.m. "I was a bit late," admits Blauzvern, smiling. "But I had a good excuse."

◆ 课文小助手

一、生词和词块释义

choppy /'tʃɑːpi/ adj. 波浪起伏的

bob /bɑːb/ vi. 上下浮沉

frantically /'fræntɪkli/ adv. 拼命地

plea /pliː/ n. 恳求

stabilize /'steɪbəlaɪz/ vt. 稳住

unresponsive /ˌʌnrɪ'spɑːnsɪv/ adj. 无反应的

deadweight /ˌded'weɪt/ n. (难以承受的) 重负

maneuver /mə'nuːvər/ vt. 控制

wedge /wedʒ/ vt. 将……挤入

haul /hɔːl/ vt. 拉

catch one's eye 引起某人注意

lose strength 丧失力气

grab hold of 抓住

thrash about 击水

give in to 向……屈服

二、话题概要

大意: 本文讲述三位平民英雄勇救跳河男子的事迹。

Para. 1: Gary Messina 注意到一位男子欲寻短见。当他靠近时,该男子跳入河中。

Para. 2: Gary Messina 和闻讯赶来的 David Blauzvern 及 John Green 一起跳入河中营救那位不会游泳、此刻正在拼命呼救的男子。

Para. 3: Blauzvern 托住男子后背,Messina 和 Green 从两边扶住男子。当他们游向河堤时,却发现无法上岸。

Para. 4: 托着 260 磅的男子,搏击激流,三位勇士很快筋疲力尽,只能尽可能沿着河堤漂流。救援船还在路上,情况十分危急。

Para. 5: 救援船最终到来,但不敢太靠近河堤。他们必须托着男子游向救援船。当他们靠近救援船时,Blauzvern 被一个回头浪吸入船底,所幸他抓住一根杆子得以自救。最终在三位勇士和船上救援人员的共同努力下,成功救起跳水者。三位勇士也平安上岸。

Para. 6: 十点半之前,他们都赶去上班了。虽然有点迟到,但这次他有很好的借口,Blauzvern 说道。

◆ 同步练习

一、长难句翻译（见文章划线处）

二、词块填空

1. He was disabled from birth, but he never felt frustrated, nor did he _____ any difficulty.

2. Then I heard Timothy's frightened roar, "Sharks," and he was _____ near me.

3. Since you can't possibly know what's coming, it's important that you keep your eyes open and be ready to _____ new opportunities.

4. Weather forecaster said the storm has weakened after the eye came ashore and said it would continue to _____ during the next day or two.

5. The beautiful flowers _____ when I am crossing the city garden.

三、佳句模仿

原文佳句	With the water flowing a good eight feet below the lip of the wall and no ladder or dock in sight, there was no way out of the river.
亮点评析	good 在这里意思为 "不少于，足足"。
写作应用	It's a good half hour's walk to the station from here. 从这儿步行到车站足足有半个多小时。

原文佳句	Somehow, he grasped a pole attached to the boat deck and hauled himself aboard.
亮点评析	attached to 是过去分词短语作后置定语，意思为 "系在……上"，修饰 a pole。另外，attached to 作后置定语还有 "附在……上，印在……上" 的意思。
写作应用	In China, packets of cigarettes come with a government health warning attached to them. 在中国，香烟的包装盒上都印有政府的健康警告。

◆ 答案

一、长难句翻译

1. 突然，他看到了什么——一位 60 岁的大个头男子正站在 4 英尺高的防汛护栏上。

2. 当他们游向朝两边绵延数个街区的混凝土防波堤时，Blauzvern 有一个可怕的预感：水面离防波堤上沿足有八英尺，又看不到梯子或码头，绝无可能上岸。

3. Green 试着将一只手和一只脚插进防波堤上的一条小裂缝中，结果在过程中划破了手脚。

4. 搏击激流的同时还要将男子托出水面很快使他们筋疲力尽，因此，他们尽可能靠近防波堤随波漂流。

5. Blauzvern 记得就在船上救援人员抓住男子，使得他刚得以松手时，自己被吸入水底。

二、词块填空

1. give in to

2. thrashing about

3. grab hold of

4. lose strength

5. catch my eye

Chapter 2

环境 / Environment

07 Dry Weather Is Helping Archaeologists Discover Ancient Sites[M]

干燥的天气帮助考古学家发现古遗址

Crops planted over ancient sites grow taller and greener in droughts, **giving away** their location.

1 As a heatwave sends most Britons **scuttling** to beaches and pub gardens, the country's archaeologists have been busy, **taking to** the skies to identify ancient sites that are not visible for most of the year. Aerial investigators from the Royal Commission on the Ancient and Historical Monuments of Wales have discovered a Roman fortlet beneath a field in Magor, along with the ruins of an ancient farm not far away in Langstone. Historic England, another public body, has **dispatched** aerial reconnaissance(勘察) teams from bases in York and Swindon to **scour** the country for Roman villas(别墅) and prehistoric forts(堡垒).

2 ①They are on the hunt for "crop marks", differences in plants' colour or height that are caused by what lies beneath the surface. Natural and man-made **grooves** in the subsoil or bedrock hold more **moisture** than the undisturbed ground around them and are usually filled with richer soils. This means that, in fields **levelled** by ploughing(耕地), crops growing over archaeological remains have access to more water and better nutrients. ②When pastures(牧场) are **parched**, as now, they stay greener and grow taller—as seen in the photograph of a prehistoric settlement near Eynsham, in Oxfordshire. **Conversely**, crops growing over old stone walls struggle to find water and wilt(枯萎) in the heat, to form what are known in the jargon(术语) as "negative" crop marks.

3 ③By getting up in the air during dry weather, archaeologists can use crop marks to identify the patterns of buried ditches or walls that once defined settlements, field boundaries or **funerary** monuments, explains Helen Winton, Historic England's aerial investigation and mapping manager. It has become the main way in which archaeologists find new sites. By some estimates, more than half of all known archaeological remains in Britain have been discovered by spotting crop marks from the sky in the past 70-odd years. ^④<u>Partly for this reason there are fewer known archaeological sites in western Scotland, which is mainly pasture, than in the country's drier eastern districts, which support more arable farming, according to Bill Hanson and Jane Drummond of Glasgow University.</u>

4　**Archivists** also **pore over** old aerial photographs in search of clues to the **whereabouts** of archaeological remains. Each year Historic England discovers and **logs** around 6,000 new sites in this way.

5　**Thanks to** the lack of rain, for archaeologists this has been one of the most fruitful summers in the past couple of decades, says Toby Driver, an aerial investigator in Wales. He plans to keep scouring the landscape before the crops ripen or the rain returns. ^⑤<u>Ms Winton from Historic England agrees, describing 2018 as "the first potential **bumper year** we have had in what feels like a long time".</u> In 2011, when the weather last **held off** for a particularly long time, her investigators discovered more than 1,500 new sites, mostly in the clay lands of eastern England. Could this summer **yield** similar results? "Fingers crossed."

◆ 课文小助手

一、生词和词块释义

scuttle /ˈskʌtl/ v. 碎步疾跑	**archivist** /ˈɑːkivist/ n. 档案管理员
dispatch /disˈpætʃ/ v. 派遣	**whereabouts** /ˈhwɛərəˌbauts/ n. 下落
scour /ˈskauə/ v. 四处搜索	**log** /lɒg/ v. 把……载入正式记录
groove /gruːv/ n. 凹槽	**yield** /jiːld/ v. 产生
moisture /ˈmɔistʃə/ n. 潮气	**give away** 暴露
level /ˈlevəl/ v. 使平坦	**take to** 向，赴
parch /paːtʃ/ v. 烤干	**thanks to** 由于
conversely /ˈkɔnvəːsli/ adv. 相反地	**pore over** 仔细研究
funerary /ˈfjuːnəˌrɛəri/ adj. 丧葬的	**bumper year** 丰收年
arable /ˈærəbl/ adj. 可耕的	**hold off** 暂时不下 (雨、雪等)

二、话题概要

大意：干旱季节，考古学家乘坐飞机从空中寻找"作物标志"和"负作物标志"，以期发现地下古遗址。

Para. 1：热浪来袭之时，考古学家们纷纷从空中寻找古遗址的迹象，并已经有所发现。

Para. 2：地下古遗址对地面农作物生长的影响在干旱季节尤其明显，它们会使得农田中出现"作物标志"和"负作物标志"，而这些标志成为了考古学家们找到古遗址的依据。

Para. 3：利用这些作物标记从空中对古遗址进行勘探是英国目前广为使用并卓有成效的勘探方法。

Para. 4：除了考古学家的空中勘探外，Historic England 的档案管理员们对于旧航拍照片的深入研究也为考古遗址的发现做出了巨大的贡献。

Para. 5：考古学家们表示有望在今年这个旱季里发现大量古遗迹。

◆ 同步练习

一、长难句翻译（见文章划线处）

二、词块填空

1. Thousands of people _____ the streets to welcome back their hero.

2. The rainy season _____ for a month, then it started to rain cats and dogs.

3. Although they are pretending hard to be young, their grey hair _____ them_____.

4. To defend him more effectively, his lawyers are _____ the small print in the contract.

5. Profits are up and, _____ its sales, the company once again climbed to the top of the Fortune 500.

三、佳句模仿

原文佳句	As a heatwave sends most Britons scuttling to beaches and pub gardens…
亮点评析	send 在这里的意思是"使快速（或猛然）移动"。此处的结构为 send + 宾语 (most Britons) + 宾语补足语 (scuttling)。
写作应用	1. Every step he took sent the pain shooting up his leg. 他每走一步，疼痛就顺腿窜上来。 2. The report sent share prices dropping a further 8p. 这份报告一公布，股价又跌了 8 便士。

◆ 答案

一、长难句翻译

1. 他们在搜寻"作物标记"，即由于地表之下存在某物，因而造成的植物色彩和高度上的不同。

2. 当牧场如现在这般遭到烈日炙烤，它们（指生长在考古遗址上的庄稼）依然更绿更高，如同在那张拍摄有牛津郡艾萨姆附近的史前居地的照片中所看到的那样。

3. 任职于 Historic England 的英国航空调查与测绘经理海伦·温顿解释道：通过在干旱天气到来时坐飞机到空中勘测，考古学家们能够利用作物标记来识别那些曾经界定了定居点、农田边界或墓地古迹，而如今却深埋于地下的沟渠或墙壁的格局。

4. 据格拉斯哥大学的比尔·汉森和简·德拉蒙德所言，部分是由于这个原因，牧场居多的苏格兰南部区域，与可耕地居多的更为干燥的苏格兰东部区域比起来，为人所知的考古遗址比较少。

5. 在 Historic England 任职的温顿女士表示赞同，她将 2018 年描述成"我们在似乎是很长一段时间之后所经历的第一个潜在的丰收年。"

二、词块填空

1. took to

2. held off

3. give away

4. poring over

5. thanks to

08 Two Polar Bear Cubs Are Spotted Playing With Plastic Sheet[M]
北极熊宝宝将塑料片当成玩具

1 These **unsettling** pictures show two adorable polar bear cubs playing with a large sheet of plastic on a remote Arctic island.

2 The **siblings** were spotted with their mother on the icy coast of Svalbard, a Norwegian archipelago (群岛) about halfway between the mainland and North Pole. ①The black plastic **stands out** against the seemingly spotless landscape as the youngsters paw (抓挠) at it, before putting it in their mouths.

3 Svalbard is hundreds of miles from continental Europe and has a population of about 2,500, yet researchers **navigating** the freezing waters found plastic waste wherever they went.

4 Claire Wallerstein was part of the Sail Against Plastic team, a group of 15 Cornish scientists, artists, filmmakers and campaigners who recently returned from an expedition to the Arctic Circle. She said: We were very lucky to be invited to take part in this unique **expedition**, and had an amazing time seeing Arctic wildlife, **stunning** glaciers and experiencing 24-hour sunlight.

5 ②"However, it was also a very **sobering** experience to see just how much plastic is **making its way** to this incredibly remote and apparently pristine (未开发的) environment." The aim of the trip was to research the impact of plastics on the **marine** environment just 600 miles (960km) from the North Pole. ③"What we found on the beaches was sadly not so very different from what we find back home", Ms Wallerstein said. ④"There was plenty of fishing waste, but the saddest thing was just how much of the waste **blighting** the Arctic is the same old disposable(一次性的) **detritus** of our daily lives—plastic bottles, cotton bud sticks, cigarette ends, wet wipes, polystyrene (聚苯乙烯) and food packaging."

6　The group sailed aboard a tall ship named the Blue Clipper, spending 10 days sampling the sea, air and beaches around the **isolated** coasts of Svalbard. Although twice the size of Belgium, Svalbard's human population is **outnumbered** by polar bears. **Ironically**, one picture captured by the group shows a team member holding a discarded plastic bag with the logo of a polar bear and the word Svalbardbutikken—a supermarket on the island.

7　The group **trawled for** microplastics (塑料微粒) and large floating plastics in the water. They also tested the air for microplastic fibres, listened for underwater noise pollution, and did beach cleans. The team found plastics on beaches at every site they surveyed, including some that must have travelled long distances.

8　Flora Rendell-Bhatti, a researcher from the University of Exeter, said: "As plastic pollution **breaks down** it is harder to identify the sources of the fragments (碎片) and fibres by eye." Our microplastic net sampled the surface waters in areas where there is currently little research. "Once the samples are analysed back in the UK, this data will indicate the levels of microplastic pollution in Arctic waters around Svalbard."

9　With **currents** reaching Svalbard from both the Atlantic and Siberia, debris can arrive from far away. Local beach cleaners have reportedly found plastic waste **traceable** even to Florida. The group said this was inevitably having an impact on Arctic wildlife.

10　⑤According to the researchers, almost 90 per cent of fulmars (管鼻藿)—a white seabird related to the albatross (信天翁)—around the island have been found to have plastic in their **guts**, with an average of 15 pieces per animal.

11　The team spent a few days in Svalbard's capital Longyearbyen (朗伊尔城) after the expedition to find out about the initiatives **under way** to clean up **hazardous** litter from the island's remote beaches.

◆ 课文小助手

一、生词和词块释义

unsettling /ʌnˈsetliŋ/ *adj.* 令人担忧的

sibling /ˈsibliŋ/ *n.* 兄弟姐妹

navigate /ˈnævigeit/ *v.* 航行

expedition /ˌekspiˈdiʃən/ *n.* 考察

stunning /ˈstʌniŋ/ *adj.* 极美的

sobering /ˈsəubəriŋ/ *adj.* 令人警醒的

marine /məˈriːn/ *adj.* 海的

blight /blait/ *v.* 破坏

detritus /diˈtraitəs/ *n.* 垃圾

isolated /ˈaisəleitid/ *adj.* 偏远的

outnumber /autˈnʌmbə/ *v.*（在数量上）压倒

ironically /aiˈrɔnikli/ *adv.* 讽刺地

discard /disˈkɑːd/ *v.* 丢弃

current /ˈkʌrənt/ *n.*（海洋或江河的）水流，潮流

traceable /ˈtreisəbl/ *adj.* 可追踪的

gut /gʌt/ *n.* 胃

hazardous /ˈhæzədəs/ *adj.* 有危害的

stands out 显眼

make its way 前往

trawl for 搜集

break down 分解

under way 进行中的

二、话题概要

大意：研究人员在北极海岸发现大量塑料，危及当地野生动物的健康。

Para. 1–3：有照片显示，两只北极熊宝宝在挪威的斯瓦尔巴特群岛一个海岸上抓挠塑料片玩，之后还将其放入口中，画面令人担忧。研究人员还发现塑料垃圾在此岛随处可见。

Para. 4–5：一位北极考察队员表示北极之美虽令人震撼，塑料之多却令人警醒。她指出：人类的生活垃圾构成了海滩垃圾的一大部分。

Para. 6–8：研究人员在斯瓦尔巴特群岛取样的过程中，甚至发现了由岛上超市丢弃的塑料袋。实际上，在他们所调查的每个海滩上都有塑料的存在，这其中包括一些远途漂流至此的塑料。研究人员对于塑料微粒的采样区域覆盖面广，故最终得到的数据将能够真实表明斯瓦尔巴特群岛的北极水域中由塑料微粒造成的污染程度。

Para. 9–10：因受海潮影响，塑料垃圾可能自远途而来，甚至是来自佛罗里达。而这无疑将对北极野生动物造成影响。研究小组已经发现几乎 90% 的管鼻藿胃中都含有大量塑料片。

Para. 11：研究小组在斯瓦尔巴特群岛的首都停留了几日，来调查该群岛目前对偏远海滩垃圾的清理措施。

◆ 同步练习

一、长难句翻译（见文章划线处）

二、词块填空

1. The police are _____ similar cases through their files.

2. Every tree, wall and fence _____ against dazzling white fields.

3. As far as we know, the substance is easily _____ by bacteria.

4. No one has claimed responsibility for the attack—and investigations are _____.

5. In 1959, the Barbie doll _____ to the New York Toy Show and receive a cool reception from the toy buyers.

三、佳句模仿

原文佳句	With currents reaching Svalbard from both the Atlantic and Siberia, debris can arrive from far away.
亮点评析	该句的原因状语部分为 With + n. + 补语的复合结构。
写作应用	1. With the wind picking up gradually, he decided that it was time to return home. 随着风力逐渐加强，他确定这是到了回家的时候了。 2. With the noise gone, he picked up his book again. 噪音停了，他把书又拿了起来。

◆ 答案

一、长难句翻译

1. 当小北极熊们对塑料又抓又挠，然后将其放到嘴里的时候，那些黑色的塑料在看起来一尘不染的风景里极其醒目。

2. "然而，这也是一次非常令人警醒的经历，因为（我们）看到那么多的塑料来到这极其偏远、显然并未开发的环境中。"

3. 沃勒斯坦女士说："令人伤心的是：我们在海滩上发现的东西和我们在家里发现的东西没有很大的不同。"

4. "那里有很多捕鱼留下的垃圾，但是最令人伤心的是破坏北极环境的绝大部分污染物依然是我们日常生活中的那些一次性垃圾——塑料瓶、棉签棒、香烟头、湿巾、聚苯乙烯和食物包装物。"

5. 据研究人员所言，几乎 90% 的生活在海岛周围的管鼻鹱（一种与信天翁有关联的白色海鸟）都被发现胃里有塑料，而且平均每只鸟的胃里就有 15 片。

二、词块填空

1. trawling for

2. stood out

3. broken down

4. under way

5. made her way

09 WeWork Says It Will Be "Meat-Free" Organization[M]

WeWork 公司声明要做"无肉"组织

Network of office spaces seeks to become more environmentally friendly

1 Some companies ask employees to reduce paper waste with less printing. Others have made their data centers run on renewable energy to help address climate change. Most offer recycling bins next to the copy machine.

2 But WeWork is trying a new **tactic** in the push toward corporate sustainability by saying it **is committed to** being "a meat-free organization." The global network of shared office spaces said in an email to employees last week that "moving forward, we will not serve or pay for meat at WeWork events and want to clarify that this includes poultry (家禽肉) and pork, as well as red meat." The company's co-founder and chief culture officer, Miguel McKelvey, said the new policy was one way it could do more to become environmentally conscious.

3 ①After the policy **garnered** headlines over the weekend, sustainability experts said it is rare—even as employers become more focused on showcasing their environmental friendliness—to see companies make a direct connection between meat and climate emissions. ②And such environmentally tied policies on employee behavior—such as tracking printing habits or financial rewards for public **transit** use—could be a sign of things to come, as employers **seek to** prove their environmental mettle (魄力) with millennial (千禧年的) workers attracted by such progressive policies.

4 ③"It's a sign of the way things are moving, as employees today expect employers to have a social and environmental **conscience**," said Virginia Hoekenga, **deputy** director of the National Association for Environmental Management, an association of corporate environmental, health, safety and sustainability leaders, most of whom work for large corporations. Companies

"understand it's a talent war out there, and employees are looking for employers that are demonstrating their commitment to environmental progress."

5   While many companies **institute** environmental policies to help with energy consumption and improve the bottom line, they are also taking measures that are more visible to workers, Hoekenga said. Many are offering financial incentives to reward public transit, composting food in the corporate cafeteria or adding green roofs to buildings to advertise their environmental awareness, even while they also take behind-the-scenes measures to reduce **toxicity**（毒性） in manufacturing or change industrial lighting to LEDs. American Airlines and Starbucks both recently said they would **phase out** plastic straws.

6   In the letter to employees, McKelvey pointed to research showing that avoiding meat has an environmental impact that could **outweigh** the use of a **hybrid** car, suggesting that WeWork could save an estimated 16.7 billion gallons of water, 445.1 million pounds of carbon dioxide emissions and more than 15 million animals by 2023 by **eliminating** meat at company events.

7   How exactly the policy would be enforced is unclear. Gwen Rocco, senior director of corporate communications at WeWork, said in an email that although the meat-free initiative does extend to expenses, the company would not comment further about how it would distinguish between, say, meat and vegetarian dishes listed on a submitted restaurant receipt.

8   WeWork's effort does not mean that employees or members who work in its facilities cannot bring their own meat, or that members can't serve meat at their own events. The effort **applies** only **to** food purchased with WeWork money, and fish is not included in its initiative.

9   While the effort was announced by WeWork leadership, employees have previously pushed for other sustainability measures, such as hosting 100 percent plastic-free events in Montreal or efforts at two buildings in London that have gone "zero plastic," Rocco said.

10 The concept of a meat-free workplace is not **unprecedented**. [4]For instance, the Physicians Committee for Responsible Medicine, a nonprofit group that promotes preventive medicine and nutrition issues, has mandated（强制执行）vegan only food in its Washington office, home to about 80 staff members, since the 1980s. Google has been experimenting with "plant-forward" recipes that **nudge** employees toward less animal protein at its offices, Fast Company reported in

2017. And an organization called Vegan Leaders in Corporate Management launched a program last year to help companies embrace vegan trends as part of their employee wellness programs.

11 The activist group PETA also has a "Meatless Monday" workplace initiative, and said in an emailed statement that it is sending a "**Compassionate** Business Award" to WeWork for the new policy. PETA's offices have been meat-free for "decades," said PETA media liaison Sofia Chauvet. Hoekenga said that WeWork's connection between meat production and climate change is surprising—"that's bold of them to be so direct"—but that food in the workplace is becoming a focus for companies in their sustainability efforts.

12 ⑤"My best guess is most of the companies I would consider in the **forefront** of corporate America have already addressed a lot of food-waste issues, and sourcing (从……处获得) locally is making its way into cafeterias," she said. Workplace menus with a conscience are "not a brand-new idea, but it's really being **pushed forward** and embraced by a younger workforce."

◆ 课文小助手

一、生词和词块释义

tactic /'tæktik/ *n.* 策略

garner /'gɑ:nə/ *v.* 得到

transit /'trænzɪt/ *n.* 交通运输系统

conscience /'kɔnʃəns/ *n.* 良知

deputy /'depjuti/ *adj.* 副的

institute /'institjut/ *v.* 实行

outweigh /ˌaut'wei/ *v.*（在重要性或意义上）超过

hybrid /'haibrid/ *adj.* 混合动力的

eliminate /i'limineit/ *v.* 根除

unprecedented /ʌn'presidəntid/ *adj.* 前所未有的

nudge /nʌdʒ/ *v.* 把……轻轻地推动

compassionate /kəm'pæʃənit/ *adj.* 表示同情的

forefront /'fɔ:frʌnt/ *n.* 前沿

be committed to 致力于

seek to do sth. 争取

phase out 逐步淘汰

apply to 适用于

push forward 推进

二、话题概要

大意：WeWork 公司提出了将在该公司的所有活动中都实行"无肉"策略，以促进生态环境的改善。

Para. 1–2: 在各个公司不尽相同的环保措施中，WeWork 公司的"无肉"策略显得很有新意。

Para. 3–4: 可持续发展专家认为 WeWork 公司的"无肉"策略相当难得，它证明了该公司领导人的环保魄力，也因其进步性吸引着千禧年代的劳动者。

Para. 5: 除了幕后措施之外，许多公司目前也实行了员工易见的环保措施，诸如经济激励。

Para. 6–8: WeWork 公司的负责人告知员工"无肉"措施对于节能、减排、保护动物都有着巨大的好处。但该公司将如何贯彻这一措施目前并不清楚。可以确定的是，除了鱼肉，WeWork 将不再出资购买其他肉类。

Para. 9: WeWork 公司的员工们之前也曾开展过其他的促进可持续发展的活动。

Para. 10: "无肉工作场所"这一概念并非前所未有，美国医师医药责任协会就一直在其华盛顿办公点实行素食主义，而谷歌公司也在尝试推行"植物优先"的菜单。一家名为"企业管理中的素食领导者"的组织也曾帮助一些公司实行素食主义，以促进员工的健康。

Para. 11: 一个名为 PETA 的行动小组也奉行了几十年的无肉办公政策。该行动小组的 Hoekenga 认为将肉食生产和气候改变联系起来着实为一个大胆的举措，但是为实现可持续发展，诸多公司将要以食物为中心了。

Para. 12: PETA 行动小组的 Hoekenga 猜测美国的重要企业中的大部分应该已经着手处

理了许多与食物浪费有关的问题，并实现了餐厅从当地进货。

◆ **同步练习**

一、长难句翻译（见文章划线处）

二、词块填空

1. The manager told us that the old machinery there would be _____ soon.

2. Despite the difficulties, it's important to _____ and complete the project.

3. Once you have acquired these skills, you must constantly _____ improve them.

4. It is stressed that these regulations _____ everyone in the company, without exception.

5. Our software company is _____ openness, innovation and the protection of privacy on the Internet.

三、佳句模仿

原文佳句	"It's a sign of the way things are moving…and sustainability leaders, most of whom work for large corporations."
亮点评析	该句的定语从句部分的结构为不定代词(most) + of + 关系代词 (whom)。在这个结构中还可能出现的其他不定代词有 few，some，any，all，none 等。
写作应用	1. We are constantly surrounded by noise, most of which is beyond our hearing range unless we hold something like a seashell close to one of our ears. 我们处在持续的杂音包围之中，其中大部分杂音我们是听不见的，除非把贝壳之类的东西靠近耳边才能听到。 2. Jerry turned to his friends for help, none of whom, however, lent him any money. 杰瑞向他的朋友们求助。然而，没有任何人借给他一点点钱。

◆ **答案**

一、长难句翻译

1. 在周末的两天里，该政策成为了头条新闻。之后，可持续发展的专家提出：即使在雇主们越来越关注如何展示他们的环保意识的当下，将肉食与温室气体的排放直接联系起来的公司也是罕见的。

2. 另外，当雇主们试图证明他们的环保魄力，而千禧年后出生的工作者们恰恰会被这样进步性政策吸引的时候，这些与环保有关的、规范员工行为的政策也许能够表明未来的发展方向。

3.“这表明了事情的发展方向，因为如今的员工们期待雇主们有社会良心和环境的良知。”国家环境管理协会副主任霍伊肯加·弗吉尼亚说。该协会是一个涉及企业环境、健康、安全和可持续发展的领导者协会，成员中的大部分来自于大企业。

4. 例如，美国医师医药责任协会是一家宣传预防性药品和营养问题的非营利性组织。它自 20 世纪 80 年代起至今，一直在其华盛顿的办公点强制执行素食政策，该办公点有 80 多名员工。

5. 她说：“我最好的估计是大部分我所认为的美国领头公司已经处理了许多与食物浪费有关的问题，并且从当地进货已逐渐成为餐厅的一项举措。”

二、词块填空

1. phased out

2. push forward

3. seek to

4. apply to

5. committed to

10 Drinking in the Last-chance Saloon[M]

北白犀最后的希望

1 Sudan, the last male northern white rhinoceros on Earth, died in March. ①He **is survived by** two females, Najin and her daughter Fatu, who live in a **conservancy in Kenya**. This pair are thus the only remaining members of the world's most endangered **subspecies** of mammal. But  all might not yet be lost. Thomas Hildebrandt of the Leibniz Institute for Zoo and Wildlife Research, in Berlin, **in collaboration with** Avantea, a biotechnology company in Cremona, Italy, is proposing **heroic** measures to keep the subspecies alive. In a paper just published in Nature, he and his colleagues say that they have created, by **in vitro fertilisation** (IVF), apparently **viable** hybrid embryos of northern white rhinos and their cousins from the south. This, they hope, will **pave the way for** the creation of pure northern-white embryos.

2 IVF seems the last hope for the northern white rhino. Though stored sperm from Sudan and several other males are available, both Najin and Fatu now seem unable to **conceive**. ②This means, if the subspecies is to be preserved, that one or both of them will have to have some eggs removed from their ovaries (卵巢) and **combined with** stored sperm in a Petri dish (培养皿).

3 Extracting rhinoceros eggs is hard. ③The animals' ovaries are over a metre deep inside them, meaning that the **extraction** procedure, which employs a **probe** with a sharp needle attached to it to suck the eggs out, is **hazardous**. But practice makes perfect, so the team started by obtaining instead some eggs from a southern white rhino, the northern's close cousin. They combined these with some of their **cache** of northern sperm and **coaxed** seven of the resulting zygotes (受精卵) through the early stages of embryonic (胚胎的) development, to the point where they could be implanted in the uterus (子宫) of a southern white, who would act as a **surrogate** mother, with a reasonable hope of success.

4 That has not yet happened. The seven embryos are now in a freezer awaiting the results of research on how best to transfer them to surrogates. In the meantime, having proved their

44

technique with these hybrids, Dr Hildebrandt and his colleagues now hope to create more embryos, this time using eggs from the two remaining female northern whites.

5　^④<u>Even if they succeed, though, it will be a long **haul** back for the northern white rhino.</u> Members of any new generation resulting from IVF will have then to be bred with each other to create **subsequent** generations. It is not so much a gene pool that Dr Hildebrandt is working with as a gene **puddle**.

6　Then there is the question of what to do with the resulting animals. Analysis of other rhinoceros species, both in Africa and Asia, points to a viable population in the wild needing to be at least 500 strong. ^⑤<u>Even if such a group could be created, and not collapse from lack of genetic diversity, releasing it into the tender mercies of what remains of Kenya's savannah (大草原) would be risky.</u> The reason the northern white has come so close to extinction—**poaching**—is unlikely to go away anytime soon.

7　Dr Hildebrandt's work is thus a half step along what **is likely to** be a very long road indeed. **Charismatic** megafauna (巨型动物) rhinoceroses may be. But whether that charisma can sustain enough effort for long enough to save the northern white is about to be tested.

◆ 课文小助手

一、生词和词块释义

conservancy /kən'sɜːvənsɪ/ *n.* 自然保护机构

subspecies /'sʌbˌspiːʃiːz/ *n.* 动植物的亚种

heroic /hɪ'rəʊɪk/ *adj.* 英雄的

viable /'vaɪəbl/ *adj.* 可存活的

conceive /kən'siːv/ *v.* 怀孕

extraction /ɪk'strækʃən/ *n.* 提取

probe /prəʊb/ *n.* 探测器

hazardous /'hæzədəs/ *adj.* 危险的

cache /kæʃ/ *n.* 储存

coax /kəʊks/ *v.* 精心摆弄

surrogate /'sʌrəgɪt/ *adj.* 代替的

haul /hɔːl/ *n.* 耗时费力的事

subsequent /'sʌbsɪkwənt/ *adj.* 随后的

puddle /'pʌdl/ *n.* 水坑

poach /pəʊtʃ/ *v.* 偷猎

charismatic /ˌkærɪz'mætɪk/ *adj.* 充满魅力的

be survived by 遗留下

in collaboration with 与……合作

in vitro fertilisation 试管受精

pave the way for 为……做准备 / 铺平道路

combine with 与……结合

be likely to 有可能

二、话题概要

大意: 在试管受精技术支持下，世界濒危动物白犀牛有了最后的希望。

Para. 1: 世界上最后一头雄性北白犀已经死去，留下了两只雌性北白犀，成为世界上最后的北白犀。Hildebrandt 博士与一个生物技术公司合作，正在使用试管受精技术创造出杂交胚胎，并为纯种北白犀胚胎制造做准备。

Para. 2–4: 对于北白犀来说试管受精是最后的希望了。尽管有一些雄性北白犀的精子被保存下来，但剩下的两头雌性北白犀似乎不能受孕。这就意味着只能通过提取卵子并与所储存的精子结合的方式来制造受精卵。然而获取犀牛的卵子并不简单，但在团队的努力下他们成功制造了七个受精卵。这七个受精卵即将放入一头雌性南白犀的子宫中。但该实验还未开始，因为该团队正在做相关研究。

Para. 5–6: 然而即使这项工程成功了，这也是一件长期费时费力的事情。如果一个物种在野外要存活，至少需要 500 只；即使这么多能够被创造出来，把他们放到大草原上也是很冒险的事情；与此同时，偷猎的行为总是不断出现。

Para. 7: Hildebrandt 博士的工作只是走到了漫漫长路的一半，是否这种大型动物的魅力能够保持下去还有待测试。

◆ 同步练习

一、长难句翻译（见文章划线处）

二、词块填空

1. He _____ his wife and two sons.

2. The experiment will_____ a real Mars expedition later this century.

3. The two playwrights worked _____ each other on the script.

4. Do remind me because I_____ forget.

5. Sickness, _____ terrible weather ruined the trip.

三、佳句模仿

原文佳句	Dr Hildebrandt and his colleagues now hope to create more embryos, this time using eggs from the two remaining female northern whites.
亮点评析	该句中，using 引导方式状语。
写作应用	We made great achievement, making use of the books he had lent to us. 通过使用他借给我们的书，我们取得了巨大的成就。

◆ 答案

一、长难句翻译

1. 他死去后遗留下来了两只雌性北白犀，Najin 和她的女儿 Fatu，这两只雌性北白犀住在肯尼亚的一个自然保护机构里。

2. 这意味着，如果这个亚种要被保存下来，那么必须从她们两只中的一只或两只的卵巢里头提取卵子并与储存在培养皿里的精子结合。

3. 这种动物的卵巢在她们身体的一米深的地方，这就意味着用带着尖尖的针的探测器去吸出卵子的提取过程是非常危险的。

4. 即使他们成功了，对北白犀来说都是一个耗时费力的事情。

5. 即使这样的一群北白犀能够被创造出来，并且没有因为缺乏基因多样化而垮掉，把他们放回到肯尼亚大草原也是十分冒险的。

二、词块填空

1. is survived by

2. pave the way for

3. in collaboration with

4. am likely to

5. combined with

11 The world Is Losing the War Against Climate Change[M]

人类正在输掉与气候变化的斗争

> Rising energy demand means use of fossil fuels is heading in the wrong direction

1 Earth is **smouldering**. From Seattle to Siberia this summer, flames have consumed swathes (大块田地) of the northern hemisphere. ①One of 18 wildfires sweeping through California, among the worst in the state's history, is generating such heat that it created its own weather. Fires that **raged** through a coastal area near Athens last week killed 91. Elsewhere people are **suffocating** in the heat. Roughly 125 have died in Japan as the result of a heatwave that pushed temperatures in Tokyo above 40°C for the first time.

2 Such **calamities**, once considered freakish (反常的), are now commonplace. Scientists have long cautioned that, as the planet warms—it is roughly 1°C hotter today than before the industrial age's first **furnaces** were lit—weather patterns will go berserk (失控的). ②An early analysis has found that this sweltering (热极了的) European summer would have been less than half as likely were it not for human-**induced** global warming.

3 Yet as the impact of climate change becomes more evident, so too does the scale of the challenge ahead. Three years after countries vowed in Paris to keep warming "well below" 2°C relative to pre-industrial levels, greenhouse-gas emissions are up again. So are investments in oil and gas. In 2017, for the first time in four years, demand for coal rose. ③**Subsidies** for **renewables**, such as wind and solar power, are **dwindling** in many places and investment has **stalled**; climate-friendly nuclear power is expensive and unpopular. It is tempting to think these are temporary setbacks and that mankind, with its **instinct** for self-preservation, will **muddle through** to a victory over global warming. In fact, it is losing the war.

4 ④Insufficient progress is not to say no progress at all. As solar panels, wind turbines (涡轮机) and other low-carbon technologies become cheaper and more efficient, their use has surged. Last year the number of electric cars sold around the world passed 1m. In some sunny and blustery (狂风大

作的) places renewable power now costs less than coal. Public concern is **picking up**. A poll last year of 38 countries found that 61% of people see climate change as a big threat.

5　Optimists say that decarbonisation (去碳化) is **within reach**. Yet, even allowing for the familiar complexities of agreeing on and enforcing global targets, it is proving extraordinary difficult.

6　One reason is soaring energy demand, especially in developing Asia. In 2006-16, as Asia's emerging economies **forged** ahead, their energy consumption rose by 40%. The use of coal, easily the dirtiest fossil fuel, grew at an annual rate of 3.1%. Use of cleaner natural gas grew by 5.2% and of oil by 2.9%. Fossil fuels are easier to **hook up** to today's **grids** than renewables that depend on the sun shining and the wind blowing. [5]Even as green fund managers threaten to pull back from oil companies, state-owned behemoths (庞然大物) in the Middle East and Russia see Asian demand as a **compelling** reason to invest.

7　The second reason is economic and political **inertia**. The more fossil fuels a country consumes, the harder it is to **wean** itself **off** them. Powerful lobbies, and the voters who back them, entrench coal in the energy mix. Reshaping existing ways of doing things can take years. In 2017 Britain enjoyed its first coal-free day since **igniting** the Industrial Revolution in the 1800s. Coal generates not merely 80% of India's electricity, but also **underpins** the economies of some of its poorest states. Panjandrums in Delhi **are** not **keen to** countenance (赞同) the end of coal, **lest** that cripple the banking system, which lent it too much money, and the railways, which depend on it.

8　Last is the technical challenge of stripping carbon out of industries beyond power generation. Steel, cement, farming, transport and other forms of economic activity account for over half of global carbon emissions. They are technically harder to clean up than power generation and are protected by vested industrial interests. Successes can turn out to be **illusory**. [6]Also, scrubbing CO_2 from the atmosphere, which climate models imply is needed on a vast scale to meet the Paris target, attracts even less attention.

9　The world is not short of ideas to realise the Paris goal. Around 70 countries or regions, responsible for one-fifth of all emissions, now price carbon. Technologists **beaver away** on sturdier grids, zero-carbon steel, even carbon-negative cement, whose production absorbs more CO_2 than it releases. All these efforts and more—including research into "solar geoengineering (地质工程)" to reflect sunlight back into space—should be redoubled.

◆ 课文小助手

一、生词和词块释义

smoulder /ˈsməʊldə/ v. 焖烧

rage /reɪdʒ/ v. 肆虐

suffocate /ˈsʌfəkeɪt/ v. 使……窒息

calamity /kəˈlæmɪtɪ/ n. 灾难

furnace /ˈfɜːnɪs/ n. 熔炉

induce /ɪnˈdjuːs/ v. 诱发

subsidy /ˈsʌbsɪdɪ/ n. 津贴

renewables /rɪˈnjuːəblz/ n. 可再生能源

dwindle /ˈdwɪndl/ v. 减少

stall /stɔːl/ v. 搁置

instinct /ˈɪnstɪŋkt/ n. 本能

forge /fɔːdʒ/ v. 创造，形成

grid /grɪd/ n. 网格

compelling /kəmˈpelɪŋ/ adj. 强有力的

inertia /ɪˈnɜːʃə/ n. 惰性

ignite /ɪgˈnaɪt/ v. 激起

underpin /ʌndəˈpɪn/ v. 巩固

lest /lest/ conj. 唯恐

cripple /ˈkrɪpl/ v. 使……受损

illusory /ɪˈljuːsərɪ/ adj. 幻觉的

scrub /skrʌb/ v. 清理

muddle through 胡乱应付过去

pick up 提高，好起来

within reach 触手可及

hook up 连接到

wean off 戒掉

be keen to 热衷于

beaver away 勤奋工作

二、话题概要

大意: 地球正被焖烧，虽然各方都在努力，但在与温室气体抗争的这一场斗争中，人类似乎并没有取得胜利。

Para. 1–2: 从西雅图到西伯利亚，大片的火苗在北半球肆虐。高温气候在北半球不断出现，已经导致很多人死亡。而这些曾经被认为是反常的气候灾难现在变得很普遍。科学家们认为，随着地球的变暖，天气模式将会失控。

Para. 3–4: 气候变化的影响变得越来越明显，人类面临的挑战也越来越大。各国在巴黎决定将地球温度保持在一定程度，但三年之后温室气体的排放再次上升。2017 年对煤的需求量增高，这是近四年来第一次出现这样的情况。在对抗气候变暖的斗争中，人类遇到了挫败，并且正在输掉这场战争。但进步不足并不代表没有进步。现在绿色能源变得更加便宜、更加高效，使用率也猛增。越来越多的人也开始关注这个问题。

Para. 5–8: 乐观主义者认为去碳化已经近在咫尺，但实际上仍然任重道远。第一个原因就是猛增的能源需求，发展中的亚洲尤为需求巨大。每年的煤炭使用量都在增加。第二个原因则是经济和政治的惰性，一个国家越多地使用化石能源，这个国家越是难以戒掉它们。最后一个原因则是将碳从各个行业中剥离出来的技术挑战。钢铁、水泥、农业、交通等行业活

动排放了大量的碳，要将碳从这些行业剥离出去，并非易事。

Para. 9: 要实现《巴黎协议》的目标我们并不缺办法：各国在为碳定价，技术人员也在勤奋工作以实现碳剥离。而这些所有的努力都应该加倍。

◆ 同步练习

一、长难句翻译（见文章划线处）

二、词块填空

1. Trade has been slack for the past year,but it is _____ now.

2. I can _____ to the library from my computer.

3. They are _____ to get everything ready for us.

4. They are in trouble, but they may be able to _____ the next five years like this.

5. I like to keep a notebook and pencil _____.

三、佳句模仿

原文佳句	An early analysis has found that this sweltering European summer would have been less than half as likely were it not for human-induced global warming.
亮点评析	这是一个复合句，后半部分的条件句将 were 放在了句首，省略了 if。
写作应用	Were she here, she would agree too. 如果她在这里，她也会同意的。

原文佳句	Around 70 countries or regions, responsible for one-fifth of all emissions, now price carbon.
亮点评析	price 在这里是 "为……定价" 的意思。
写作应用	The car is priced at £28 000. 这辆车定价 2.8 万英镑。

◆ 答案

一、长难句翻译

1. 在加利福尼亚历史上最大的十八场野火中，有一场导致极高的温度，以至于在该州形成了其特殊的天气。

2. 早期的分析发现，如果不是人类导致的全球变暖，这热极了的欧洲夏天出现的概率有可能减小一半。

3. 对可再生能源，如风能、太阳能等的补贴在许多地方都正在减少，投资也被搁置了；而对气候友好的核能，是又昂贵，又不受到欢迎。

4. 进步不充分并不代表完全没有进步。

5. 即使有绿色基金会的管理人员威胁说要从石油公司撤出，中东地区和俄罗斯的国有大型企业把亚洲对石油的需求作为一个投资的强有力的理由。

6. 同时，根据气候模式，要达到《巴黎协定》中的目标需要大量地把二氧化碳从大气中去除，但这一工作却越来越不受关注。

二、词块填空

1. picking up

2. hook up

3. beavering away

4. muddle through

5. within reach

12 Climate Change: The Long Hot Summer[A]

气候变化：夏天炎热且漫长

1　Sodankyla, a town in Finnish Lapland just north of the Arctic Circle, **boasts** an average annual temperature a little below freezing. Residents eagerly await the brief **spell** in July when the region enjoys something **akin to** summer. On July 18th thermometers (温度计) showed 32.1°C, which is 12°C warmer than typical for the month and the highest since records began in 1908. But Sodankyla is not the only place that is **sizzling**. Sweden has suffered **a rash of** forest fires, **sparked** by unusually hot and dry weather. Japan has declared its heatwave to be a natural disaster. <u>①That seems positively **nippy compared with** Quriyat in Oman, which recorded a 24-hour minimum temperature of 42.6°C a few days earlier.</u>

2　Heatwaves bring problems, especially in the developing world. Crops are **ravaged**, food spoils and workers become less productive. Studies have linked rising temperatures to violent crime and civil strife (内乱). And heat can kill **on its own**. In 2003 more than 70,000 Europeans may have died as a direct result of an **infernal** summer.

3　That was seen as a once-a-millennium heatwave at the time. <u>②**By comparison**, notes Geert Jan van Oldenborgh of the Royal Netherlands Meteorological Institute (荷兰皇家气象研究所), outside of northern Europe the summer of 2018 looks **unremarkable**, so far, in terms of temperature.</u> The Netherlands, for instance, can expect scorchers every couple of years. Except, he adds, a century ago that might have been once every 20 years.

4　<u>③No consequence of global warming is as **self-evident**</u> as higher temperatures. Earth is roughly 1°C hotter today than it was before humanity started **belching** greenhouse gases into the atmosphere during the Industrial Revolution. <u>④If this so-called thermodynamic effect (热力学效应) were all there was to it, temperatures now considered unusually hot would become more typical and those regarded as uncommonly cold, uncommoner still.</u> But climate being a complicated thing, there is more to it.

5　Weather patterns can change because the colder poles warm faster than **balmier** lower latitudes

(纬度). As the thermal (热的) difference between the two **diminishes**, so does the velocity (速度) of the jet stream (急流), a westerly wind which blows at an altitude of around 10km. That means the weather it carries can **stay in place** for longer. Sometimes, it **offsets** the thermodynamic effects, leading to cooler temperatures than might be expected.

6　When and by how much is a matter of hot debate among climate scientists. It is hard to **pin** any particular heatwave, drought or flood **on** the effects of man-made pollution. ⑤<u>**Freak** events happen; the highest temperature ever recorded on Earth was 56.7°C in Death Valley, California, but that was on July 10th 1913, when concentrations (浓度) of carbon dioxide in the atmosphere were much lower.</u>

7　By using clever statistics to compare the climate's actual behaviour with computer simulations (计算机模拟) of how it might have behaved **in the absence of** human activity, researchers can calculate how mankind has made a particular weather event more likely. The first such study, co-authored by Dr Stott in 2004, found that the likelihood of the 2003 European summer had doubled as a result of human activity. Since then similar "event attribution" (事件归因) research has **burgeoned**. A year ago Carbon Brief, a web portal (门户网站), identified a total of 138 peer-reviewed (同行评议) papers in the field, covering 144 weather events. Of 48 heatwaves, 41 contained humankind's **imprint** in the data.

8　⑥<u>Besides **scrutinising** past weather, many of the studies **look ahead**—in particular at how the likelihood of future extreme events changes depending on how seriously countries take their commitment in Paris in 2015 to limit global warming to "well below" 2°C **relative to** pre-industrial levels.</u>

9　The picture that emerges is **bleak**. It looks even more alarming if you **factor in** humidity (湿度). Human beings can tolerate heat with sweat, which **evaporates** and cools the skin. That is why a dry 50°C can feel less **stifling** than a **muggy** 30°C. If the wet-bulb temperature exceeds 35°C, even a fit, healthy youngster **lounging** naked in the shade next to a fan could die in six hours.

10　At present, wet-bulb temperatures seldom exceed 31°C. In 2016 Jeremy Pal of Loyola Marymount University and Elfatih of the Massachusetts Institute for Technology found that if carbon emissions continue **unabated**, several cities in the Persian Gulf, including Abu Dhabi and Dubai, could exceed wet-bulb levels of 35°C by the end of the century. A follow-up study **reckoned** that, by 2100, parts of South Asia, which is much more **populous** than the sheikhdoms (酋长国) and a lot poorer, could suffer a wet-bulb level of 34.2°C every 25 years.

11   The effects could be **devastating**. The World Bank has warned that rising temperatures and changing monsoons (雨季) could cost India 2.8% of GDP per person by 2050 and affect the living standards of 600m Indians in areas identified as **hot spots**. The global cost of productivity lost to heat has been estimated at $2trn by 2030.

12   The **toll** on human lives is hard to imagine. But at least people can learn from past mistakes. Thanks to better government responses, particularly in care for the elderly, in 2012 Europe survived a summer hotter still than 2003 with fewer **casualties**. As Indians get richer more will be able to afford air-conditioning; even those in shantytowns (棚户区) can paint their corrugated-iron (波状钢) roofs white to reflect sunlight. If only the world could **take in** a similar lesson about the importance of stopping climate change **in the first place**.

◆ 课文小助手

一、生词和词块释义

boast /bəʊst/ vt. 有（值得自豪的东西）

spell /spel/ n. （持续的）一段时间

sizzling /ˈsɪzlɪŋ/ adj. 酷热的

spark /spɑːk/ vt. 引发

nippy /ˈnɪpɪ/ adj. 寒冷的

ravage /ˈrævɪdʒ/ vt. 毁坏

infernal /ɪnˈfɜːnəl/ adj. 极讨厌的

unremarkable /ˌʌnrɪˈmɑːkəbl/ adj. 不显著的

scorcher /ˈskɔːtʃə(r)/ n. 大热天

self-evident adj. 显而易见的

belch /beltʃ/ v. （大量）喷出

balmy /ˈbɑːmɪ/ adj. 温暖惬意的

diminish /dɪˈmɪnɪʃ/ v. 减少

offset /ˈɒfset/ vt. 抵消

freak /friːk/ adj. 反常的

burgeon /ˈbɜːdʒən/ v. 激增

imprint /ɪmˈprɪnt/ n. 印记

scrutinise /ˈskruːtɪnaɪz/ vt. 仔细查看

bleak /bliːk/ adj. 暗淡的

evaporate /ɪˈvæpəreɪt/ v. 挥发

stifling /ˈstaɪflɪŋ/ adj. 令人窒息的

muggy /ˈmʌgi/ adj. 闷热潮湿的

lounge /laʊndʒ/ v. 懒洋洋地站（或坐、躺）着

unabated /ˌʌnəˈbeɪtɪd/ adj. 不减的

reckon /ˈrekən/ vt. 认为

populous /ˈpɒpjʊləs/ adj. 人口众多的

devastating /ˈdevəsteɪtɪŋ/ adj. 毁灭性的

toll /təʊl/ n. 毁坏

casualty /ˈkæʒʊəltɪ/ n. 伤亡人员

akin to [something] 与某事物相似

a rash of （涌现的）令人不快的事物

compared with 与……相比

on one's own 单独

by comparison 相比之下

stay in place 呆在原地

pin...on... 把……归咎于

in the absence of 缺乏

look ahead 展望未来

relative to 相对于

factor in 将……考虑进去

hot spot 多事之地

take in 领会

in the first place 起初

二、话题概要

大意：各地气候变暖引发各种问题甚至灾害，这样的天气可能会成为新常态，数据表明人类活动难辞其咎。

Para. 1：各地夏季气温普遍高于往年最高气温，有些地区甚至因为气候干燥、天气炎热引发森林大火。

Para. 2：持续热浪，尤其在发展中国家，引发许多问题，如庄稼歉收、工人效率低下、

暴力犯罪和内乱，甚至炎热本身夺人性命。

Para. 3: 持续热浪在过去是千年一遇，而相比之下，荷兰每隔几年就有大热天，一个世纪前大热天的频率是每 20 年一次。

Para. 4: 气候问题本身就很复杂，远非热力学效应能解释。

Para. 5: 天气模式可能发生变化，因为较冷的两极地区比温和的低纬度地区升温快。

Para. 6: 气温何时变化以及变化的幅度大小，是气候科学家们热议的一个话题。很难把某次热浪、干旱或洪水归咎于人为污染带来的影响。

Para. 7: 通过灵活使用数据比较气候的实际行为和无人类行为干扰下电脑模拟的气候行为，研究者们可以推测人类怎样使某种天气事件更可能发生。第一个此类研究发现，2003 年欧洲热浪发生的几率因为人类活动而翻倍。此后，类似的"事件归因"研究层出不穷。数据中，人类的印记几乎无处不在。

Para. 8–10: 除了研究过去的天气，许多研究着眼预测未来的天气走向。未来前景黯淡，如果考虑湿度的因素，则更令人担忧。如果不减少碳排放，到本世纪末，波斯湾一些城市的气温可能超过湿球温度 35 摄氏度，即便健康的年轻人裸身在树荫下吹着风扇休息，也可能因受不了湿热而在 6 小时内身亡。

Para. 11–12: 气候变暖的影响可能是毁灭性的，既可能损耗国家的国内生产总值，也会影响人民的生活水平，还会降低全球生产力，对人类生命的伤害更是难以估算。唯愿人类当初就意识到阻止气候变化的重要性。

◆ 同步练习

一、长难句翻译（见文章划线处）

二、词块填空

1. Listening to his life story is _____ reading a good adventure novel.

2. The case was dismissed _____ any definite proof.

3. Please mark the position of the sun _____ the earth on the map.

4. Remember to _____ staffing costs when you are planning the project.

5. There has been _____ burglaries in the area over the last month.

6. You can't _____ the blame _____ her—she wasn't even there when the accident happened.

三、佳句模仿

原文佳句	Sweden has suffered a rash of forest fires, sparked by unusually hot and dry weather.

亮点评析	suffer 这里有"深受其害"之意思，a rash of 表示"大量不好的东西出现"，spark 是名词时，作"火花"讲，这里作动词用，表示"引发"，刚好这里是森林大火，过去分词短语的使用更是妙笔生花。
写作应用	Nearby villagers suffered a violent brush fire, sparked by a discarded cigarette. 一个乱扔的烟头引起了一场猛烈的灌木丛火灾，附近的村民们深受其害。

原文佳句	Residents eagerly await the brief spell in July when the region enjoys something akin to summer.
亮点评析	await 一词多用于正式文本，符合文章特点，spell 这里表示"一段时间"，when 引导定语从句。句子简洁，但表现力丰富。
写作应用	Job candidates patiently await their turns to be called to the interview room where they will fully exhibit their talents. 求职者们耐心等待，直到被喊进面试室，充分展示各自的才华。

◆ 答案

一、长难句翻译

1. 那与阿曼的 Quriyat 相比肯定是有点冷啦，因为 Quriyat 几天前创下 24 小时内最低温度 42.6 摄氏度的记录。

2. 相比之下，荷兰皇家气象研究所的 Geert 注意到，迄今为止，2018 年北欧以外的夏季就气温而言，看起来不那么显著。

3. 全球变暖的影响就数气温不断升高是不言自明的了。

4. 如果这所谓的热力学效应可以解释一切的话，那么现在异常高的气温可能变得更典型，而那些被认为罕见的寒冷可能会更罕见。

5. 反常的事情时有发生；地球上有记录的最高气温是 56.7 摄氏度，发生在加利福尼亚的死谷，但那是 1913 年 7 月 10 日，当时大气中二氧化碳的浓度低多了。

6. 除了研究过去的天气，许多研究着眼预测未来，尤其是未来各国兑现 2015 年巴黎承诺的认真程度影响极端天气事件变化的可能性，2015 年各国在巴黎承诺将全球变暖的温度控制在相对于前工业水平时期的 2 摄氏度以下。

二、词块填空

1. akin to

2. in the absence of

3. relative to

4. factor in

5. a rash of

6. pin; on

13 Don't Despair—Climate Change Catastrophe Can Still Be Averted[A]

不要绝望——气候变化灾难仍可能避免

The future looks fiery and dangerous, according to new reports. But political will and grassroots engagement can change this.

Wild fire in Athens, Greece.

1　This is the summer when, for many, climate change got real. The future looks fiery and dangerous. Despair is in the air. ①Now a new scientific report makes the case that even fairly modest future carbon dioxide emissions could set off a cascade of catastrophe, with melting permafrost (永冻层) releasing methane (甲烷) to ratchet up global temperatures enough to drive much of the Amazon to die off, and so on in a chain reaction around the world that pushes Earth into a terrifying new hothouse state from which there is no return. Civilisation as we know it would surely not survive.

2　One common way of thinking about climate change is the lower the future carbon dioxide emissions, the less warming and the less havoc we will face as this century progresses. This is certainly true, but as the summer heatwave and the potential hothouse news remind us, the shifts in climate we will experience will not be smooth, gradual and linear (直线的) changes. They may be fast, abrupt, and dangerous surprises may happen. However, an unstoppable globally enveloping cascade of catastrophe, while possible, is certainly not a probable outcome.

3　Yet, even without a hothouse (温室) we are on track to transform Earth this century. The world, after 30 years of warnings, has barely got to grips with reducing carbon dioxide emissions. ②They need to rapidly decline to zero, but after decades of increases, are, at best, flatlining, with investments in extracting new fossil fuels (矿物燃料) continuing, including last month's scandalous announcement that fracking (水力压裂) will be allowed in the UK. Temperatures have increased just 1℃ above preindustrial levels, and we are on course for another 2℃ or 3℃ on top of that. Could civilisation weather this level of warming?

4 The honest answer is nobody knows. ③Dystopia（反乌托邦）is easy to **envisage**: for example, Europe is not coping well with even modest numbers of migrants, and future flows look likely to increase **substantially** as migration itself is an adaptation to rapid climate change. How will the cooler, richer parts of the world react to tens of millions of people escaping the hotter, poorer parts?

5 ④However, taking a step back from the **gloom**, we face the same three choices **in response to** climate change as we did before this **scorching** summer: reduce greenhouse gas emissions (**mitigation**), make changes to reduce the **adverse** impacts of the new conditions we create (adaptation), or suffer the consequences of what we fail to mitigate or adapt to. It is useful to come back to these three options, and settle on the **formula** that serious mitigation and wise adaptation means little suffering.

6 Despite this basic advice being decades old, we **are heading for** some mitigation, very little adaptation, and a lot of suffering. Why is this happening? This is because while the diagnosis （诊断）of climate change being a problem is a scientific issue, the response to it is not. Leaving fossil fuels in the ground is, for example, a question of regulation, while investing in renewable energy is a policy choice, and modernising our housing stock（住宅）to make it energy efficient is about overcoming the **lobbying** power of the building industry. Solving climate change is about power, money, and political will.

7 And that means talking about climate change and engaging in politics at all levels. One way to put climate change centre stage in the next general election could be to approach the candidates of key marginal seats（边缘席位）to discuss whether they would support serious climate-related legislation（立法）. In return hundreds of supporters of climate legislation would door-knock（挨家挨户征求选票）and leaflet（散发传单）these constituencies（选区选民）to support them. ⑤A serious grassroots conversation would occur, it would become an election issue, and a large group of people outside parliament（议会）and inside it would **be poised to** lobby for the necessary transformative legislation on mitigation and adaptation.

8 Thinking about climate change as a practical political problem helps avoid despair because we know that huge political changes have happened in the past and continue to do so. The future is up to us if we act **collectively** and engage in politics. To **quote** Antonio Gramsci: "I'm a pessimist because of intelligence, but an optimist because of will." Looked at this way, we can see the politics as a battle between a future shaped by fear versus a future shaped by hope.

9   That hope is built on a better story of the future and routes to enact it. Given the colossal wealth and the scientific knowledge available today, we can solve many of the world's pressing problems and all live well. Given that our environmental impacts are so long-lasting, the future is the politics we make today.

◆ 课文小助手

一、生词和词块释义

despair /dɪ'speə(r)/ *v./n.* 绝望

avert /ə'vɜːt/ *vt.* 避免（危险、坏事）

fiery /'faɪərɪ/ *adj.* 火一般的

modest /'mɒdɪst/ *adj.* 不太大（或贵、重要等）的

havoc /'hævək/ *n.* 灾害

envelop /ɪn'veləp/ *vt.* 裹住

flatline /'flætlaɪn/ *vi.* 没有起色

extract /ɪk'strækt/ *vt.* 提取

weather /'weðə(r)/ *vt.* 经受住

envisage /ɪn'vɪzɪdʒ/ *vt.* 想象

substantially /səb'stænʃəlɪ/ *adv.* 大大地

gloom /gluːm/ *n.* 忧郁

scorching /'skɔːtʃɪŋ/ *adj.* 酷热的

mitigation /ˌmɪtɪ'geɪʃən/ *n.* 减轻

adverse /'ædvɜːs/ *adj.* 不利的

formula /'fɔːmjʊlə/ *n.* 方案

lobby /'lɒbɪ/ *v.* 游说（从政者或政府）

collectively /kə'lektɪvlɪ/ *adv.* 共同地

quote /kwəʊt/ *vt.* 引用

pessimist /'pesɪmɪst/ *n.* 悲观主义者

versus /'vɜːsəs/ *prep.* 与……相对

enact /ɪ'nækt/ *vt.* 上演

colossal /kə'lɒsəl/ *adj.* 巨大的

pressing /'presɪŋ/ *adj.* 紧急的

in the air 可感觉到

make the case that... 阐明

set off 引发

a cascade of 瀑布般的

ratchet up 逐步增加

die off 慢慢枯死

on track 步入正轨

get to grips with 开始理解并着手处理难题

on course for （因为已开始做而）很可能做成（或做）

on top of 除……之外

in response to 回应

be heading for sth. 很可能遭受（不幸）

be poised to 准备好

二、话题概要

大意: 未来看似火气冲天、灾难重重，但是政治决心和全民参与还是可以改变一切。

Para. 1: 今夏，气温如此火爆，气候变化绝非虚言。到处弥漫着人类的绝望。气温节节升高，有可能把人类带入一条不归路，文明也将随之毁灭。

Para. 2: 未来的气候变化可能会来势汹汹、毫无规律。

Para. 3–4: 本世纪，人类已步入正轨致力于改变地球，气温相对于前工业水平时期仅仅上升了1摄氏度，有可能在此基础上气温还会再上升2到3摄氏度，可是人类文明能经受住吗？这个问题无人能回答。人类陷入恶劣困境的场景倒是不难想象。

Para. 5: 摆在人类面前的还是那三个选择：减排；调适；坐以待毙。人类要少受罪，是时候确定方案，认真减排，明智调适。

Para. 6–7: 人类一直在减排，也做出不大的调适，但处处受难，原因何在？诊断环境变化问题是科学的分内之事，但对环境变化的应对却非科学所能及，而是关乎权力、金钱和政治意愿的大事。这就意味着全民要关注气候变化，在政治层面参与应对气候变化。

Para. 8–9: 视气候变化为实际的政治问题，有助于规避绝望情绪。未来究竟是充满希望还是充斥恐怖，取决于我们是否集体行动，全民参与政治斗争。希望建立在对未来的美好愿景之上，更是建立在实现美好愿景的具体路线上。凭借巨大的社会财富和发达的科学技术，未来气候如何，就看今天的政治了。

◆ 同步练习

一、长难句翻译（见文章划线处）

二、词块填空

1. We are all in this life together, and helping others achieve their goals can get our own_____.

2. But the bank warned that it was too early to judge whether China was _____ a lasting recovery, despite an even better forecast of 7.7% growth in 2010.

3. The couple looks as though they're _____ divorce.

4. I should have the report ready for you by this afternoon. I just need to _____ this new software update first.

5. It is a fact of the information age that too many movements spring up like beautiful flowers but quickly_____.

6. As the band plays, and with romance_____, Mr. Li recalls how he came to Panzhihua.

三、佳句模仿

原文佳句	Despite this basic advice being decades old, we are heading for some mitigation, very little adaptation, and a lot of suffering.
亮点评析	despite 后使用现在分词短语表让步，后面 some, very little 和 a lot of 依次出现，突出了量上的对比。
写作应用	Despite various efforts being made, we are experiencing some puzzlement, very little satisfaction, and a lot of motivation. 尽管做出的努力各种各样，我们的体验是一些困惑、些许满足和十足的动机。

原文佳句	I'm a pessimist because of intelligence, but an optimist because of will.
亮点评析	pessimist 和 optimist 形成对照，but 后面构成省略，句子言简意赅。
写作应用	I'm a loser because of arrogance, but a winner because of modesty. 傲慢使人失败，谦虚促人成功。

◆ 答案

一、长难句翻译

1. 现在，一份最新的科学报道指出，未来即使相当不起眼的二氧化碳的排放也可能引发一系列灾难，永冻层融化释放出甲烷逐渐推高全球气温，高温甚至可能使亚马逊河日渐干枯，如此等等，在全球形成一个链锁反应，将地球变成一个可怕的不可逆转的温室热球。

2. 二氧化碳的排放必须立即降为零，但是几十年来，二氧化碳的排放量一直只增不减，现在至多也就是维持不变，而对提取矿物燃料的投资活动从未中断，上个月甚至大言不惭地宣布英国将允许使用水力压裂法开采石油。

3. 不难想象未来反乌托邦的场景，比如，欧洲甚至处理不好少量的难民，未来难民的流入量很可能会大大增加，因为迁徙本身就是对气候快速变化的一种调适。

4. 然而，撇开忧郁的前景，就气候变化而言，我们还和以前一样，面前有三个选择：减少温室气体排放（减排），做出改变以减少人类制造的种种新情况带来的负面影响（调适），或者承担因未能减排或调适而带来的后果。

5. 一次严肃的草根谈话应该会发生，它应该成为选举的一个话题，议会内外的一大群人应该做好准备，在减排和调适方面，进行必要的立法改革游说。

二、词块填空

1. on track

2. on course for

3. heading for

4. get to grips with

5. die off

6. in the air

14　Global Warming May Become Unstoppable Even if We Stick to Paris Target[M]

即使我们恪守巴黎目标，全球变暖也可能不可遏止

1　[1]We could be **on the verge** of **triggering** a series of **cascading** tipping points（临界点）that result in the planet warming 4 or 5°C hotter than the pre-industrial **benchmark**.

2　That, at least, is the view of a group of 16 climate scientists, who have **spelled out** a **scenario** in which sea levels would be 10 to 60 metres higher than today. This warming would continue even if we **ceased** pumping CO_2 into the atmosphere—and the **threshold** could be as low as 2°C.

3　[2]If they are right, it means that the supposed "safe" limit for global warming **set out** in the Paris agreement might be **anything but**. "Two degrees may actually be very dangerous," says Johan Rockstrom of Stockholm University, who is one of the 16.

4　For most of the past half billion years, Earth was much hotter than today, with no permanent ice at the poles: the hothouse Earth state（地球温室状态）. [3]Three million years ago, as carbon dioxide levels fell, it began **oscillating** between two cooler states: ice ages（冰河时代）in which great ice sheets covered much land in the northern hemisphere, and **interglacials** like the present.

5　The aim of the Paris agreement is to limit warming to 2°C by 2100. But if Rockstrom is right, we might be **on the brink of** pushing the planet out of the present interglacial state and into the hothouse earth state. This means it might not be possible to stabilise global temperature at this level.

6　Even if we manage to limit warming to 2°C by 2100—we are currently **on course for** 3 or 4°C by 2100—warming would continue over the next few centuries even if all our greenhouse gas emissions ceased.

7　"The first cluster（组）of tipping points in the climate system **is centered around** 2°C warming," says team member John Schellnhuber of the Potsdam Institute for Climate Impact Research. "The **perturbation** could push the planetary machinery out of the glacial cycle."

8   ④The team stress that they are pointing out a potential danger that needs study, not that they have shown **conclusively** that this will happen. "We are discussing a possibility, not a probability, and ask the scientific community to **put** our scenario **to the test**," says Schellnhuber. ⑤Indeed, other climate scientists that *New Scientist* spoke to—who did not wish to be named—expressed scepticism at its findings although others thought it was reasonable.

9   "It is **plausible** that if we **exceed** some temperature threshold we will place Earth in a different climate state," says Jeffrey Kiehl of the National Center for Atmospheric Research in the US, who studies climate change in the past and present, and was not involved in the study.

◆ 课文小助手

一、生词和词块释义

trigger /ˈtrɪɡə(r)/ *vt.* 引起

cascade /kæˈskeɪd/ *vi.* 大量落下

benchmark /ˈbentʃmɑːk/ *n.* 基准

scenario /sɪˈnɑːrɪəʊ/ *n.* 设想

cease /siːs/ *vt.* 停止

threshold /ˈθreʃhəʊld/ *n.* 阈

oscillate /ˈɒsɪleɪt/ *vi.* 摇摆

interglacial /ˌɪntəˈɡleɪsjəl/ *n.* 间冰期

perturbation /ˌpɜːtəˈbeɪʃən/ *n.* 小变异

conclusively /kənˈkluːsɪvli/ *adv.* 确凿地

plausible /ˈplɔːzəbl/ *adj.* 有道理的

exceed /ɪkˈsiːd/ *vt.* 超过

on the verge of 濒于

spell out 解释明白

set out 阐明

anything but 决不

on the brink of 濒于

on course for (因为已开始做而) 很可能做成 (或做)

centre around 把……当作中心

put sth. to the test 使受检验

二、话题概要

大意: 全球变暖似乎不可遏止,专家们对此评说不一。

Para. 1–2: 一群 16 人组成的科学家警告说,我们可能即将触发一系列层叠的临界点,导致地球气温比前工业时代的基准气温高 4 到 5 摄氏度。即使人类停止排放二氧化碳,气候变暖仍会继续。

Para. 3: 这也意味着巴黎协定中为全球变暖设定的所谓 "安全" 界限也许一点都不安全。

Para. 4: 过去的五亿年中,地球比今天热多了,三百万年前,地球在冰河时代和间冰期两种凉爽的状态间波动。

Para. 5–7: 巴黎协定旨在到 2100 年将气候变暖幅度控制在 2 摄氏度以内。照前述科学家的说法,将全球气温稳定在目前水平已不可能。气候系统的第一组临界点大约是变暖 2 摄氏度。2 摄氏度的变化足以将地球这个大机器推出冰川周期。

Para. 8–9: 16 位科学家强调,他们只是指出一个潜在的危险,还有待科学界的检验。也有不愿透露姓名的科学家对此并不认同。一直研究气候变化,但并未参与该项研究的美国大气研究中心的 Jeffrey Kiehl 认为这一观点是有道理的。

◆ 同步练习

一、长难句翻译(见文章划线处)

二、词块填空

1. The show was _____ being canceled due to low ratings.

2. It wasn't cheap._____.

3. If he wins today, he is _____ the Grand Slam (大满贯).

4. Discussions were _____ developments in Eastern Europe.

5. The government has so far refused to _____ its plans.

三、佳句模仿

原文佳句	We could be on the verge of triggering a series of cascading tipping points (临界点) that result in the planet warming 4 or 5℃ hotter than the pre-industrial benchmark.
亮点评析	on the verge of 在句子中表示"濒临，即将"，trigger 一词形象生动，有"一触即发"之意思，cascading 一词本意是"像瀑布一样落下"，that 引导定语从句。
写作应用	We could be on the verge of triggering a series of cascading chain reactions that result in the entire society trapped in a dilemma for lack of trust. 我们有可能即将引发一系列链锁反应，并使整个社会因为缺乏信任而陷入某种困境。

原文佳句	The team stress that they are pointing out a potential danger that needs study, not that they have shown conclusively that this will happen.
亮点评析	The team stress that…not that… 该句型用于表述观点。
写作应用	They stress that they are putting forward a potential solution that needs to be put into practice, not that they can guarantee that it will solve the problem once for all. 他们强调，他们只是提出了一个有待付诸实践的可能的解决方案，并不意味着他们保证这个方案会彻底解决这个问题。

◆ 答案

一、长难句翻译

1. 我们可能即将触发一系列层叠的临界点，导致地球气温比前工业时代的基准气温高 4 到 5 摄氏度。

2. 如果他们是正确的，这也意味着巴黎协定中为全球变暖设定的所谓"安全"界限也许一点都不安全。

3. 三百万年前，伴随着二氧化碳水平的下降，地球开始在两个更凉爽的状态之间波动：一个是冰河时代，北半球大部分陆地被巨大的冰川覆盖，一个是像现在这样的间冰期。

4. 该团队强调，他们指出的只是一个潜在的危险，还有待于进一步研究，并不是说他们确定这一定会发生。

5. 的确，虽然其他科学家觉得这是可以理解的，但是，新《科学家》杂志采访过的其他气候科学家——不便透露姓名——对这一研究发现表示怀疑。

二、词块填空

1. on the verge/brink of

2. Anything but

3. on course for

4. centred on/around

5. spell out

Chapter 3

健康 / Health

15 A Few Drinks Might Help Stave off Dementia[M]

小饮防痴呆

1 Light drinking helps prevent **dementia**（痴呆）, and now we may know why: **it revs up** the brain's waste **disposal** system.

2 Brain cells are surrounded by a network of ultra-thin tubes that **flush** toxins（毒素）and cell waste products away. Work in mice shows that low levels of alcohol **stimulate** this system, while higher amounts **hinder** it. ①If the findings **apply to** people, the low levels would **be equivalent to** about two units of alcohol a day, which is about a pint of beer or a medium glass of wine.

3 Alcohol has been getting a bad press lately. **Excessive** drinking causes liver damage and has **been linked with** several kinds of cancer. In the UK, the recommendation for how much it is safe to drink has been cut, with both men and women advised to stick to 14 units or fewer a week. The latest UK government report said even drinking at very low levels carries some risk. However, this relates to a slightly higher rate of cancers that are fairly rare—such as those of the oesophagus（食管癌）.

4 ②When it comes to more common conditions, such as dementia, total **abstention** from alcohol carries a slightly higher risk than low to moderate drinking. But it was unclear why. The reason may be the brain's waste disposal system, known as the glymphatic system（淋巴系统）, which was only discovered in 2012. We know it **ramps up** its activity during sleep. Among the toxins it clears is a protein called beta-amyloid（β-淀粉样蛋白）, which makes up the sticky plaques（斑块）found in the brains of people with Alzheimer's disease（阿尔茨海默病）. Some studies have suggested that long-term sleep **disruption** may **contribute to** Alzheimer's by causing amyloid build-up.

5 ③Iben Lundgaard of the University of Rochester in New York and her colleagues looked at the effects of alcohol on this network, by **injecting** a dye（染料）into mouse brains then removing them half an hour later to see how much had got into the tubes. Low **doses** of alcohol **boosted** the amount cleared by 40 per cent compared with mice that had no alcohol. Intermediate（中级的）and high doses had the opposite effect, cutting it by about 30 per cent. It is unclear how much that would affect people's risk of Alzheimer's. Roxana Carare of the University of Southampton, UK,

says that the reason a low dose of alcohol has this effect may be because it raises the heart rate, and the pumping of blood helps drive fluid through the glymphatic system. "But there's a lot we still don't know about the normal functioning of the glymph system. We don't know how this translates to humans."

6　④At the Federation of European Neuroscience Societies meeting in Berlin last month, Lundgaard said that light drinking does seem to benefit the glymphatic system, but that more data would be needed before people make decisions about how much they drink based on this work, especially as it was in mice: "I think that would be a little bit too soon." ⑤Lundgaard says that as well as considering how alcohol affects their risk of Alzheimer's, people might also want to consider the effect on cancer.

◆ 课文小助手

一、生词和词块释义

disposal /dɪ'spəʊz(ə)l/ *n.* 处理

flush /flʌʃ/ *vt.* 冲洗

stimulate /'stɪmjʊleɪt/ *vt.* 刺激

hinder /'hɪndə/ *vt.* 阻碍

excessive /ɪk'sesɪv/ *adj.* 过多的

abstention /əb'stenʃ(ə)n/ *n.* 戒绝

disruption /dɪs'rʌpʃn/ *n.* 中断

inject /ɪn'dʒekt/ *vt.* 注入

dose /dəʊs/ *n.* 剂量

boost /buːst/ *vt.* 提高

rev up 加快转速

apply to 适用于

be equivalent to 相等于

be linked with 与……有关

when it comes to 当谈及

ramp up 提升

contribute to 导致

二、话题概要

大意: 通过小白鼠试验，有关学者初步了解到了通过轻度饮酒可以在一定程度上预防痴呆症，但具体作用机制尚未探明，仍需大量试验数据支持。

Para. 1: 小白鼠试验表明，轻度饮酒刺激了大脑废物处理系统，从而有助于预防痴呆症。

Para. 2: 通过小白鼠试验推断出适用于人类的轻度饮酒度量标准。

Para. 3: 即使少量饮酒也存在健康风险。

Para. 4: 研究者对于戒酒比少量饮酒更易引起痴呆等常见疾病的可能性推测。

Para. 5: 研究者进行小鼠大脑试验以探究酒精对人们患痴呆的影响，并总结分析。

Para. 6: 学者提出试验结论仍需更多数据的支撑，酒精与癌症的关系也在人类思考范围之中。

◆ 同步练习

一、长难句翻译（见文章划线处）

二、词块填空

1. Knowledge must _____ training, practical experience and strict adherence to safety.

2. Yet the majority of these employees have no voice, especially_____ their own safety.

3. Among these reasons for the accident, one should be emphasized that mechanism failure _____ it dramatically.

4. Make the best use of available resources by _____ the highest priority projects

5. Changing her job like that_____ giving her the sack.

三、佳句模仿

原文佳句	In the UK, the recommendation for how much it is safe to drink has been cut, with both men and women advised to stick to 14 units or fewer a week.
亮点评析	with both men and women advised to stick to 属于 with + 名词（或代词）+ 过去分词 的复合结构，作伴随状语。
写作应用	Sat in my room for a few minutes with my eyes fixed on the ceiling. 我在房间坐了一会儿，眼睛盯着天花板。

原文佳句	Lundgaard says that as well as considering how alcohol affects their risk of Alzheimer's, people might also want to consider the effect on cancer.
亮点评析	as well as 与动词连用时，其后可用 V-ing 形式，尤其 as well as 位于句首时，此时相当于 in addition to。
写作应用	It means facing difficulties without denial, as well as fully enjoying the beauty of each moment. 它意味着不拒绝面对困难，同样也完全地享受目前每一秒钟的美好。

◆ 答案

一、长难句翻译

1. 如果研究结果适用于人类，那么足以预防痴呆症的低水平的酒精则相当于每天两单位的酒精，即一品脱的啤酒或一中等杯的葡萄酒。

2. 至于更常见的疾病，如痴呆症，完全戒酒的风险略高于低至中度饮酒。

3. 纽约罗切斯特大学的 Iben Lundgaard 和她的同事们研究了酒精对这一网络的影响，方法是将一种染料注入小鼠大脑，然后半小时后将其取出，看看有多少进入试管。

4. 上个月，在柏林举行的欧洲神经科学协会联合会会议上，Lundgaard 说，轻度饮酒确实对淋巴系统有好处，但在人们根据这项研究决定他们喝多少酒之前，还需要更多的数据，尤其是在老鼠身上试验得出的数据。

5. Lundgaard 说，除了考虑酒精如何影响他们患老年痴呆症的风险外，人们可能还要考虑酒精对癌症的影响。

二、词块填空

1. be linked with

2. when it comes to

3. contributed to

4. applying to

5. is equivalent to

16 Vision Restored With Virtual Reality[M]

虚拟现实助力视力恢复

1 A virtual reality headset has restored sight to people who are legally blind. [1]While it didn't cure the physical cause of their blindness, the device let people with **severe** macular degeneration（黄斑变性）**resume** activities like reading and gardening—tasks they previously found impossible.

2 Macular degeneration is a common, age-related condition. It affects around 11 million people in the US and around 600,000 people in the UK. Damage to blood **vessels** causes the central part of the eye, called the macular, to **degrade**. This leaves people with a blind spot in the centre of their vision, and can make those with the condition legally blind. "You can still see with your periphery（边缘）, but it's difficult or impossible to recognise people, to read, to perform everyday activities," says Bob Massof at Johns Hopkins University in Maryland.

3 The new system, called IrisVision, uses VR to make the most of peripheral vision（周边视觉）. The user puts on a VR headset that holds a Samsung Galaxy phone. It records the person's surroundings and displays them in real time, but the user can **magnify** the image as many times as they need for their peripheral vision to become clear. Doing so also helps to effectively reduce or **eliminate** their blind spot.

4 "Everything around the blind spot looks, say, 10 times bigger, so the **relative** size of the blind spot looks so much smaller that the brain can't **perceive** it anymore," says Tom Perski at IrisVision, who also has severe macular degeneration. When he first started using the device it was an emotional experience. "I sensed that I could see again and the tears started coming," he says. If I were to look at my wife—and I'm standing 4 or 5 feet away—my blind spot is so large I can't see her head at all," says Perski. But when he uses IrisVision the **magnification** causes the blind spot to be relatively much smaller, so that it no longer covers his wife's whole head, just a small part of her face. "If I just move that blind spot I can see her whole face and her expression and everything," he says.

5 The software also **automatically focuses on** what the person is looking at, **enabling** them **to** go from reading a book on their lap to looking at the distance without adjusting the magnification or **zoom manually**. ②Colours are given a boost because many people with macular degeneration **have trouble** distinguishing them, and users can place a magnification bubble over anything they want to see in even more detail, for example to read small print.

6   ③In a trial, 30 people used the system for two weeks, **filling out** questionnaires on their ability to complete daily activities before and after the period. "They can now read, they can watch TV, they can **interact with** people, they can do gardening. They can do stuff that for years was not even a consideration," says David Rhew at Samsung Electronics Americas. According to Rhew, the vision of participants was all but restored with the headset. "④The baseline rate of vision in the individuals came in at 20/400, which is legally blind, and with the use of this technology it improved to 20/30, which is **pretty** close to 20/20 vision," he says.

7   The results were presented at the Association for Research in Vision and Ophthalmology（眼科学）annual meeting. The headset is now being used in 80 ophthalmology centres around the US, and the next step is to adapt the software to work for other vision disorders.

8   Melissa Chun, at the Stein Eye Institute at the University of California, Los Angeles, is one of those who has been working with the system. "My patients who have used it like that it is an all-in-one. They read with it, watch television, see faces of friends and family," says Chun, although some have commented that it is heavy for long periods of use. ⑤Many people with macular degeneration regularly use eight to ten different tools, such as telescopes and magnifying glasses, to help them with daily life, but IrisVision can replace them all, says Perski.

◆ 课文小助手

一、生词和词块释义

severe /sɪˈvɪə/ *adj.* 严重的

resume /rɪˈzjuːm/ *vt.* 恢复

vessel /ˈves(ə)l/ *n.* 血管

degrade /dɪˈgreɪd/ *vi.* 退化

magnify /ˈmægnɪfaɪ/ *vt.* 放大

eliminate /ɪˈlɪmɪneɪt/ *vt.* 消除

relative /ˈrelətɪv/ *adj.* 相对的

perceive /pəˈsiːv/ *vt.* 察觉

magnification /ˌmægnɪfɪˈkeɪʃ(ə)n/ *n.* 放大

automatically /ˌɔːtəˈmætɪklɪ/ *adv.* 自动地

zoom /zuːm/ *n.* 变焦

manually /ˈmænjuəli/ *adv.* 手动地

boost /buːst/ *n.* 推动

pretty /ˈprɪtɪ/ *adv.* 相当地

focus on 集中

enable...to... 使……能够

have trouble doing 有困难

fill out 填写

interact with 互动

二、话题概要

大意： 一种 VR 耳机实现了在无法改变失明原因的前提下帮助黄斑变性患者恢复与视力相关的日常活动。目前该项目正在对其系统完善推广中，以适用于其他视力障碍患者。

Para. 1: 黄斑变性患者的福音——一种 VR 耳机的问世使他们得以进行与视力相关的日常活动。

Para. 2: 指出黄斑变性患者的致病因子，其对患者日常生活的不良影响。

Para. 3: IrisVision 系统帮助患者改善视觉的作用机理。

Para. 4: 使用过该设备的患者对其的体会与评价

Para. 5: 设备的相关人性化设计。

Para. 6: 设备小范围测试结果反馈。

Para. 7: 通过测试的耳机问世，将要大范围推广进行改善。

Para. 8: 学者评价认为该设备集合了可有效帮助患者的多种工具功能。

◆ 同步练习

一、长难句翻译（见文章划线处）

二、词块填空

1. But rather dwell on the sadness of our parting, we'll_____ our hopes for a brighter future—for him and for us.

2. Indeed some fields are expanding so quickly that even the experts in that field _____ keeping up.

3. They know what they should do or say, they just _____ doing it or saying it.

4. So we should not underestimate the "pleasure" of _____ a screen when we puzzled over why it seems so appealing to young people.

5. You'd better check whether you have _____ all the blanks before you hand it in.

三、佳句模仿

原文佳句	While it didn't cure the physical cause of their blindness, the device let people with severe macular degeneration resume activities like reading and gardening—tasks they previously found impossible.
亮点评析	While it didn't cure...while 的意思为"虽然，尽管"，引导让步状语从句。...they previously found impossible 作为定语从句修饰 tasks，同时 tasks 又作为 activities 的同位语。
写作应用	While it may be more convenient to possess a car, it is also expensive and troublesome at times. 虽然拥有一辆汽车可能更方便，但有时它也很昂贵和麻烦。

原文佳句	The software also automatically focuses on what the person is looking at, enabling them to go from reading a book on their lap to looking at the distance without adjusting the magnification or zoom manually.
亮点评析	what the person is looking at, what 引导宾语从句，enabling them to go... 现在分词作伴随状语。
写作应用	This book will teach you the scientific way to tap the realm of Infinite Power within you, enabling you to get what you really want in life. 这本书会教给你一种科学的方法，来开发你内在拥有"无穷力量"的这个领域，使得你能够实现你在生活中真正的期望。

◆ 答案

一、长难句翻译

1. 虽然它不能治愈失明的物理性原因，但该装置让患有严重黄斑变性的人恢复了阅读和园艺等活动——这些活动他们以前认为是不可能的。

2. 辨色度得到了提升，因为许多黄斑变性患者很难分辨颜色，并且用户可以在他们想要看到的任何细节的东西上放置一个放大气泡，例如阅读小字体。

3. 在一项试验中，30 人使用该系统两周，填写了调查问卷，说明他们在此期间前后完成日常活动的能力。

4. 他说："这些人的视力基线率为 20/400，这在法律上是失明的。使用这项技术后，视力基线率提高到了 20/30，这与 20/20 的视力基线率相当接近。"

5. Perski 说，许多黄斑变性患者经常使用 8 到 10 种不同的工具，如望远镜和放大镜，来帮助他们的日常生活，但 IrisVision 可以取代所有这些工具。

二、词块填空

1. focus on

2. have trouble

3. have trouble

4. interacting with

5. filled out

17　You Can Catch up on Sleep Debt on Weekends, Study Says[M]

睡眠不足，周末可补

1　Sleeping in on a day off feels **marvelous**, especially for those who don't get nearly enough rest during the workweek. But are the extra weekend winks (瞌睡) worth it? It is a question that psychologist Torbjorn Akerstedt, director of the Stress Research Institute at Stockholm University, and his colleagues tried to answer in a study published Wednesday in the Journal of Sleep Research.

2　Akerstedt and his colleagues tracked more than 38,000 people in Sweden over 13 years, with a focus on their weekend vs. weekday sleeping habits. This **peek at** weekend slumber (睡眠) **fills in** an "**overlooked**" gap in sleep science, Akerstedt said. Previous sleep studies asked people to count their hours of sleep for an average night, without distinguishing between workdays and days off. ①In the new study people under the age of 65 who slept for five hours or less every night, all week, did not live as long as those who **consistently** slept seven hours a night.

3　But weekend snoozers (酣睡者) lived just as long as the well-slept. ②People who slept for fewer than the recommended seven hours each weekday, but caught an extra hour or two on weekends, lived just as long as people who always slept seven hours, the authors reported. "It seems that weekend **compensation** is good" for the sleep-needy, Akerstedt said, though he cautioned that this was a "**tentative** conclusion" of this new research. ③Epidemiologists (流行病学家) described the result as a **plausible** finding, if not a **statistically** robust one, that deserves more investigation.

4　Michael Grandner, director of the Sleep and Health Research Program at the University of Arizona's College of Medicine, who was not involved with this work, warned that sleep is not like a financial **transaction**. ④We can't **deposit** sleep over the weekend and expect to cash them out later. A superior **metaphor**, he said, is a diet. ⑤For the sleep-deprived, sleeping in on a weekend is like eating a salad after **a series of** hamburger dinners—healthier, sure, but from "one perspective the damage is done."

5　In September 1997, thousands of Swedes filled out 36-page health questionnaires as part of a fund-raiser for the Swedish Cancer Society. The study's authors followed 38,015 survey participants over 13 years to track their **mortality** rates. Between 1997 and 2010, 3,234 of these subjects died, most as a result of cancer or heart disease. That's roughly six deaths per 1,000 people per year. **By comparison**, the world mortality rate in 2010 was nearly eight in 1,000. ⑥The researchers tried to **account for** the usual gremlins (捣蛋鬼) that influence sleep: alcohol **consumption**, coffee **intake, naps**, smoking, shift work, and similar factors, and used statistical methods to control for their effect. "The only thing that we don't have control over is latent (潜在的) disease," Akerstedt said, meaning diseases that went undetected in a person's life.

6 Akerstedt and his colleagues grouped the 38,000 Swedes by self-reports of sleep **duration**. Short sleepers slept for less than five hours per night. Medium sleepers slept the typical seven hours. Long sleepers, per the new study, snoozed for nine or more hours. (The "consensus recommendation," per the American Academy of Sleep Medicine and Sleep Research Society, is seven-plus hours a night for adults ages 18 to 60.) The researchers further divided the groups by **pairing** their weekday and weekend habits.A short-short sleeper got less than five hours a night all week long. They had increased mortality rates. A long-long sleeper slept nine or more hours every night. They too had increased mortality rates. The short-medium sleepers, on the other hand, slept less than five hours on weeknights but seven or eight hours on days off. Their mortality rates were not different from the average.

◆ 课文小助手

一、生词和词块释义

marvelous /ˈmɑːvələs/ *adj.* 了不起的	**consumption** /kənˈsʌm(p)ʃ(ə)n/ *n.* 消费
overlook /əʊvəˈlʊk/ *vt.* 忽视	**intake** /ˈɪnteɪk/ *n.* 摄取
consistently /kənˈsɪstəntli/ *adv.* 一贯地	**nap** /næp/ *n.* 小睡
compensation /kɒmpenˈseɪʃ(ə)n/ *n.* 补偿	**duration** /djʊˈreɪʃ(ə)n/ *n.* 持续的时间
tentative /tãtatiːv/ *adj.* 暂定的	**pairing** /ˈpeərɪŋ/ *n.* 配对
plausible /ˈplɔːzɪb(ə)l/ *adj.* 貌似可信的	**catch up on** 弥补
statistically /stəˈtɪstɪkli/ *adv.* 统计上地	**peek at** 窥探
transaction /trænˈzækʃ(ə)n/ *n.* 交易	**fill in** 填补
deposit /dɪˈpɒzɪt/ *vt.* 存款	**a series of** 一系列的
metaphor /ˈmetəfə/ *n.* 暗喻	**by comparison** 相比之下
mortality /mɔːˈtælɪtɪ/ *n.* 死亡率	**account for** 解释

二、话题概要

大意：学者通过多年以来的持续性追踪发现，尽管周末补眠可能对身体造成某些其他方面的伤害，但是总的说来，对于工作日睡眠时间相对较少的人来说，周末补眠利大于弊。

Para. 1: 学者就"周末补眠是否值得"这一问题展开创新性探究。

Para. 2: 其研究的学术价值及区别于传统的调查方法。

Para. 3: 试验初步得出的周末补眠对睡眠不足的人有益的结论，这令学者抱有谨慎的乐观。

Para. 4: 有学者表达了不同的看法，认为即便周末补充睡眠，但睡眠不足所造成的伤害已经既成事实。

Para. 5: 学者试图根据一份健康状况，解释一些可能影响睡眠的因素并使用统计学手段进行控制。

Para. 6: 分组实验结果发现，睡眠时间相对较短但是会在周末进行补眠的受试者与正常睡眠时间的受试者的健康状况基本相同。

◆ 同步练习

一、长难句翻译（见文章划线处）

二、词块填空

1. Industry, it turned out, _____ only ten percent of the smog in the city.

2. Many African counties, particularly fragile states, have taken longer to _____ infrastructure and have considered lower-cost technologies.

3. The first stars in our universe are long gone, but their light still shines, giving us a_____ what the universe looked like in its early years.

4. Please_____ this form and show me your passport.

5. Life is just _____ present moments, and the choices we make in those moments.

6. _____, their own shallow life, their boring days, were becoming unbearable.

三、佳句模仿

原文佳句	This peek at weekend slumber (睡眠) fills in an "overlooked" gap in sleep science, Akerstedt said.
亮点评析	fill in a gap: 填补空白，取其比喻 (metaphoric) 意义。
写作应用	Last year they filled in the gaps in the fields of science and technology. 他们在去年填补了一项科学技术领域的空白。

原文佳句	Epidemiologists (流行病学家) described the result as a plausible finding, if not a statistically robust one, that deserves more investigation.
亮点评析	if not a statistically robust one，为省略句，补充完整即为 if it is not a statistically robust one。连词 if not 用于条件句可以用真实语气，也可以用虚拟语气，但是，句子中只要有 but for，该句子必须用虚拟语气。
写作应用	Sometimes, that standard is quite difficult, if not impossible, to achieve. 有时即便有可能达到那个标准，那也是非常困难。

◆ 答案

一、长难句翻译

1. 在这项新的研究中，65 岁以下整个星期每晚睡 5 小时或少于 5 小时的人，他们的寿命都不如那些每晚睡 7 小时的人长。

2. 作者报告称，每个工作日睡眠时间少于推荐的 7 个小时，但周末多睡了一两个小时的人，其寿命与那些总是睡了 7 个小时的人一样长。

3. 流行病学家将这一结果描述为一个看似合理的发现，即使不是一个统计上可靠的发现，也值得更多的研究。

4. 我们不能如存钱一样在周末储存睡眠，指望以后再把睡眠兑现。

5. 对于睡眠不足的人来说，周末睡懒觉就像吃完一系列汉堡包晚餐后的沙拉——更健康，但无疑从"一个角度来看，损害已经造成了。"

6. 研究人员试图解释影响睡眠的常见因素：饮酒、咖啡摄入量、午睡、吸烟、倒班工作和类似因素，并使用统计方法对其效果进行控制。

二、词块填空

1. accounted for

2. catch up on

3. peek at

4. fill in

5. a series of

6. By comparison

18 Goodbye, Loneliness; Hello, Happiness[M]

揖别孤独，拥抱幸福

1   At a colloquium (谈论会) last month at the Harvard T.H. Chan School of Public Health, Nobel Prize-winning economist Angus Deaton spoke of a global rise in preventable deaths by suicide, alcoholism-related liver disease, and addiction, calling them "deaths of **despair**." [①]From the perspectives of public health and medicine, we recognize the out-sized role that loneliness and social **isolation** play in those deaths of despair.

2   This is not an American public health issue alone. Globally, the World Health Organization now lists social support networks as one of the factors that determine health, while the United Kingdom recently created a minister of health to address loneliness as a public health **priority**.

3   Researchers **define** social isolation as something with objective, quantifiable markers such as living alone, having few social network ties, or a dearth (缺乏) of social contacts. Loneliness is more **subjective**. It is something we **perceive**; we feel the absence of the social connections we desire. It's lack of companionship, or lack of **intimacy** with others.

4   Social connections have a **profound** influence on risk for mortality and **are associated with** a 30 percent increased risk of early death. **In fact**, loneliness can have long-term effects on health and is as lethal (致命的) as smoking 15 cigarettes a day. But health, and certainly happiness, are more than the absence of illness. Loneliness saps **vitality**, impairs productivity, and **diminishes** enjoyment of life. [②]Loneliness affects more than one-third of American adults, especially people facing such challenges as the loss of a loved one, major illness, the return from military service, or marginalization (边缘化) because of minority or immigrant status. People suffering from chronic or major illness can be lonely and isolated as these disorders progress, a burden often shared by their caregivers. External factors also **are to blame**. Research indicates that Internet and social media engagement exacerbates (加剧) feelings of loneliness, depression, and anxiety.

5   As a society, we **thrive** when we are connected. Strong social bonds play a causal (因果关系的) role in long-term health and well-being. Social connections, in a very real way, are keys to happiness and health. If there is any doubt that people **crave** knowledge about the secrets to happiness and

health, consider this: An academic's 2015 YouTube video on the lessons learned from a Harvard research study has been viewed nearly 21 million times. "The surprising finding is that our relationships and how happy we are in our relationships has a powerful influence on our health. Taking care of your body is important but tending to your relationships is a form of self-care too," said Dr. Robert Waldinger, a professor of psychiatry at Harvard Medical School and director of the Harvard Study of Adult Development, an ongoing research project since 1938.

6　If our Holy Grail is happiness and health, how do we **combat** loneliness and isolation? First, the media's **coverage** of the topic is welcome. As global awareness rises, the stigma of feeling lonely and isolated is **drastically** reduced. ③We in public health must **be especially sensitive to** how loneliness affects specific at-risk populations, including the sick, older adults, college students, veterans (退伍军人), and the marginalized. Second, solutions founded on evidence-based programming must **acknowledge** loneliness and isolation as public health issues. Public health professionals need to make connected communities achievable. That means **empowering** workplaces, schools, community centers, places of worship, and even the local coffee shop with programs and tools that bring people together in meaningful ways. And primary care providers need to consider loneliness to be a modifiable (可修改的) risk factor for ill health. And let's not overlook **innovative** approaches. Next month, for example, the UnLonely Film Festival and Conference in New York will showcase successful programs that are **chipping away** at social isolation. Such initiatives aren't complex or expensive. ④Former surgeon general Dr. Vivek Murthy introduced a five-minute exercise during staff meetings called "Inside Scoop," which allowed staffers (职员) to share photos **highlighting** meaningful personal stories. He noted how this personal sharing reduced stress and increased both connections to others and to the group's **mission**. Finally, the critical nature of social relationships should be included in national public health priorities, taking its place with **obesity**, **substance** abuse, and physical inactivity. ⑤Public health researchers and practitioners must continue to study and promote effective responses to loneliness and isolation—**in particular,** how to roll back those heartbreaking, preventable deaths of despair.

◆ 课文小助手

一、生词和词块释义

despair /dɪˈspeə/ n. 绝望

isolation /ˌaɪsəˈleɪʃ(ə)n/ n. 孤立

priority /praɪˈɒrɪtɪ/ n. 优先考虑的事

define /dɪˈfaɪn/ vt. 定义

subjective /səbˈdʒektɪv/ adj. 主观的

perceive /pəˈsiːv/ vi. 感知

intimacy /ˈɪntɪməsɪ/ n. 亲密关系

profound /prəˈfaʊnd/ adj. 意义深远的

vitality /vaɪˈtælɪtɪ/ n. 活力

diminish /dɪˈmɪnɪʃ/ vt. 使减少

thrive /θraɪv/ vi. 茁壮成长

crave /kreɪv/ vt. 渴求

combat /ˈkɒmbæt/ vt. 与……对抗

coverage /ˈkʌv(ə)rɪdʒ/ n. 新闻报道

drastically /ˈdræstɪkəli/ adv. 大幅度地

acknowledge /əkˈnɒlɪdʒ/ vt. 承认

empower /ɪmˈpaʊə/ v. 允许

innovative /ˈɪnəvətɪv/ adj. 创新的

highlight /ˈhaɪlaɪt/ vt. 突出

mission /ˈmɪʃ(ə)n/ n. 使命

obesity /ə(ʊ)ˈbiːsɪtɪ/ n. 肥胖

substance /ˈsʌbst(ə)ns/ n. 物质

be associated with 与……有关

in fact 事实上

be to blame 应承担责任

be sensitive to 对……敏感

chip away 削弱

in particular 尤其

二、话题概要

大意：作为一种社会性动物，人如果长期孤立游离于整个社会之外，那么由此而导致的"绝望的死亡"在所难免。学者针对近年来在全球范围内持续发生的类似事件进行了相关分析研究并提出解决措施。

Para. 1: 孤独和社会孤立导致了逐年加重的"绝望的死亡"。

Para. 2: 该问题在全球范围内被认知并引起重视。

Para. 3: 研究者对"社会隔离"进行定义。

Para. 4: 孤独对人的一系列消极影响。

Para. 5: 说明社会关系与人健康成长的密切关系。

Para. 6: 简述克服孤独与孤立的 4 个小提示 (tips)。

◆ 同步练习

一、长难句翻译（见文章划线处）

二、词块填空

1. In this section, we'll create a new interface that will _____ this import.

2. For any place, but_____ for any city to live, you must have faith in it, in its reality and significance.

3. People occasionally tell you, "Do that in your free time," but_____ there's no such thing as "free" time.

4. Children_____ disapproval and adjust their behaviour accordingly.

5. Our rough edges must_____ to bring out the image of Christ.

三、佳句模仿

原文佳句	From the perspectives of public health and medicine, we recognize the out-sized role that loneliness and social isolation play in those deaths of despair.
亮点评析	the out-sized role that loneliness and social isolation play in... 是定语从句，其中 role 作为先行词，余下的动词和介词成为定语从句的谓语部分，即 play (the role) in。
写作应用	The role that he played in the activity was pretty important. 他在活动中扮演的角色很重要。

原文佳句	But health, and certainly happiness, are more than the absence of illness.
亮点评析	"More than + 名词"表示"不仅仅是"。"More than + 形容词"等于"很"或"非常"的意思，如：The heat there was more than he could stand. 那儿的炎热程度是他所不能忍受的。
写作应用	Literacy is more than the ability to read and write and some of your competition skills. 文化素养远远不止一个人的读写能力以及一个人的某些竞争技能。

◆ 答案

一、长难句翻译

1. 从公共卫生和医学的角度来看，我们认识到孤独和社会孤立在那些"绝望的死亡"中所起的巨大作用。

2. 孤独感影响了超过三分之一的美国成年人，尤其是因为少数民族或移民身份而面临诸如失去亲人，重大疾病，退伍归来或边缘化等挑战的人。

3. 在公共卫生方面，我们必须特别关注孤独感如何影响特定的高危人群，包括病人、老年人、大学生、退伍军人和边缘化人群。

4. 前外科医生 Vivek Murthy 博士在员工会议上介绍了一项名为 "Inside Scoop" 的五分钟

练习，该项目允许员工分享特别有意义的个人故事的照片。

5. 公共卫生研究人员和从业人员必须继续研究和有效应对孤独和孤立感，特别是如何扭转那些令人心碎、可预防的"绝望的死亡"。

二、词块填空

1. be associated with

2. in particular

3. in fact

4. are sensitive to

5. be chipped away

19　Dentists Can Smell Your Fear[E]

牙医可以嗅出你的恐惧

1　Keep calm. ①Dentists can smell when a patient is anxious and it makes them more **prone to** errors, according to a study of **dental** students.

2　The finding is the first real-world evidence that chemical signals in our body **odour** can betray our emotions and influence the behaviour of those around us, says Valentina Parma at the International School for Advanced Studies in Trieste, Italy.

3　Many lab experiments have found that the odours of people who are feeling emotions— particularly negative ones like **disgust** and fear—can influence our **perception** of them. This happens **even though** we can rarely pinpoint (查明) why or describe what we are smelling.

4　To find a more realistic setting for investigating this effect, Parma's team **turned to** dentistry, since the people dentists treat are often anxious. ②The researchers asked 24 student volunteers to each donate a T-shirt they had worn during a stressful exam, and another worn at a calm lecture. The team doused the T-shirts with a chemical that **masks** body odour, so that no one could **consciously** smell it. A separate group of 24 dental students said they couldn't **detect** any difference between the two sets of shirts. Next, examiners **graded** the dental students as they carried out treatments on mannequins dressed in the donated T-shirts. The students scored significantly worse when the mannequins were wearing T-shirts from stressful contexts. Mistakes included being more likely to damage teeth next to the ones they were working on (Chemical Senses, doi.org/cpz4). ③Parma thinks the **scent** of anxiety could be **triggering** the same emotion in those who **subconsciously** smell it. "It's quite **fascinating**," says Pamela Dalton at Monell Chemical Senses Center in Philadelphia. "It helps us understand how we can communicate without language."

5　The phenomenon **is likely to** occur in other settings, too. ④Doctors might also be able to smell their patients' fear, for instance, and sitting close to an especially nervous person during an exam might impact your grades, says Parma. **In addition**, body odours may influence work performance, if you are within **sniffing** distance of your boss or colleagues.

6 ⑤Parma does not know whether qualified dentists are as **vulnerable** to signals in body odours as students, and plans to investigate this in future.

7 Even if the effect is confirmed in more experienced dentists, there is probably little a patient can do to mask their body's chemical signals. "I don't think we'll be able to develop an anti-anxiety deodorant（除臭剂）, unless we find the **molecule** responsible," says Parma.

8 ⑥Instead, Parma hopes that training dentists and medical professionals to be aware of the body odour effect and to manage their anxiety might improve patient care.

◆ 课文小助手

一、生词和词块释义

dental /'dent(ə)l/ *adj.* 牙科的

odour /'əʊdə/ *n.* 气味

disgust /dɪs'gʌst/ *n.* 嫌恶

perception /pə'sepʃ(ə)n/ *n.* 看法

mask /mɑːsk/ *vt.* 掩饰

consciously /'kɒnʃəslɪ/ *adv.* 有意识地

detect /dɪ'tekt/ *vt.* 察觉

grade /'greɪd/ *vt.* 分等级

scent /sent/ *n.* 气味

trigger /'trɪgə/ *v.* 引起

subconsciously /sʌb'kɒnʃəsli/ *adv.* 潜意识地

fascinating /'fæsɪneɪtɪŋ/ *adj.* 吸引人的

sniff /snɪf/ *vt.* 嗅

vulnerable /'vʌlnərəbl/ *adj.* 易受伤害的

molecule /'mɒlɪkjuːl/ *n.* 分子

prone to 有……倾向的

even though 即便

turn to 转向

be likely to 有可能……

in addition 此外

二、话题概要

大意：研究表明，资历尚浅的牙医易受患者焦虑时的气味影响而出错，由于尚未探明其分子反应机制，故难以研制抗味剂。但是学者认为可通过相应的训练以达到应对目的。

Para. 1: 研究表明，牙医闻到患者焦虑时的气味使他们更易犯错。

Para. 2: 相关学者表示，我们身体里的化学信号会泄露我们的情绪并影响我们身边人的行为。

Para. 3: 实验表明，体味能影响我们对情绪的感知，即使我们不能准确描述所闻到的焦虑情绪。

Para. 4: 学者针对牙科学生展开试验调查，试验表明穿着来自焦虑环境下的 T 恤的牙医更易犯错。

Para. 5: 在许多其他环境下气味对人的影响也同样适用。

Para. 6: 对于有资历的牙医是否也会受影响这点尚不清楚，但未来会展开研究。

Para. 7: Parma 认为除非可以发现这种分子反应机制，否则难以研制出有效药物。

Para. 8: Parma 认为，通过对医师和医护人员的相关培训可改善负面体味的影响。

◆ 同步练习

一、长难句翻译（见文章划线处）

二、词块填空

1. People who have heart attacks _____ despair.

2. He originally acted as a fence for another gang before _____ burglary himself.

3. _____, previous successes make you and your team victims of the "old way" of doing things.

4. He's the best teacher, _____ he has the least experience.

5. Someone allergic to milk_____ react to cheese.

三、佳句模仿

原文佳句	The team doused the T-shirts with a chemical that masks body odour, so that no one could consciously smell it.
亮点评析	mask: 掩饰。so that 引导目的状语从句。
写作应用	The healthy trade figures mask a much gloomier picture. 繁荣的贸易数据背后掩盖着贸易极不景气的真相。

◆ 答案

一、长难句翻译

1. 一项针对牙科学生的研究显示，当患者焦虑时，牙医会闻到它们的味道并且更容易出错。

2. 研究人员让 24 名学生志愿者每人各自捐赠一件他们在压力大的考试中穿的 T 恤，另一件是在心平气和的讲座中穿的。

3. Parma 认为，焦虑的气味可能会在那些下意识地闻到焦虑的气味的人身上触发同样的情绪。

4. 例如，医生也可能能闻到患者的恐惧（气味），并且在考试中坐在一个特别紧张的人旁边可能会影响你的成绩，Parma 说。

5. Parma 不知道合格的牙医是否像学生一样容易受到体味信号的影响，并计划在将来对此进行调查。

6. 相反，Parma 希望通过培训牙医和医疗专业人士，使他们能够意识到体味的影响，并控制他们的焦虑情绪，这可能会改善病人的护理。

二、词块填空

1. are prone to

2. turning to

3. In addition

4. even though

5. is likely to

20 Medicare Might Save Billions, if Law Is Changed[M]

法律若调整，医疗保险会大幅节省

1 By allowing the federal government to negotiate with drug makers, Medicare and its **beneficiaries** could save an estimated $2.8 billion in a single year for the top 20 most commonly prescribed medicines（处方药）, according to a new analysis by Democrats on the Senate Homeland Security and Governmental Affairs Committee.

2 ①In crunching（分析）the numbers, the committee staff found that other government agencies that are permitted to negotiate with drug companies, such as the Department of Veterans Affairs and the Department of Defense, were able to secure pricing that rose at "significantly lower rates" than **wholesale** prices for the most widely prescribed brand-name drugs in Medicare Part D.

3 The report arrives as the Trump administration **grapples with** high costs for medicines, a pocketbook issue for many Americans. ②The White House developed a **blueprint** to address the problem, but allowing Medicare to negotiate with drug makers—which is currently prohibited by law—is not among the various ideas being considered, since the pharmaceutical industry objects. Supporters, though, say the need to negotiate is **intensifying**.

4 In 2016, for example, Medicare **accounted for** 29 percent of all **retail prescription** spending, which **amounted to** $95.4 billion, and this is expected to rise to $202.5 billion in 2026. ③The projected increase is **attributed to** an increasing number of seniors **enrolling** in Medicare, including Part D, which the report noted is the largest federal drug purchasing program. ④Many health plans that have contracts to administer Part D drug coverage do negotiate prices with manufacturers, but there are concerns that the process "often **results in inconsistent** drug prices for **identical** drugs among Part D plans," according to the report. For this reason, the committee's minority staff examined the pricing obtained by other federal agencies. ⑤After adjusting for **inflation**, the average price for drugs in the Part D program rose from $151.58 to $241.09 between 2012 and 2017, which amounted to an increase of 59 percent, compared with an increase in the average negotiated federal drug price from $104.10 to $149.88, or a 44

percent increase, for the same drugs during the same time period, according to the report. Even when applying the average **rebate** amount, which is 17.5 percent, for Part D brand-name drugs that is published by the Centers for Medicare and Medicaid Services, and increasing negotiated federal prices by $13.46 to cover various fees, the report found that Medicare could save $2.8 billion in one year. Moreover, negotiated prices for seven of the 20 most commonly prescribed drugs were less than half of the wholesale prices.

5　"When we don't let Medicare negotiate for better prices, it puts the profits of big pharma (大制药厂) ahead of the interests of...seniors," said Senator Claire Mc-Caskill, Democrat of Missouri, who ordered the report, in a statement. "Getting **bulk** discounts is something every business does, and the fact that the federal government is prohibited from doing it for Medicare is unconscionable (不合情理的)."

6　There are some caveats (警告). For instance, the list price for the Nitrostat nitroglycerin was $108.76 and the negotiated federal price was $46.24, but as the report noted, Nitrostat accounted for only 0.2 percent of prescriptions among those 20 most commonly prescribed brand-name drugs in Medicare Part D, so the effect was "**minimal**."

7　A spokeswoman for Pharmaceutical Research and Manufacturers of America, the industry trade group, wrote to say that the report ignores the robust negotiations already occurring in Medicare Part D that generate significant savings. ⑥The Congressional Budget Office has **consistently** stated that negotiations would not achieve lower prices than the current negotiation and competition in Part D without restricting access to the medicines seniors rely upon. That restriction is exactly what has happened with the VA pricing system that this report **holds up** as a model.

◆ 课文小助手

一、生词和词块释义

beneficiary /ˌbenɪˈfɪʃ(ə)rɪ/　*n.* 受益人

wholesale /ˈhəʊlseɪl/　*adj.* 批发的

blueprint /ˈbluːprɪnt/　*n.* 计划

intensify /ɪnˈtensɪfaɪ/　*vt. vi.* 变激烈

retail /ˈriːteɪl/　*adj.* 零售的

prescription /prɪˈskrɪpʃ(ə)n/　*n.* 药方

enrol /ɪnˈrəʊl/　*vi.* 注册

inconsistent /ˌɪnkənˈsɪst(ə)nt/　*adj.* 不一致的

identical /aɪˈdentɪk(ə)l/　*adj.* 同一的

inflation /ɪnˈfleɪʃ(ə)n/　*n.* 通货膨胀

bulk /bʌlk/　*n.* 大块

rebate /ˈriːbeɪt/　*n.* 折扣

minimal /ˈmɪnɪm(ə)l/　*adj.* 最低的

consistently /kənˈsɪstəntli/　*adv.* 一贯地

grapple with 努力克服

account for 占……比例

amount to 总计为

be attributed to 归因于……

result in 导致

hold up as 推崇为

二、话题概要

大意: 《我不是药神》所折射的高药价不能承受之痛，在美国也在所难免。最近参议院民主党人提出一份分析报告，通过允许联邦政府与制药商谈判，联邦医疗保险(Medicare)及其受益人可以在一年内为最常见的处方药节省约 28 亿美元之多。这对于普通民众来说或许是个好消息，毕竟钱袋子是硬道理，尽管有人担心有些相同药物价格不一致。

Para. 1: 参议院的一份分析报告认为，政府参与制药商谈判可以节省大量资金。

Para. 2: 报告分析发现，政府参与谈判能够确保医疗保险 D 中最广泛规定的品牌药品的价格以"明显低于批发价"的价格上涨。

Para. 3: 尽管目前法律禁止医疗保险与制药商谈判，但谈判的必要性正在增加。

Para. 4: 报告援引各种数据表明协商谈判价格的优势。

Para. 5: 有关人士对目前采购制度的批评："获得大宗折扣是每个企业都会做的事情，联邦政府被禁止为医疗保险提供折扣，这是不合情理的。"

Para. 6: 报告中建议的谈判制度存在弊端：如亚硝酸盐在医保 D 部分中的 20 种最常用的名牌药品中只占处方药的 0.2%，所以效果是"最少。"

Para. 7: 制药商与政府部门的担忧。

◆ 同步练习

一、长难句翻译（见文章划线处）

二、词块填空

1. His poor performance may _____ lack of motivation rather than to reading

difficulties.

2. He _____ the problem for an hour before he solved it.

3. As the old saying goes, there is no _____ tastes.

4. But even these limited civil service pensions often don't_____ much.

5. Software today is too often designed to please too many users, _____ low user satisfaction.

三、佳句模仿

原文佳句	After adjusting for inflation, the average price for drugs in the Part D program rose from $151.58 to $241.09 between 2012 and 2017, which amounted to an increase of 59 percent, compared with an increase in the average negotiated federal drug price from $104.10 to $149.88, or a 44 percent increase, for the same drugs during the same time period, according to the report.
亮点评析	本句主干结构为 the average price…rose from…to…。which amounted to 为定语从句。After adjusting for... 以及 compared with... 都作状语成分。
写作应用	The unemployed rose from 75million in June, 2016 to 78 million in July, 2016, which amounted to an increase of 4 percent. 失业人数从 2016 年 6 月的 7500 万增加到 2016 年 7 月的 7800 万，增幅达 4%。

◆ 答案

一、长难句翻译

1. 在分析这些数据时，委员会的工作人员发现，其他获准与药品公司进行谈判的政府机构，如退伍军人事务部和国防部，能够确保医疗保险 D 部分中最广泛使用的品牌药品的价格以"明显低于批发价"的价格上涨。

2. 白宫制定了解决这一问题的蓝图，但允许医疗保险与制药商谈判——目前法律禁止——并不在考虑中的各种想法之列，因为制药业对此持反对态度。

3. 预计增加的原因是参加医疗保险的老年人数量增加，包括 D 部分，报告指出这是最大的联邦药物采购计划。

4. 该报告称，许多签订合同管理 D 部分药品覆盖范围的健康计划确实与制造商谈判价格，但人们担心，这一过程"往往导致 D 部分计划中相同药品的药品价格不一致"。

5. 报告称，扣除通胀因素后，D 部分项目的药品平均价格在 2012 年至 2017 年期间从 151.58 美元升至 241.09 美元，增幅为 59%，而同期同一批药品的平均协商联邦药品价格从 104.10 美元增至 149.88 美元，涨幅为 44%。

6. 国会预算办公室一直表示，如果不限制老年人所依赖的药品的获取，谈判就无法实现低于目前 D 部分谈判和竞争的价格。这一限制正是与 VA 定价制度所发生的情况一样，这份报告将其作为一种模式。

二、词块填空

1. be attributed to

2. grappled with

3. accounting for

4. amount to

5. resulting in

21 Alzheimer's Link to Herpes Virus in Brain[M]

阿尔兹海默症与大脑病毒有关

1　The presence of viruses in the brain has been linked to Alzheimer's disease in research that challenges conventional theories about the onset of dementia (痴呆).

2　①The results, based on tests of brain tissue from nearly 1,000 people, found that two **strains** of herpes (疱疹) virus **were** far more **abundant in** the brains of those with early-stage Alzheimer's than in healthy controls. However, scientists are divided on whether viruses are likely to be an active **trigger**, or whether the brains of people already on the path towards Alzheimer's are simply more **vulnerable** to infection.

3　"The viral genomes (基因组) were detectable in about 30% of Alzheimer's brains and **virtually undetectable** in the control group," said Sam Gandy, professor of neurology (神经学) at the Icahn School of Medicine at Mount Sinai, New York and a co-author of the study.

4　②The study also suggested that the presence of the herpes viruses in the brain could influence or control the activity of various genes linked to an increased risk of Alzheimer's.

5　The scientists did not **set out** to look for a link between viruses and dementia. Instead, they were hoping to **pinpoint** genes that were unusually active in the brains of people with the earliest stage of Alzheimer's. ③But when they studied brain tissue, comparing people with early-stage Alzheimer's and healthy controls, the most striking differences in gene activity were not found in human genes, but in genes belonging to two herpes virus strains, HHV6A and HHV7. And the abundance of the viruses **correlated with clinical** dementia scores of the donors.

6　"We didn't go looking for viruses, but viruses **sort of** screamed out at us," said Ben Readhead, assistant professor at Arizona State University-Banner Neurodegenerative Disease Research Center and lead author.

7　Gandy said the team were initially "surprised and **sceptical**" about the results, based on brain tissue from the Mount Sinai Brain bank, and so repeated the study using two further brain banks—in total 622 brains with signs of Alzheimer's and 322 healthy control brains—

and detected the very same genes. "We've tried to be **conservative** in our interpretation and **replicated** the results in three different brain banks, but we have to at least recognise that these diseased brains are carrying these viral genomes," he added.

8   ④The scientists could not prove whether viruses actively **contribute to** the onset of disease, but they discovered a **plausible** mechanism for how this could happen. Some of the herpes genes were found to be **boosting** the activity of several known Alzheimer's genes.

9   David Reynolds, chief scientific officer of Alzheimer's Research UK, said this element was significant. "Previous studies have suggested that viruses might be linked with Alzheimer's, but this detailed analysis of human brain tissue takes this research further, indicating a relationship between the viruses and the activity of genes involved in Alzheimer's, as well as brain changes, molecular (分子的) signals, and symptoms **associated with** the disease," he said.

10   However, others were more sceptical. Prof John Hardy, a geneticist at University College London, said: "There are some families with mutations in specific genes who always get this disease. It's difficult to **square** that **with** a viral aetiology (病因学). I'd urge an extremely cautious interpretation of these results."

11   ⑤The viruses highlighted are not the same as those that cause cold sores, but much more common forms of herpes that nearly everyone carries and which don't typically cause any problems. The study in no way suggests that Alzheimer's disease is **contagious** or can be passed from person to person like a virus—or that having cold sores increases a person's risk of dementia. Poor quality sleep could increase Alzheimer's risk, research suggests.

12   There are currently 850,000 people living with dementia in Britain, and the number is **projected** to rise to a million by 2025 and 2 million by 2050. But despite hundreds of drug trials during the past decade, an effective treatment has not yet **emerged**.

13   "While these findings do potentially open the door for new treatment options to explore in a disease where we've had hundreds of failed trials, they don't change anything that we know about the risk and **susceptibility** of Alzheimer's disease or our ability to treat it today," said Gandy.

◆ 课文小助手

一、生词和词块释义

strain /'streɪn/ *n.* 类型；品质

trigger /'trɪgər/ *n.* 诱发；起因

vulnerable /'vʌlnərəbl/ *adj.* 易受影响（或攻击）的

virtually /'vɜːtjuəli/ *adv.* 几乎；实际上

undetectable /ˌʌndɪ'tektəbl/ *adj.* 看不见的；察觉不出的

pinpoint /'pɪnpɔɪnt/ *v.* 准确指出

clinical /'klɪnɪkəl/ *adj.* 临床的

sceptical /'skeptɪkəl/ *adj.* 怀疑的，持怀疑态度的

conservative /kən'sɜːvətɪv/ *adj.* 保守的，传统的

replicate /'replɪkeɪt/ *v.* 重复；复制

plausible /'plɔːzəbl/ *adj.* 貌似真实（或可信）的

boost /buːst/ *v.* 改善；提高

contagious /kən'teɪˌdʒəs/ *adj.* （疾病）接触性传染的

projected /prə'dʒektɪd/ *adj.* 计划的，预计的

emerge /ɪ'mɜːdʒ/ *v.* 出现，浮现

susceptibility /səˌseptɪ'bɪlɪti/ *n.* 易受影响（或伤害、感染）

be abundant in 大量的；丰富的

set out 开始；着手

be correlated with 有相互关系的

sort of 有几分地

contribute to 贡献；有助于

be associated with 与……相关

square…with… （使）与……一致，与……相符

二、话题概要

大意：与传统理论不同，最近的研究表明，阿尔兹海默症与大脑病毒相关。

Para. 1–2: 大脑病毒出现与阿尔兹海默症相关，这项研究颠覆了传统老年痴呆症的理论。

Para. 3–7: 病毒的基因组在 30% 的阿尔兹海默症大脑里可以探测到，而在控制组却探测不到。

Para. 8–9: 科学家们不能证明这些病毒有效地造成疾病的发作，但是他们发现了疾病发作方式的合理解释机制。

Para. 10–11: 但是其他学者持怀疑态度。伦敦大学的基因学家 John Hardy 教授，认为许多患病家族的具体基因产生突变。

Para. 12–13: 目前英国有 85 万痴呆症患者，预计到 2025 年会增加到 100 万，到 2050 年增加到 200 万。

◆ 同步练习

一、长难句翻译（见文章划线处）

二、词块填空

1. China covers a vast territory and _____ natural resources.

2. We _____ to find the truth behind the mystery.

3. What if we believe this is an important goal because it is significantly _____ success, happiness and well-being?

4. I'm _____ worried about Jenny.

5. Fresh air and exercise can _____ good health.

6. His social problems were _____ heavy drinking.

7. We must remember that the interests of the farmers need to be _____ those of consumers.

三、佳句模仿

原文佳句	However, scientists are divided on whether viruses are likely to be an active trigger, or whether the brains of people already on the path towards Alzheimer's are simply more vulnerable to infection.
亮点评析	However 使上下文连接顺畅，be divided on 在这表示"意见不一致"，on 后面接 whether 引导的宾语从句。
写作应用	1. However, adolescents are divided on whether it is reasonable to go abroad for further study. 但是，青少年们就是否出国留学深造意见不一致。 2. However, experts are divided on how the electronic devices have influence on the development of teenagers. 但是，专家们就电子设备如何影响孩子们的发展意见不一。

原文佳句	But when they studied brain tissue, comparing people with early-stage Alzheimer's and healthy controls, the most striking differences in gene activity were not found in human genes, but in genes belonging to two herpes virus strains, HHV6A and HHV7.
亮点评析	when 引导状语，非谓语动词"comparing"表示比较，striking 意思是"令人印象深刻的"，belonging to 是非谓语动词作定语成分。
写作应用	1. Comparing the study with previous one, the striking differences in subjects are that they show more obedience to authority. 将本项研究与之前相比，令人印象深刻的是受试者更屈服于权威。 2. When psychologists discuss about the conclusion, comparing Chinese kids with foreign ones, the most striking difference in them are that they react differently to the same topic. 当心理学家讨论结论时，将中国孩子与国外孩子比较，令人印象最为深刻的是他们对同一主题的不同反应。

◆ 答案

一、长难句翻译

1. 基于对近 1000 个人的脑组织研究结果显示，早期的阿尔兹海默症病人脑中的两种疱疹病毒要比健康人大脑中的多。

2. 该项研究也表明大脑中疱疹病毒会影响或控制各种基因活动，这些基因与阿尔兹海默症发病增长相关。

3. 但是当他们研究脑组织，将早期阿尔兹海默症患者与健康控制组相比，基因活跃度的显著差异不存在于人类基因里，而在 HHV6A 和 HHV7 病毒里。且病毒数量与捐献者临床痴呆程度呈正比关系。

4. 科学家们不能证明这些病毒有效地造成疾病的发作，但是他们发现了疾病发作方式的合理解释机制。

5. 凸显的病毒与唇疱疹并不一样，而是更为常见的病毒，几乎人人都会携带，并不会引起任何问题。

二、词块填空

1. is abundant in

2. set out

3. correlated with

4. sort of

5. contribute to

6. associated with

7. squared with

22 What Love at First Sight Really Is[M]

一见钟情的真相

1   ①You may remember your eyes meeting across a crowded room and your life changing forever. But was it really love **at first sight**?

2   ②One in three people say they have **fallen in love** as soon as they **laid eyes on** someone. However, a study suggests the phenomenon probably doesn't exist.

3   ③"People think of love at first sight as a lightning strike as soon as they see a person," says Florian Zsok at the University of Zurich, Switzerland.

4   ④Until now, research into the experience has mostly **focused on** people who are in relationships, which is likely to **distort** our understanding of it. Such people are more likely to remember the beginning of that relationship in an **exaggeratedly** positive light.

5   ⑤So Zsok and his colleagues conducted a series of experiments in which volunteers saw new people for the first time. Each person **filled in** a survey and was asked how they felt about the people they saw or met.

6   The first experiment was designed to **mimic** online dating. In it, 282 volunteers were shown pictures on the internet of six people of the same **gender** they found attractive, and were then surveyed on their feelings about them. Around half the volunteers were in relationships. They were also asked about the early days of those relationships. A similar experiment involved showing 50 volunteers nine pictures.

7   Zsok and his team also studied the reactions of 64 people who met each other face-to-face, either at a bar, during speed dating or at a food-based event designed to allow people to meet in groups of four.

8   Of the 396 volunteers across all **arms** of the study, 32 reported experiencing love at first sight

However, none of these people matched, says Zsok. "There was no **reciprocated** love."

9 Analysing the surveys showed that people are most likely to report love at first sight when they find someone physically attractive. ⑥We **tend to** associate a range of positive **attributes** to good-looking people, a phenomenon known as the **halo effect**. This might help explain why people think they are falling in love with someone at first sight, says Zsok.

10 "What you feel is **lust** at first sight and is largely **subconscious**," says Anna Machin at the University of Oxford. "⑦Love is an attachment that comes later. It is more complex and involves conscious reflection on a relationship."

11 In reality, it is unlikely that people ever form this kind of connection upon meeting one another, says Zsok. "⑧People like this romantic idea, but you have to **read between the lines**."

12 So why do so many people feel like it has happened to them? People often **misremember** the early stages of what is now a successful relationship, says Machin. "It's an unconscious attempt to **underpin** a relationship," she says. "⑨Telling someone 20 years **down the line** that you loved them at first sight is a lovely thing to say and a good way to maintain a relationship."

13 But Sandra Langeslag at the University of Missouri-St Louis disagrees. ⑩The fact that some people said they felt love at first sight means it does exist, as long as you use a broad definition of what love is, she says. "A lot of people **refer to** the deep love you experience in a relationship, but I would call **infatuation** and **sexual** desire a type of love."

◆ 课文小助手

一、生词和词块释义

distort /dɪ'stɔ:t/ v. 扭曲；使变形

exaggeratedly /ɪg'zædʒəreɪtɪdli/ adv. 夸大地；夸张地

mimic /'mɪmɪk/ v. 模仿

gender /'dʒendər/ n. 性别

arm /ɑːm/ n. 部分

reciprocate /rɪ'sɪprəkeɪt/ v. 回应

attribute /'ætrɪbjuːt/ n. 特性；特质

lust /lʌst/ n. 对（某人）有强烈的情欲

subconscious /sʌb'kɒnʃəs/ adj. 潜意识的，下意识的

misremember /mɪsrɪ'membə(r)/ v. 记错

underpin /ʌndə'pɪn/ v. 加强；巩固

infatuation /ɪnˌfætju'eɪʃən/ n.（通常短期）热恋，着迷

sexual /'seksjuəl/ adj. 性的

at first sight 乍看之下；一看到……就

fall in love 爱上

lay eyes on 看到，瞧见；注视

focus on 聚焦于；致力于

fill in 填（写）

tend to 趋向

halo effect 光圈效应

read between the lines 领会言外之意

down the line 在将来；今后

refer to 谈到；提到

二、话题概要

大意： 文章通过实验研究，阐述了对"一见钟情"现象和其他学者的不同看法。

Para. 1: 你也许记得你的眼睛扫过人群拥挤的房间，你的生活永久改变的那一刻。但是，它真的是一见钟情吗？

Para. 2–4: 三分之一的人说他们一看见某一个人时就立刻陷入爱河。但是一项研究表明这种现象很可能并不存在。"人们将一见钟情想象成为一见到某人时如同被闪电击中一般。"瑞士苏黎世大学的 Zsok 说道。直到现在，对这项体验的研究主要集中于彼此有关系的人，那将有可能扭曲我们对现象的理解。这些人更有可能以夸大积极的方式回忆关系的开始。

Para. 5–6: Zsok 和他的同事们开展了一系列实验，在这些实验里志愿者们见的是第一次见面的新人。每个人都填写调查表，询问他们对第一次见到或遇到的人感觉如何。设计的第一个实验是模仿网络约会。在这个实验里，研究者向 282 名志愿者展示了 6 张他们认为有魅力且相同性别人的照片，然后调查他们对这些照片的感觉如何。大约有一半志愿者是相互有关系的。他们也被问及他们之间关系的早期情况。相似的实验里向 50 名志愿者展示了 9 张照片。

Para. 7–8: Zsok 与其同事也研究了 64 名面对面人的反应，这些人在酒吧、快速约会或允许四人一组地参加宴会相聚。在这项研究的各部分中，396 名志愿者中，其中 32 名报告说曾经历过一见钟情。但是，这些人当中没有与之相匹配的，Zsok 说道。"他们没有对应的爱。"

Para. 9: 调查分析显示当人发现身体具有魅力时，他们最后可能报告说一见钟情。我们往往将一系列积极特质与相貌较好的人联系起来，这种现象被称为光圈效应。这也许有助于解释为何人们认为他们一眼就爱上某人，Zsok 说道。

Para. 10: "你感觉到的是第一眼下强烈的情欲，很大部分是潜意识的，"，牛津大学学者 Anna 说道。"爱情是随之而来的附加品。它更为复杂，包含对关系有意识的反思。"

Para. 11: 在现实中，人们一经相遇就形成这样的联系是不可能的，Zsok 说道。"人们喜欢这种浪漫的想法，但你必须领会其中言外之意。"

Para. 12: 所以为何很多人感到这种情况确实发生在他们身上过？人们经常记错良好关系的初始阶段，Machin 说道。"通过无意识努力强化关系"，她说道。"20 年之后，你告知某人曾对他（她）一见钟情是一件说起来美妙的事情，也是一种维持关系的好的方法。"

Para. 13: 但密苏里州大学的学者 Sandra 却不同意这个看法。一些人说一见钟情的事实意味着它确实存在，只要你使用爱情的宽泛定义，她说道。"许多人指的是你在一种关系中经历的深爱，但我将着迷和性欲称为一种爱情。"

◆ 同步练习

一、长难句翻译（见文章划线处）

二、词块填空

1. _____ the house appeared to be empty than it really is.

2. They _____ when they were students in high school.

3. I knew when I _____ that car that it was the car for me.

4. We're going to _____ the relationship between freedom and necessity.

5. Many people find it difficult to _____ a form.

6. He _____ get angry when people disagree with him.

7. It was unwise in your speech to _____ rising unemployment.

三、佳句模仿

原文佳句	Until now, research into the experience has mostly focused on people who are in relationships, which is likely to distort our understanding of it.
亮点评析	mostly 在这里的意思是"主要地"；focused on 表示"集中于"；who 与 which 分别引导定语从句；likely 是形容词表示可能性。
写作应用	Nowadays, readers have mostly focused on books that are written in plain language, which is likely to hinder their English from advancing. 现如今读者们大都聚焦于使用浅显英语写成的书籍，阻碍了他们英语水平进一步发展。

原文佳句	Analysing the surveys showed that people are most likely to report love at first sight when they find someone physically attractive.
亮点评析	analysing 是动名词做主语；at first sight 表示"一见钟情"；when 引导状语从句。
写作应用	Comparing all accident report indicates that women drivers are far more likely to have accidents than men drivers, when they are nervous. 比较所有的车祸数据表明，女司机发生车祸的可能性要远远大于男司机，当他们都紧张时。

◆ 答案

一、长难句翻译

1. 你也许记得你的眼睛扫过人群拥挤的房间，你的生活永久改变的那一刻。

2. 三分之一的人说他们一看见某一个人时就立刻陷入爱河。

3. 人们将一见钟情想象成为一见到某人时如同被闪电击中一般。

4. 直到现在，对这项体验的研究主要集中于彼此有关系的人，那将有可能扭曲我们对现象的理解。

5. 所以 Zsok 和他的同事开展了一系列实验，在这些实验里志愿者们见的是第一次见面的新人。

6. 我们往往将一系列积极特质与相貌较好的人联系起来，这种现象被称为光圈效应。

7. 爱情是随之而来的附加品。它更为复杂，包含对关系有意识的反思。

8. 人们喜欢这种浪漫的想法，但你必须领会其中言外之意。

9. 20 年之后，你告知某人曾对他（她）一见钟情是一件说起来美妙的事情，也是一种维持关系的好的方法。

10. 一些人说一见钟情的事实意味着它确实存在，只要你使用爱情的宽泛定义，她说道。

二、词块填空

1. At first sight

2. fell in love

3. laid eyes on

4. focus on

5. fill in

6. tends to

7. refer to

Chapter 4

经济 / Economy

23 Who's Left to Employ? Tight Job Market Scoops up Those on the Margin[M]

还剩下谁能雇？火爆的劳务市场将边缘人群一抢而光

*A tight job market means opportunity—including for Americans with prison records, disabilities, or health challenges. And their participation could strengthen the economy **in the long run**.*

1 Almost **like clockwork**, a growing US economy **cranks out** new jobs. In July, it added 157,000 positions, the US Labor Department reported Friday; in June, 248,000. But with unemployment near 20-year lows and some analysts **appealing for** "full employment", are there enough available people to keep filling them?

2 Population growth can **account for** about a third to a half of the new hires. But to keep the economy growing, people not currently working need to **come off the sidelines** to reenter the workforce. And that's what's happening. [①]The story of who and how is a sometimes messy process, with people struggling with issues from health to criminal backgrounds getting jobs, losing them, and then gaining the courage to try again.

3 It's also a tale of progress and hope. Seated around tables shaped in a U, a dozen men and women are taking an **intensive** two-week course here at JVS CareerSolution, learning how to find work despite a background of addiction or criminal activity.

4 There's general agreement here that the economy is strong and that it's a good time to look for a job. But there are **complications**.

5 Massachusetts' CORI, or Criminal Offender Record Information, is a barrier for many in the class. Mark, a former mechanic, was recently rejected for jobs at two garages because of his criminal background. "You try to change your life," he says, "and it's not working."

6 [②]Get-tough policies across America, often **resulting in** prison terms for minor **infractions**, are sometimes credited for reducing the nation's crime rate. But an unintended side effect has been to **marginalize** many Americans, mostly men and often minorities, which often keeps them from reentering the workforce. And that's one reason that, worryingly, the share of people in the labor force has been declining in recent years.

7　However, the overall labor participation rate has been sliding partly because a growing share of Americans are retirees. What concerns economists is that the rate has been falling even among Americans in their **prime** working years (ages 25 to 54). For women, it's been falling since 2000; for men, since 1953.

8　The hopeful sign is that in the past three years, the participation rate has **rebounded** strongly, especially for women. ③In July, participation among prime working-age women **ticked** up to a seasonally adjusted 75.5 percent, an eight-year high, according to the Department of Labor. For men, it **dipped** to 88.8 percent—higher than the all-time low of 88 percent reached in 2015, but the lowest level so far this year. The question is whether the rebound is simply a return to the trend after the damaging effect of the Great **Recession** or the start of a rise that will **reverse** the long-term slide. The next six months should provide a clearer answer.

9　Reportedly, employers appear to be willing to overlook a background of criminal activity or substance abuse."This is my first time in recovery," says Toi, one of two women in the JVS CareerSolution group. "I have been in a couple job interviews but they haven't worked so well. That's why I came here. Basically, I'm just trying to find my way." JVS CareerSolution boasts that 92 percent of those who complete its two-week course either get a job or further training to acquire job skills—Toi's challenge.

10　But it's often a difficult process, with backward as well as forward steps."I was an EMT [emergency medical technician] for years; I left there because of my drinking," says one man who doesn't give his name. "I think about it all the time. I see an ambulance and I think: 'I should be doing that instead of flipping eggs.' " Of the people in the group, he says: "It's not bad people, it's just big bad mistakes."

11　Another big barrier to labor participation is health. Almost 30 percent of prime-age Americans not in the labor force say a disability keeps them from looking for work, according to the study. ④Even though the recession-linked dramatic increase in disability cases is largely over, many would-be workers struggle with health issues.

12 Ashlee Smith worked as a personal care assistant until last year, when she **was diagnosed with** multiple sclerosis (多发性硬化症). ⑤<u>She quit her job and has since **strung together a series of** administrative positions, which don't require a lot of physical movement, through a temp (办公室里的临时雇员) agency.</u> But her lack of administrative experience has made it hard to land a full-time job. "I need something more permanent," she says, typing in her personal data to apply for services at JVS CareerSolution. "The job market is really good, but it's very much according to your past experience."

◆ 课文小助手

一、生词和词块释义

crank /kræŋk/ *vt.* 用曲柄启动（机器等）

intensive /ɪn'tensɪv/ *adj.* 密集的

complication /ˌkɒmplɪ'keɪʃən/ *n.* 复杂的
情况

infraction /ɪn'frækʃn/ *n.* （对规则、法律
等的）违背，违犯

marginalize /'mɑːdʒɪnəl(ə)laɪz/ *vt.* 使……
边缘化

prime /praɪm/ *adj.* 最佳的

rebound /rɪ'baʊnd/ *vi.* 反弹

tick /tɪk/ *vt.* 留下记号

dip /dɪp/ *vi.* 下降

recession /rɪ'seʃ(ə)n/ *n.* 【经济】衰退，
萧条

reverse /rɪ'vɜːs/ *vt.* 使……逆转

diagnose /'daɪəgnəʊz/ *vt.* 诊断

scoop sth. up 把……抢购一空

on the margin(s) 处于边缘地位

in the long run 从长久来看

like clockwork 可预见地；有规律地

crank out 大量粗制滥造

appeal for 呼吁

come off the sidelines 不再袖手旁观

account for 占有……比例

result in 导致……结果

be diagnosed with 被确诊患有……

string sth. together 把……拼在一起

a series of 一系列

二、话题概要

大意：势头正旺的美国经济前所未有，给有残疾和其他健康问题的适龄劳动力带来机会的同时，就个人而言，其就业状况仍然前景未卜。

Para. 1：不断增长的美国经济提供了诸多就业岗位。由于失业率为 20 年以来的最低点，是否有充足的劳动力来填补这些岗位就成了问题关键。

Para. 2–5：人口增长数量只占新就业人数的 1/3 到 1/2 不等，这就要求离岗人员重新进入劳动力大军。因健康、酗酒、吸毒或犯罪前科等问题就业后失业，如此循环往复的人群喜忧参半。喜的是就业前景大好，忧的是曾经的犯罪记录给他们痛改前非的志向带来了巨大障碍。

Para. 6–8：严苛的收监政策将大多数男子，往往是少数族裔，挤出了劳动力大军，但这只是近几年来人力资源份额持续下降的一个原因。总体就业率一直在下滑的部分原因还包括越来越多的美国人都退休了。但在过去的三年里，就业率，尤其是妇女就业率，强劲反弹。这是经济大萧条后的复苏还是对长期下滑态势的彻底扭转有待观望。

Para. 9–10：由于就业市场趋紧，一些雇主似乎愿意既往不咎。用一位曾担任过急救大夫的酒鬼的话来说，他这类人不是坏人，只不过犯了大错。但就业培训过程实属不易，受训人

员有进有退。

Para. 11–12: 影响就业率的另一障碍就是健康问题。有 30% 的就业黄金年龄段人员皆因此被拒门外。

◆ **同步练习**

一、长难句翻译（见文章划线处）

二、词块填空

1. The most important thing for women to do is ＿＿＿＿ and understand their voice matters.

2. Everything is going ＿＿＿＿, so we should be ready to start construction by the end of the month.

3. He was worried a lot about the subject he's teaching, as in the end-term exam, the passing grades merely ＿＿＿＿ half of the grades he himself has given.

4. NBA basketball star cards were well-received, and fans ＿＿＿＿ the trading cards in the first few hours of the sale.

5. Workers have played an important role in the past, but for the moment, they're ＿＿＿＿ of Chinese society.

三、佳句模仿

原文佳句	There's general agreement here that the economy is strong and that it's a good time to look for a job.
亮点评析	这里 that 引导的是两个并列同位语从句，说明先行词 agreement 的具体内容。
写作应用	She started taking money in the mistaken belief that she would not be discovered and that this would be her last time to do it. 她开始拿走钱，错误地以为她不会被发现，这也是她最后一次做。

原文佳句	But an unintended side effect has been to marginalize many Americans, mostly men and often minorities, which often keeps them from reentering the workforce.
亮点评析	mostly men and often minorities 作 many Americans 的同位语，which 引出非限制性定语从句，指代整个主句 an unintended side effect has been to marginalize many Americans。

<table>
<tr><td>写作应用</td><td>When deeply absorbed in work, which he often was, he would forget all about worldly routines, basically eating and sleeping.
这是他常见的情况，一沉浸在工作中，他就会忘记一切世俗的繁缛，基本就是吃和睡。</td></tr>
</table>

◆ 答案

一、长难句翻译

1. 有健康或犯罪前科等问题的各色人等找到工作，又失去，再鼓起勇气尝试一番，这是一个什么人如何找工作的故事，有时是一个剪不断理还乱的过程。

2. 通行全美的强硬政策因降低了全国的犯罪率而备受赞誉，但往往造成因轻微违法行为而获刑的结果。

3. 据劳工部统计，就业黄金年龄段女性的就业率在季节性调整后冲高至 75.5%，为八年来的最高点；而黄金就业年龄段男性的就业率则降至 88.8%——略高于 2015 年所达到的最低值，今年以来的最低层次。

4. 尽管由经济萧条造成的残疾激增情况已经不复存在，但是许多准备务工的人却在为健康问题而苦苦挣扎。

5. 她辞掉了工作，在专门介绍临时工的代理机构帮助下，从此开始从事一系列无需太多体力活动的行政工作。

二、词块填空

1. come off the sidelines

2. like clockwork

3. accounted for

4. scooped up

5. on the margins

24 Why the Sharing Economy Still Hasn't Reached Its Potential[H]

为何共享经济尚未充分发挥其潜能？

1   Next month, the travel marketplace AirBnb will turn ten years old—marking a major milestone for the Sharing Economy.

2   These platforms have now grown into a massive, global industry facilitating hundreds of millions of **transactions** every day. While its corporate roots are in the United States, the Sharing Economy is booming in dense urban environments everywhere—with China **taking the lead**. Nearly every country now has some version of it, but still, they are only **scratching the surface** of what is possible.

3   Trillions of dollars of **assets** remain **underutilized** and the original mission to create a cleaner, cheaper, and more just world **has yet to** be achieved. In order for the Sharing Economy to reach the next stage of growth it will need to directly confront the issues of uneven quality. To do that, it needs to borrow an approach from the industries it has **set out** to **disrupt**.

4   We need trade groups, institutions, and firms working at a global level to conduct **audits**, set standards, and spread information about how to operate effectively. But it's not **a matter of** building more bureaucracy（官僚机构）to move the industry forward. Instead, it's about introspection（内省）and cooperation.

5   Take for example the issue of background checks and reputation scores. As we've seen **over and over again**, there are still major problems to be resolved in this area. **Screening** users **relies** heavily **upon** the quality of identity information available. [1]Third party services that help with the process are **rife with** their own issues and rating systems are **opaque**, inconsistent, and easily **gamed**. There is thousands of startups and companies around the world all trying to solve the same problem at the same time.

6   Everyone is running their own experiments, but nobody is collecting the results. Imagine

instead if these organizations **were to** address the problem by coming together to spread best practices, establish data-sharing **protocols**, and **codify** procedures to increase safety and trust. <u>②By handling common pain points, we can grow the market while achieving higher acceptance amongst consumers and less **skepticism** from regulators.</u>

Here are five key areas where I see cooperation leading to a stronger industry:

7 Reducing **fraud** and **harassment**: Nothing is more **toxic** to a platform than when somebody is put in danger because of a preventable **oversight**. Right now frauds exist across multiple platforms, but that information stays secret. <u>③To lessen this companies can privately share black-listed accounts, create ways to make ratings **portable**, and develop open-source fraud detection techniques.</u>

8 Rethinking employment **interfaces**: From invoicing, to payments, to human resources—we are **in the midst of** redefining the processes of work. Smart contracts can **automate** payments, massive amounts of data can be used for insurance products, and the app is becoming your boss. But technology needs to be **taken advantage of** carefully here. Companies like Uber use psychological tricks to keep their drivers on the road, and that can be harmful. <u>④The industry needs to create **ethical** guidelines to determine the healthy balance between **constructive** gamification (游戏化) and complete **manipulation**.</u>

9 Managing and maintaining assets: We're all a little uneasy about sharing and using physical items when we can't **check out** their condition. This makes many businesses extremely expensive. The industry would be much better off if our need to trust wasn't so necessary. Software, sensors, and cryptographic tokens (加密令牌) can all play a part in forming a new level of **transparency** where an object can be tracked and examined **in real time**.

10 **Integrating with** cultural and legal systems: Instead of **overrunning** local governments with lobbyists (游说者), companies should shift their **tactics**. The industry has been accepted by the public—and a heavy-handed approach isn't as necessary anymore. But our expectations of what these companies need to do have also changed; we are no longer tolerating platforms that avoid taxes and liability (义务). <u>⑤The industry should **embrace regulation** by collectively developing suggestions and publishing resources for how to balance innovation, accountability (问责制),</u>

and local sensibilities (敏感度).

11 Reducing environmental damage: The promise of the Sharing Economy was to make the world more sustainable—instead it's stimulating consumption, degrading consumer behaviors, and creating an enormous amount of waste as a by-product. Companies should **work out** tactics together on how they could reduce packaging, materials, and **emissions**. This is not an altruistic (利他的) effort, it's **in their own interest**—they need to get ahead of this problem before the debt becomes too large.

12 When the industry was dominated by startups and marked by fierce competition, survival was the key consideration. But things have changed now, and the needs are different. [6]If we want to reach the next billion users, we'll need a **different** set of strategies **than** the ones that got us here so far.

◆ **课文小助手**

一、生词和词块释义

transaction /træn'zækʃ(ə)n/ *n.* 交易

assets /'æsets/ *n.* (复数) 资产

underutilize /ʌndə'juːtilaiz/ *vt.* 未充分利用

disrupt /dɪs'rʌpt/ *vt.* 扰乱

audit /'ɔːdɪt/ *n.* 审计

screen /skriːn/ *vt.* 筛选

opaque /ə(ʊ)'peɪk/ *adj.* 不透明的

game /ɡeɪm/ *vt.* 钻（制度的）空子

protocol /'protə,kɒl/ *n.* （电脑间数据共享的）协议

codify /'kəʊdəfaɪ/ *vt.* 将（法律、条例等）编撰成典籍

skepticism /'skɛptɪ,sɪzəm/ *n.* 怀疑的态度

fraud /frɔːd/ *n.* 诈骗

harassment /'hærəsm(ə)nt/ *n.* 骚扰

toxic /'tɒksɪk/ *adj.* 有毒的

oversight /'əʊvəsaɪt/ *n.* 疏忽

portable /'pɔːtəb(ə)l/ *adj.* 【程序】跨平台的

interface /'ɪntəfeɪs/ *n.* 界面

automate /'ɔːtəmeɪt/ *vt.* 使……自动化

ethical /'eθɪk(ə)l/ *adj.* 合乎道德的

constructive /kən'strʌktɪv/ *adj.* 起改进作用的

manipulation /mə,nɪpjʊ'leɪʃ(ə)n/ *n.* 操纵

transparency /træn'spær(ə)nsɪ/ *n.* 透明度

overrun /əʊvə'rʌn/ *vt.* 肆虐于某处

tactic /'tæktɪk/ *n.* 策略

embrace /ɪm'breɪs; em-/ *vt.* 欣然接受

regulation /regjʊ'leɪʃ(ə)n/ *n.* 管控

emission /ɪ'mɪʃ(ə)n/ *n.* （复数）排放物

take the lead 领先

scratch the surface 仅触及问题的表面

have yet to do sth. 尚未开始做某事

set out to do sth. （怀着特定目的）开始，着手

be a matter of doing sth. 是做某事的问题

over and over again 反复不断地

rely upon 有赖于

be to do sth. 必须做某事

be rife with sth. 到处充斥着（坏事）

in the midst of sth. 在某事的进行过程中

check sth. out 查证；核实

take advantage of 利用

in real time 实时地

integrate with sth. 与某物相融合

work sth. out 制定出

in one's own interest 给某人带来好处或利益

be different than 与……有所不同

二、话题概要

大意: 截至目前，共享经济各自为政，鸡肋众多。文章作者号召全球共享企业进行合作，互惠互利，充分发掘行业潜能。作者还提出了五点可行性建议。

Para. 1–2: 扎根于美国的共享经济平台遍布全球人口密集的城市中。尽管各个国家有不

同版本，但他们都只触及了共享经济的皮毛。

Para. 3: 为使共享经济健康发展，共享产品质量有失均衡的问题亟待解决，这就需要从深受其影响的行业中借鉴方法。

Para. 4: 各商贸集团、机构和公司需在全球层面上进行合作，共同进行审计、制定行业标准，传播运营经验。

Para. 5–6: 以背景考核和信用评分为例，与身份信息相关的鸡肋众多，全球各个平台正设法解决。如果各个机构能够联手，传播最佳经营方法，做到数据共享，程序规范化，则会增加平台的安全感和信任感。

Para. 7–11: 将共享行业做强做大的五个关键点：减少诈骗和骚扰案件；重新考量工作界面；管理并维护资产；与文化和法律体系相融合；减少对自然环境的破坏。

Para. 12: 以初创企业为主体、相互竞争为特点、生存为要务的共享行业已成为历史；新形势下的共享经济需要变革。

◆ 同步练习

一、长难句翻译（见文章划线处）

二、词块填空

1. The country is _____ an economic crisis.

2. After last night's win, Johnson has _____ in the championship table.

3. There is nobody standing up to be a witness. We'll need to _____ his story.

4. The amount of aid that has been offered is hardly going to _____ of the problem.

5. They accepted our proposal without much reservation, as it's _____ to cooperate with us.

6. It's a good idea to use Microsoft Excel as statistical software. The computer may analyze the data _____ as it comes in.

三、佳句模仿

原文佳句	But it's not a matter of building more bureaucracy to move the industry forward. Instead, it's about introspection and cooperation.
亮点评析	这是一种将两件事情对比开来加以阐述的句式，用以强调"非 A 而 B"。
写作应用	Addiction is not a matter of disease. Instead, it's about willpower. 上瘾并非疾病问题；相反，是意志力问题。

原文佳句	Imagine instead if these organizations were to address the problem by coming together to spread best practices, establish data-sharing protocols, and codify procedures to increase safety and trust.

亮点评析	不定式 be to do sth. 用于 if 条件句中，带有情态意义，用来表示目的。Imagine if... 是带有条件句的祈使句，意为"想象一下，如果……想要……结果会怎样"。
写作应用	Imagine if you are to obtain all the recordings, books and movies you're supposed to see. 想象一下，如果你获得了你想要的所有的记录、书和电影。

◆ 答案

一、长难句翻译

1. 帮助进行用户筛选的第三方服务平台充斥着他们自己的问题，加之评级系统规则不透明、前后不统一、漏洞百出。

2. 通过解决常见的痛点问题，我们可以扩大市场，同时在消费者中获得更高程度的认可，而来自监管机构的怀疑也就愈发减少。

3. 为了减少诈骗肆虐所带来的副作用，公司可以私下分享黑名单户头，想办法让评级系统可以跨平台使用，并开发开放源代码的诈骗检测技术。

4. 共享行业需要制定道德准则，在将产品游戏化以改进服务和对产品进行全程操纵之间找到合理的平衡点。

5. 这一行业应该加以管理，集体拿出方案，并公布可利用资源以平衡创新、问责制和地方敏感性问题。

6. 如果我们想要再拿下十亿用户，我们需要一套不同的策略，而不是我们到目前为止一直采用的办法。

二、词块填空

1. in the midst of

2. taken the lead

3. check out

4. scratch the surface

5. in their own interests

6. in real time

25　Slumping Milk Prices Force Dairy Farmers to Think Outside the Barn[E]

牛奶价格的暴跌迫使奶农们另觅它法

Dairy farmers have seen low milk prices before, but the current downturn has been severe in its duration. As some dairy farms fail, others are finding new paths forward.

1　Mr. Edge sold most of his cows at an auction last month, undone by a stretch of low milk prices that has lasted 3½ years and put dairy farmers across the country in danger.

2　①Overproduction worldwide has **turned out a glut of** milk, driving prices below what farmers say it costs them to produce it, for months at a time. Farmers are used to fluctuations in milk prices, but previous downturns have usually lasted only a year or 18 months.

3　The US Department of Agriculture predicts that milk prices will rise this year and into next. But no one expects a big increase. The Trump administration's trade debates and the prospect of trade wars involving agricultural products have only deepened the uncertainty.

Running as fast as we can

4　As this downturn reaches the middle of the fourth year, many farmers are struggling just to **hang on**, borrowing against land and equipment to pay their bills, **betting** the farm **that** prices will turn.

5　"Once you've invested a million dollars in a milking parlor (挤奶间), you're going to milk cows," says Sarah Lloyd, a farmer in Wisconsin Dells. The result, she says, is that "my husband and I are **on the treadmill** and we're running as fast as we can. That's **happening to** a lot of families."

6　Not all farmers are struggling. Some have managed to **pay down debts**. And, as in other types of farming, large operations often enjoy economies of scale (规模经济). Big farms can run milking parlors **around the clock** and negotiate discounts for things like feed (饲料) and **breeding** services.

7　Wisconsin alone lost about 5 percent of its dairy farms between 2016 and 2017. Just 15 miles west of Edge's farm, William and Kelle Calvert had gone into debt to buy a 450-acre farm, and gave up **dairying** because they were afraid of losing everything. They sold their cows to save the farm. Now they **cash-crop** corn, soybeans（黄豆）, and hay（甘草）and raise a few animals for other people.

Finding new pathways

8　②The milk crisis has also inspired farmers to think harder about new strategies with their dairy herds（乳牛群）, including alternatives to conventional dairying. Some are advocating rotational grazing（循环放牧）, a method that involves sending cows out to pastures（牧场）rather than **confining** them in big barns, as many dairy farms do. Grazing requires a lower investment in buildings, machinery and feed, and dairy experts say it offers a small economic advantage over conventional dairying.

9　Organic milk production has for decades offered a profitable alternative for smaller farms, and although organic milk prices have fallen recently, too, organic producers haven't suffered as much as conventional producers.

10　Other farmers are trying to diversify, raising beef cattle or producing milk for a niche market（缝隙市场）. Some have **switched to** milking goats or sheep; the number of goat and sheep farms in Wisconsin almost doubled between 2015 and 2017. Richard Cates, who directs the Wisconsin School for Beginning Dairy and Livestock Farmers, says he "can't imagine" **starting out as** a conventional dairy farmer these days. "You have to be innovative and creative," he says. "You have to do what other people are not doing."

11　The Marcoot Jersey Creamery, in Greenville, Ill., is one example. It grew out of a common **predicament**: an older farmer thinking of selling his cows. Instead, he and two daughters started a cheese-making operation on the farm in 2010. Today Marcoot has 14 employees and about 100 cows. ③It makes 20 varieties of cheese, which it sells at an on-farm store and ships to scores of restaurants and grocery stores in the Midwest.

A model in Canada?

12　④As farmers struggle, agricultural agencies in dairy states are trying to help, offering financial advice, credit **mediation** services, and access to professional advice.

13 A growing number of Midwestern dairy farmers are showing an interest in policies that would raise milk prices by controlling production. They've **looked to** Canada, which has a supply management system that **imposes** quotas（配额）**on** farmers (and barriers on imports from countries like the United States).

14 "It has kept prices stable," says Alan Ker, director of the Institute for the Advanced Study of Food and Agricultural Policy at the University of Guelph in Guelph, Ont. "It takes out a lot of risk for farmers."

15 This spring, hundreds of farmers attended meetings in Michigan and Wisconsin to hear about the Canadian system directly from Ontario dairy farmers. "As farmers especially, we need to take a look at why we keep producing more and more when there's no market for it," says Mr. Von Ruden, who helped organize the meetings.

◆ 课文小助手

一、生词和词块释义

treadmill /ˈtredmɪl/ *n.* 跑步机

breed /briːd/ *vt.* 饲养

dairy /ˈdeərɪ/ *vi.* 生产乳品；*adj.* 产乳的

cash-crop /ˈkæʃ ˌkrɒp/ *vt.* 种植(经济作物)

confine /kənˈfaɪn/ *vt.* 监禁

predicament /prɪˈdɪkəm(ə)nt/ *n.* 困境

mediation /ˌmiːdiˈeɪʃən/ *n.* 斡旋

impose /ɪmˈpəʊz/ *vt.* 强制

turn out 生产出

a glut of sth. 某物供过于求

hang on (克服艰难险阻)坚持下来

bet sth. that 用某物打赌，坚信……

on the treadmill 上了贼船(重复做繁重无聊的工作)

happen to sb./sth. 发生在某人、某物身上

pay down debts 以分期付款方式还清债务

around the clock 昼夜不停地

switch to 转变到

start out as 从……开始起步

scores of 大批的

look to 关注

impose sth. on sb./sth. 把……强加于……

二、话题概要

大意： 过去几年中牛奶价格持续走低，将一些奶农挤出了祖传产业。而另外一些奶农不仅仅限于在大棚里挤牛奶，他们开始关注奶酪制作或转而饲养山羊或绵羊。还有一些奶农寄希望于出台政策，效仿加拿大配额生产体系，以稳定奶价。

Para. 1–3： 奶价低于成本价，每次都持续数月。对于价格波动，奶农已习以为常，但以前行情走低只持续一年或一年半，不像眼下，已经历经三年半，全美奶农处境岌岌可危。农产品贸易战使事态愈发难料。

Para. 4–7： 金蝉脱壳：当低价行情进入第四个年头中期时，许多奶农以农场或挤奶设备作抵押来付账，马不停蹄地辛勤劳作。但一些大农场却享受着规模经济效益，昼夜不停地挤奶，为饲料和奶牛繁殖业务而讨价还价。还有一些奶农售出奶牛以保农场。目前他们靠种植经济作物或为他人饲养动物为生。

Para. 8–11： 另辟蹊径：将牛群放养的循环放牧法因投资小，较传统乳制品生产有着经济上的优势。有机奶的生产为小型农场提供了利润来源，有机奶厂家没有像传统奶厂家那样惨淡经营。其他养殖户通过饲养肉牛和生产特供牛奶来使产品多样化。他们深深懂得，只有不囿于传统才是生存之道。

Para. 12–15： 仿效加拿大模式？在农业部门提供各种咨询服务的同时，中西部越来越多的养殖户渴望像加拿大看齐，建立供应管理机制，采取养殖配额管理或限制进口的措施来提高奶价。

◆ **同步练习**

一、长难句翻译（见文章划线处）

二、词块填空

1. Doctors have been working on him _____, but his condition is still critical.

2. For further cooperation, we need to _____ the future and forget about our past problems.

3. The new environmental protection law would encourage companies to _____ cleaner fuels.

4. The Star _____ a small weekly newspaper, but has later become a well-known daily publication.

5. Without the support of my parents I would have cracked up completely, but I managed to _____.

三、佳句模仿

原文佳句	Some are advocating rotational grazing, a method that involves sending cows out to pastures rather than confining them in big barns, as many dairy farms do.
亮点评析	带有定语从句 that involves sending cows out to pastures rather than confining them in big barns 的名词 a method 是名词短语 rotational grazing 的同位语；而 as many dairy farms do 为非限定性定语从句，其中，关系代词 as 指代其前定语从句中的一部分，即 sending cows out to pastures rather than confining them in big barns。
写作应用	Mother Nature is protesting at the sin committed by us humans, the pollution that we've been creating for the last century, as we might not realize. 大自然母亲正在抗议我们人类所造的孽，即上世纪以来我们不断制造的污染，而这点我们很有可能并没有意识到。

原文佳句	As this downturn reaches the middle of the fourth year, many farmers are struggling just to hang on, borrowing against land and equipment to pay their bills, betting the farm that prices will turn.
亮点评析	主句 many farmers are struggling just to hang on 后有两个现在分词短语：第一个作方式状语，说明主句谓语动作的方式；而后一个作主句谓语动作的伴随状语。
写作应用	The winds blew across the sea, pushing little waves into bigger and bigger ones, rocking the sampan like a cradle. 大风掠过海面，朵朵小波花给吹成了波浪，越滚越大，把舢板晃得像只摇篮。

◆ 答案

一、长难句翻译

1. 世界范围内的生产过剩导致牛奶供过于求，促使其售价低于奶农所言的成本价，这种状况每次都持续数月。

2. 牛奶危机也促使农民们更加认真地考虑为他们的奶牛牧群制定新策略，包括替代传统的乳制品生产。

3. Marcoot 新泽西奶油厂自产 20 种奶酪在农场小店销售并装船运往中西部多家饭店和超市。

4. 当养殖户们奋力抗争时，乳品生产州的助农机构也在想方设法，努力提供金融咨询、信用调解服务和专业咨询。

二、词块填空

1. around the clock

2. look to

3. switch to

4. started out as

5. hang on

26 Sun, Sea and Surgery[M]

阳光、大海和手术

*More people are going **under the knife** abroad.*

1 In the tiny Croatian town of Zabok patients arrive **in their thousands** each year from across Europe and the Middle East, seeking replacement hips or knees at the St Catherine hospital, which **specializes in** orthopaedic (矫形的) work. Some come for treatment they cannot get at home, and others to escape long waiting-lists for public health care or high prices for private operations. Croatia is one of a number of treatment hotspots in the medical-tourism industry. Babies are made in Barbados, sexes are changed in Bangkok, teeth are replaced in Hungary or Mexico and hair is transplanted in Turkey.

2 [1]Precise numbers are hard to **pin down**, partly because of differences between countries in what is **counted as** medical tourism. Some national statistics include a mere spa visit or a tourist who falls sick.

3 Rising numbers of middle-class patients in Asian and African countries mean more people willing to spend if they cannot find what they need at home. [2]And consumers are **incentivised** to travel by substantial price differences across borders for the same treatment. The average heart-valve (心脏瓣膜) replacement, for example, costs €30,000 ($35,000) in Germany but only €15,000 next door in Austria, with little or no drop in quality. A hip operation can be had for €12,000 in Britain, €10,000 in Turkey and only €4,725 in Poland.

4 Governments are **responding to** rising demand. South Korea, Malaysia and Dubai have all **invested** heavily **in** creating regional centres of medical **expertise** to attract foreign patients. The Dubai Healthcare City seeks to attract patients from Gulf nations who have in the past been sent **further afield** by their health systems, to Europe or America. Some **niche** areas are showing particularly strong growth. Mr Pollard says that international travel for in vitro fertilisation (IVF) (体外受精) is increasing rapidly because many wealthy countries have restricted access to free treatment. A number of European countries, such as Germany, offer only three rounds of IVF and limit access to those with medical conditions or to younger women.

5 [3]Medical tourism is still blocked, however, **by a lack of** detailed, reliable information on the quality of hospitals and clinics and of their doctors and surgeons, notes Valorie Crooks, a professor of geography at Simon Fraser University in British Columbia. International hospitals are often confirmed by the Joint Commission, a non-profit organisation that awards **accreditation** to medical-services providers. ④These aside, patients have had to rely solely on reputation or on **intermediaries** that **grease the wheels of** medical travel. Patients often do not realise that these"facilitators" may be working only with certain clinics; some receive unrevealed **commissions**. If things go wrong, patients may **have little recourse to** help. Doctors have long complained about people who return from treatment abroad with **complications**.

6 Two newish online firms, Qunomedical and Medigo, both based in Berlin, hope to improve matters. They allow patients to search for medical treatments from **a large selection of** providers, offering clear information about pricing and the quality of staff and services. Both take fees from the hospitals and clinics that they list, as published on their websites; Medigo also earns money from patients and corporate customers **in the form of** fees. Patients write reviews, and human advisers are available to help with choosing where to receive treatment. Such information should make foreign medical treatments more appealing.

7 But making money out of medical tourism can still be hard. Variations in exchange rates can instantly make a destination less appealing. The market for "scalpel(外科手术刀) safaris" in South Africa has proved **volatile**, say people in the business, due to currency **fluctuations**. Sometimes demand fails to materialise. When work first started on a 2,000-bed hospital called Health City Cayman Islands, the $2bn project was expected to attract more than 17,000 foreign patients annually, mostly from America. But when the first wing of the hospital opened in 2014, the International Medical Travel Journal reported that fewer than 1,000 overseas patients arrived in its first year. ⑤One reason was that its backers based estimations of customer numbers on a **flawed** study, according to a **subsequent** investigation by a government public-accounts committee. Fewer American patients came than expected partly because health insurers were not interested in sending people overseas.

8 **In time**, health-care providers are likely themselves to travel to serve patients. Vikram Kapur, a partner at Bain & Company, says that China has in the past been an exporter of patients but now American hospitals, such as Johns Hopkins, the Cleveland Clinic and the University of Pittsburgh Medical Center, are undertaking joint ventures with local Chinese hospitals to deliver services to patients **closer to** their homes. **One way or another**, health care is becoming more **footloose**.

◆ 课文小助手

一、生词和词块释义

incentivise /ɪnˈsentɪvaɪz/ v. 用物质奖励来激励

expertise /ˌekspɜːˈtiːz/ n. 专门技术

niche /nˈiːʃ/ n. (需求某种产品或服务的)特殊领域

accreditation /əˌkredɪˈteɪʃən/ n. 鉴定合格

intermediary /ˌɪntəˈmiːdɪərɪ/ n. 中间人

commission /kəˈmɪʃ(ə)n/ n. 佣金

recourse /rɪˈkɔːs/ n. 求助对象

complication /ˌkɒmplɪˈkeɪʃn/ n. 并发症

volatile /ˈvɒlətaɪl/ adj. 不稳定的

fluctuation /ˌflʌktʃuˈeɪʃən/ n. 波动

flawed /flɔːd/ adj. 有瑕疵的

subsequent /ˈsʌbsɪkw(ə)nt/ adj. 随后的

footloose /ˈfʊtluːs/ adj. 不受约束的

under the knife 接受手术

be in one's/the thousands 成千上万地

specialize in 专攻

pin sth. down 明确说明或确定某事

be counted as 被视为

respond to sth. 对某事作出回应

invest in sth. 投资于

further afield 到远方

by a lack of 由于缺乏

grease the wheels (of sth.) 使(某事)顺利发展

have little recourse to sth. 难以诉诸于

a large selection of 品种繁多的

in the form of 以……形式

in time 最终，迟早

be close to sb./sth. 靠近某人 / 某物

one way or another 无论如何

二、话题概要

大意: 越来越多的人出国挨刀——医疗资源的合理配置使跨境就医因价格低廉、医治迅速和独到的专业技术而风靡全球。但对国外医疗机构缺乏了解也使得一些患者深受其害。此外，国际行情的变化多端也处处影响着医疗旅游业的发展。但是，宽松的市场准入机制有望让患者在国内就能享受到世界一流的医疗服务。

Para. 1: 基于不同国家的医疗专业特长，患者纷纷跨境求医，有的因为缺乏某种医疗技术，有的为了逃避公共保健体制中的长久等候，还有的为了躲避高昂的手术费。

Para. 2: 由于各个国家的统计口径不一，跨境求医人数难以确定。

Para. 3: 跨境求医的原因：亚非国家中产阶级愿意花钱享受国内缺乏的医疗技术；即便国内有某种技术，但巨大的价差也激励着患者出国求医。

Para. 4: 面对日益增长的需求，政府投巨资兴建专科医疗区域中心以吸引国外患者。

Para. 5: 由于对国外医疗机构和医师资质缺乏了解，患者很容易上当受骗，而且投诉无门。

Para. 6: 总部设在柏林的两家网上公司提供大量有关定价、医护人员资质和医疗服务质量的明确信息供患者选择。这两家公司都与网上公布的医疗机构有经济往来，其中一家也向患者收取服务费。

Para. 7: 汇率的波动以及人寿保险政策等诸多国际因素无时无刻不在影响着医疗旅游，这一行业的钱也不好赚。

Para. 8: 将来，医护人员很有可能出国走穴，给患者就近提供服务。不管怎样，健康保健业市场准入政策将越来越宽松。

◆ 同步练习

一、长难句翻译（见文章划线处）

二、词块填空

1. More and more women are choosing to go _____ to improve their appearance.

2. If we cannot _____ exactly what we are supposed to be managing, how can we manage it?

3. The clients have been reluctant to sign on for another year, so the boss is offering a cash incentive to help _____.

4. At present, you're tired of your parents' repeated instruction. _____, you will come to realize how much they care about you.

5. _____, petrol cars aren't going to be around forever on account of climate change and finite oil supplies.

三、佳句模仿

原文佳句	Both take fees from the hospitals and clinics that they list, as published on their websites.
亮点评析	句中 as 作为关系代词指代前面整个主句并引出非限定性定语从句。另外，as 引导的限制性或非限制性定语从句若含有被动结构 "be 动词 + 过去分词"，be 动词往往被省略。
写作应用	The actress acts skillfully, as shown in the movie. 正如电影里的显示，女演员表演精湛。

原文佳句	Fewer American patients came than expected partly because health insurers were not interested in sending people overseas.
亮点评析	当主句中含有形容词或副词的比较级时，其比较对象需要用 than 引出。因 than 兼具关系代词和连词的功用，故其引导的比较状语从句中含有被动结构 "be 动词 + 过去分词" 时，容易引起争议的 be 动词往往被省略。

写作应用

Tesla doubled its loss in the second quarter but burned less cash than expected, as the rush of new Model 3 sales helped ease some pressure as the electric-car maker seeks to deliver a profit later this year.

特斯拉第二季度的亏损增加了一倍，但其现金消耗低于预期，因为新车型 3 的畅销缓解了一部分压力，而这恰恰发生在特斯拉试图在今年下半年实现盈利之际。

◆ 答案

一、长难句翻译

1. 一部分原因是国与国之间在把什么视为是医疗旅游方面存在差异，所以难以给出精确的统计数字。

2. 相当大的价格差促使消费者越境去接受相同的治疗。

3. 加拿大英属哥伦比亚大学西蒙弗雷泽大学的地理学教授 Valorie 补充说，由于不掌握有关医院和诊所以及全科和外科医生资质的详尽而可靠的信息，所以医疗旅游仍然受到了制约。

4. 如果撇下这些国际医院不谈，患者一直以来就不得不单纯依靠医院的声望或推行医疗旅行的中介机构的说辞了。

5. 政府公共账户管理委员会的后续调查表明，其中一个原因是赞助商对就医人数的预估是建立在一份有虚假成分的研究报告上的。

二、词块填空

1. under the knife

2. pin down

3. grease the wheels

4. In time

5. One way or another

27 Open Offices Can Lead to Closed Minds[M]

开放式办公室可致心理封闭

Some workplace designs are more about cost-cutting than collaboration

1　"Loneliness is a crowded room," as Bryan Ferry of the band Roxy Music once **warbled**, adding that everyone was "all together, all alone". The **open-plan office** might have been designed to **make his point**. That is not the **rationale** for the layout (布局)，of course. The supposed aim of  open-plan offices is to ensure that workers will have more contact with their **colleagues**, and that the resulting **collaboration** will **lead to** greater **productivity**.

2　Ethan Bernstein and Stephen Turban, two Harvard Business School academics (专业学者)，**set out** to test this proposition (见解).

3　①The authors surveyed interactions between colleagues in two unnamed multinational companies which had switched to open-plan offices. They did so by recruiting workers to wear "sociometric (社会测量)" **badges**. These used infra-red sensors (红外传感器) to detect when people were interacting, microphones to determine when they were speaking or listening to each other, another device to monitor their body movement and **posture** and a Bluetooth sensor to capture their location.

4　②At the first company, the authors found that face-to-face interactions were more than three times higher in the old, **cubicle**-based office than in an open-plan space where employees have clear **lines of sight** to each other. **In contrast**, the number of e-mails people sent to each other increased by 56% when they switched to open-plan. In the second company, face-to-face interactions decreased by a third after the switch to open-plan, whereas e-mail traffic increased by between 22% and 50%.

5　Why did this shift occur? The authors suggest that employees value their privacy and find new ways to preserve it in an open-plan office. They shut themselves off by wearing large headphones to **keep out** the **distractions** caused by nearby colleagues. Indeed, those who champion open-plan offices seem to have forgotten the importance of being able to **concentrate on** your work.

6 Employees also find other ways of communicating with their fellow workers. ③Rather than have a chat in front of a large audience, employees simply send an e-mail; the result (as measured at one of the two companies surveyed) was that productivity declined.

7 ④Cubicles do not offer a great work environment either; they are still noisy and **cut off** employees **from** natural light. But at least workers have more of a chance to give their work area a personal touch（特色）. Allowing plenty of room for pictures of children, office plants, **novelty** coffee mugs—these are ways of making people feel more relaxed and happy in their jobs.

8 ⑤Such comforts are completely denied when companies shift to "hot-desking（无固定办公桌式办公）", as 45% of multinationals plan by 2020, according to CBRE, a property firm, up from 30% of such companies now. Workers **roam** the building **in search of** a desk, like commuters hunting the last rush-hour seat or tourists looking for a poolside **lounger**. If you planned to spend a morning quietly reading a research paper or a management **tome**, tough luck; the last desk was **nabbed** by Jenkins in accounts（财务部）.

9 Hot-desking is a clear message to low-level office workers that they are seen as **disposable cogs** in a machine. Combine this with the lack of privacy and the office becomes a depressing place to work. Workers could stay at home but that **negates** the intended benefits of collaboration that open-plan offices bring.

10 The drive for such offices is **reminiscent of** the British enthusiasm for residential tower blocks（塔式大楼）after the second world war. One British wartime survey found that 49% wanted to live in a small house with a garden; only 5% wanted a flat. But flats they got. Architects, who fancied themselves as visionaries（有远见之人）like Howard Roark, the "hero" of Ayn Rand's *The Fountainhead*, competed to create concrete temples for the masses to occupy. As David Kynaston, in his book *Austerity Britain* describes, the desires of the actual residents were dismissed.

11 The real reason post-war architects built flats rather than homes is that it was a lot cheaper. And the same reason, not the supposed benefits of **mingling with** colleagues, is why open-plan offices are **all the rage**. More workers can be **crammed** into any given space.

12 Some people like them, of course, just as some like living in tower blocks. The only option for everyone else is to **kick up a stink** until **executives change their minds** and provide some personal space. **In other words**: workers of the world, unite. So you can separate again.

◆ 课文小助手

一、生词和词块释义

warble /'wɔ:bəl/ *vi.* 用颤音高声唱

rationale /ˌræʃən'ɑ:l/ *n.* （决定、信念等）的依据

colleague /'kɒli:g/ *n.* 同行

collaboration /kəˌlæbə'reɪʃn/ *n.* 合作

productivity /ˌprɒdʌk'tɪvɪti/ *n.* 生产率

badge /bædʒ/ *n.* 徽章

recruit /rɪ'kru:t/ *vt.* 招募

posture /'pɒstʃə/ *n.* 仪态

cubicle /'kju:bɪk(ə)l/ *n.* 小隔间

distraction /dɪ'strækʃ(ə)n/ *n.* 使人分心的东西

novelty /'nɒv(ə)lti/ *n.* 新颖

roam /rəʊm/ *vt.* 闲逛

lounger /'laʊndʒə/ *n.* 躺椅

tome /təʊm/ *n.* （学术性或理论性的）大部头作品

nab /næb/ *vt.* 抢占

disposable /dɪ'spəʊzəb(ə)l/ *adj.* 一次性的

cog /kɒg/ *n.* 轮齿

negate /nɪ'geɪt/ *vt.* 使……无效

austerity /ɒ'sterɪti/ *n.* 朴素

cram /kræm/ *vt.* 把……塞满

stink /stɪŋk/ *n.* 恶臭

executive /ɪg'zekjʊtɪv/ *n.* 行政管理人员

open-plan office 开敞式办公室

make one's point 使某人的论点为人所信服

lead to 导致

set out to do sth. 着手做某事

line of sight 视线

in contrast 与此相反

keep sth. out 遮挡某物

concentrate on 集中精力于

cut sth. off from sth. 把……与……隔绝

in search of 寻找

reminiscent of 使人联想到

mingle with （在社交场合）与……周旋、交际

all the rage 风靡一时

kick up a stink 大吵大闹

change one's mind 改变某人的想法

in other words 换言之

二、话题概要

大意：开放式和无固定办公桌式等新兴办公场所的设计方案，与其说是为了增进合作，提高效率，不如说是为了节约成本。员工应团结起来予以抵制。

Para. 1: 推行开放式办公室的初衷就是使员工彼此多接触，多合作，以便提高劳动生产率。

Para. 2–4: 有两位专家让受试者佩戴社会测量仪，在两家跨国公司里对此主张进行了调研，结果发现，开放式办公室并不利于员工面对面交流，他们更喜欢发邮件而非在大庭广众之下来沟通。

Para. 5–6: 事与愿违的原因是员工在开放式办公环境中更注意保护个人隐私，所以他们宁愿发邮件；再者，他们喜欢闹中取静以便在工作中能聚精会神。

Para. 7: 隔断式办公室虽然也吵，也见不到自然光，但可以按个人偏好装扮属于自己的空间，可以在工作中更具幸福感。

Para. 8–9: 在"无固定办公桌式办公"环境中，底层员工没有隐私权，感觉自己可有可无，办公室也毫无吸引力可言。他们可以呆在家，但最初实行开放式办公的合作意义就荡然无存了。糟糕的是有 45% 的跨国公司表示要在 2020 年前采用"无固定办公桌式办公"。

Para. 10–11: 第二次世界大战时期，一些建筑学家自认为有远见卓识，背弃了居民的诉求，为了省钱，盖起了一幢幢水泥筒子楼让百姓居住，而这也是为什么开放式办公室风靡一时的原因——无论多大的空间都可以塞进更多的人，这与开放式办公室当初所设想的优势——与同事打成一片——截然不同。

Para. 12: 萝卜青菜各有所爱。留给众人的唯一选择只能是大吵大闹直到高管改变策略，给员工私密空间。也就是说：全世界打工者联合起来，为自己的一方寸土而斗争。

◆ 同步练习

一、长难句翻译（见文章划线处）

二、词块填空

1. Ok, you've _____. There's no need to keep going on about it.

2. Local residents are _____ over the new parking charges.

3. Accessible only by air, our town is _____ the rest of the country.

4. You might as well take full advantage of the wedding. Go out of your way to _____ others.

5. For today's children, take-out eating, worn jeans and online studying are _____.

6. The cannon can be linked to the _____ of the gunner so that it points in the same direction that he looks in.

三、佳句模仿

原文佳句	These used infra-red sensors to detect when people were interacting, microphones to determine when they were speaking or listening to each other, another device to monitor their body movement and posture and a Bluetooth sensor to capture their location.
亮点评析	谓语动词 used 后有 4 个并列宾语，而每个宾语后又都有一个动词不定式作目的状语。前两个不定式后又跟有 when 引导的从句作宾语。

写作应用	The way space is used to enable the individual to achieve privacy, to build homes or to design cities is culturally influenced. 如何使用空间来让个人获得隐私、建造房子或设计城市，这是受文化影响的。 We use space to enable individuals to achieve privacy, communities to share resources and the social security system to come to each other's rescue. 我们使用空间来让个人获得隐私，让团体共享资源，让每一个人都能得到社会安全体系的援救。

原文佳句	In the second company, face-to-face interactions decreased by a third after the switch to open-plan, whereas e-mail traffic increased by between 22% and 50%.
亮点评析	并列连词 whereas 连接了两个描写数值变化的并列句，使之形成鲜明对比。句中有关数值变化的句式 increase/decrease by between...to... 可以效仿。
写作应用	The largest changes occurred from 2008 to 2011, when small cigar consumption decreased by 86.4%, from 5.9 billion to 0.8 billion, whereas large cigar consumption increased by between 110% and 126.3% according to different geological areas. 2008 年到 2011 年发生了最大的变化，而这期间，小雪茄消费减少了 86.4%，也就是从 59 亿减少到 8 亿，然而根据不同的地理环境，大雪茄消费增加范围在 110% 到 126.3%。

◆ 答案

一、长难句翻译

1. 这两位作者调研了两家匿名跨国公司同事之间的互动情况，而这两家公司都已经换成了开敞式办公室。

2. 在第一家公司作者发现，与雇员间能彼此看得很清楚的开放式空间相比，在传统的、小隔断式的办公室，面对面互动要高出三倍有余。

3. 员工们并没有在大庭广众之下聊天，而只是发邮件。（正如在上述两家跨国公司做调研时在其中一家所测评的那样）其结果就是生产率下降。

4. 小隔断也并没有提供良好的工作环境，里面也是吵吵嚷嚷，也是见不到自然光，但至少员工有机会给自己的工作区域增添些许个性情调。

5. 根据房地产公司 CBRE 的数据，当公司转向"无固定办公桌式办公"时，这种舒适的办公条件就被完全剥夺了，因为到 2020 年，有 45% 的跨国公司计划这样做，而现在只有 30% 的公司采取这种方式办公。

二、词块填空

1. made your point

2. kicking up a stink

3. cut off from

4. mingle with

5. all the rage

6. line of sight

Chapter 5

科普 / Science

28 How to Stop Information Overload[M]
如 何 中 止 信 息 超 载

1 　①Information overload is a creature that has been growing on the Internet's back since its beginnings. The bigger the Internet gets, the more information there is. The more quality information we see, the more we want to consume it. The more we want to consume it, the more overloaded we feel. This has to stop somewhere.

2 　The sole fact that there's more and more information published online every single day is not the actual problem. When we see some half-completed blog (博客) posts we don't even consider reading, we just skip to the next thing. But when we see something truly interesting—maybe even epic (史诗)—we want to consume it.No matter what topic we're interested in, there are always hundreds of quality blogs publishing entries every single day or every other day. **Not to mention** all the forums, message boards, social news sites, and so on. ②The amount of epic content on the Internet these days is so big that it's actually impossible for us to digest it all. But we try anyway. That's when we feel overloaded. Information overload is a plague (灾祸). There's no vaccine, there's no cure. It's quite easy to convince yourself that you really need something just because of poor self-control.

3 　③When you try to consume more and more information every day, you start to notice that even though you've been reading tons of articles, watching tons of videos and listening to tons of podcasts, the stream of incoming information seems to be infinite. Therefore, you convince yourself that you need to be on a constant careful search for new information if you want to be able to accomplish anything in your life, work and/or **passion**. The final result is that **you** are consuming too much information, and taking too little action because you don't have enough

time for it.Be sure that you don't need every piece of advice possible to live your life, do your work or enjoy your passion.

4　How to recognize the part of information that you really need? Start with setting goals. If you don't have your goals, you'll be just running around grabbing every possible advice and thinking that it's "just what you've been looking for." Setting goals is a much more **profound** task than just a way to **get rid of** information overload. Now by "goals" I don't mean things like "get rich, have kids, and live a good life". I mean something much more within your immediate grasp. Something that can be achieved in the near future—like within a month (or a year) at most.

5　Know what to skip when facing new information. ④Once you have your goals, plans, strategies and tasks, you can use them to decide what information is really **crucial**. First of all, if the information you're about to read **has nothing to do with** your current goals and plans, then skip it. You don't need it. If it does, then ask yourself these questions: Will you be able to put this information into action immediately? Does it have the potential to maybe **alter** your nearest actions/tasks? Is it so incredible that you absolutely need to take action on it right away? If the information is not actionable in a day or two, then skip it. Digest only what can be used immediately. If you have a task that you need to do, consume only the information necessary for getting this one task done, nothing more.You need to be focused in order to have clear judgment, and be able to decide whether some piece of information is required or unnecessary.

6　Everybody knows that every pill has a MED—Minimal (最少的) Effective Dose, and after that specific dose, no other positive effects occur, only some negative side effects if you overdose big. Consuming information is somewhat similar. You need just a **precise** amount of it to help you to achieve your goals and put your plans into life.Everything more than that amount won't improve your results any further.

7　Don't procrastinate (耽搁) by consuming more information. Probably one of the most common causes of consuming ridiculous amounts of information is the need to procrastinate. ⑤We don't **feel like doing** what really needs to be done—the important stuff—so instead we find something else, and convince ourselves that "that thing" is equally important. Which is just not true.Don't consume information just **for the sake of** it. It gets you nowhere.

◆ 课文小助手

一、生词和词块释义

passion /'pæʃn/ *n.* 热情，激情   not to mention 更不必说

profound /prə'faʊnd/ *adj.* 极深的   get rid of 摆脱

crucial /'kru:ʃl/ *adj.* 重要的   have nothing to do with 与……无关

alter /'ɔ:ltə/ *v.* 改变   feel like doing sth. 喜欢做某事

precise /prɪ'saɪs/ *adj.* 精确的   for the sake of 为了……起见

二、话题概要

大意：本文主要说明信息超载的含义、信息超载的问题所在以及如何中止信息超载。

Para. 1: 信息超载的含义及形成的情况。

Para. 2: 感到信息超载。信息超载的严重性以及其产生的原因。

Para. 3: 信息超载阻止你采取行动，所以你得明确你不需要每一条建议来过你的生活，做你的工作或者享受你的激情。

Para. 4: 在如何识别你真正需要的信息的方面，首先从设定长远目标开始。

Para. 5: 面对新信息时，学会取舍。

Para. 6: MED（最小有效剂量）的原理。

Para. 7: 不要因为使用更多的信息而耽搁。

◆ 同步练习

一、长难句翻译（见文章划线处）

二、词块填空

1. It is true that plenty of people end up in jobs that _____ what they studies in their universities.

2. You are not allowed to go swimming alone _____ your safety.

3. You should be well aware of that it is not easy to _____ the bad habit.

4. I've changed my idea, I don't _____ going out tonight, I want to spend time to stay with my family.

三、佳句临摹

原文佳句	The amount of epic content on the Internet these days is so big that it's actually impossible for us to digest it all.
亮点评析	so...that... 引导结果状语从句

| 写作应用 | He is so confident that he is not afraid of making a speech in front of many people.
他非常自信以至他不怕在众人面前发表演说。 |

◆ 答案

一、长难句翻译

1. 信息超载是一种从互联网诞生以来就一直在增长的互联网的产物。

2. 现在互联网上的史诗内容是如此之大以至于我们根本不可能消化所有这些内容。

3. 当你每天都要使用越来越多的信息时，你会发现，即使你已经阅读了大量的文章，观看了大量的视频，听了大量的播客，但源源不断的信息似乎是无限的。

4. 一旦你有了你的目标、计划、策略和任务，你就可以用它们来决定哪些信息是至关重要的。

5. 我们不想做真正需要做的事情——（这是）重要的事情——所以我们找到了其他的东西，并说服自己"那件事"同样重要。

二、词块填空

1. have nothing to do with

2. for the safe of

3. get rid of

4. feel like

29 Admit It, Older People—You Are Addicted to Your Phones, too[E]

承认吧，老年人们——你们也对手机上瘾了

Over-reliance on mobiles isn't just the scourge of the young, and it has a damaging effect on families

1   "Leaving the room to wait until my father is finished with his 'serious business' (ie Farmville), has now become the norm." My mother likes to sit with her legs crossed on the sofa, glasses balanced on her nose, while she scrolls through her iPhone. I don't know whether she is commenting on a friend's family photo album, crushing candy or liking a **meme** with the caption: "Tonight's forecast: 99% chance of wine", but I do know that this is not the first time I catch her like this. My father opts for the "I'll be with you shortly" line, which he delivers with a very serious look on his face as he aggressively taps away on his phone. I have learned by now that this is my cue to leave him alone for the next 10 minutes. As much as they don't like admitting it, both of my parents are just as addicted to their phones as I am.

2   Growing up, we are constantly reminded that young people are the **demographic** most affected by technology. We are the "**antisocial** social club", those who prefer to text our friends in the same room rather than having to make eye-contact with them. <u>①We are the "**digital natives**", ruining the English language because we favour using heart-eye emojis to tell someone we **fancy** them, instead of spelling it out.</u> We are "generation mute", unable to bear phone calls because apparently the awkwardness of calling someone up is just too real. <u>②And even though I can recognise myself in some of the never-ending studies that reveal to us the extent of our social media addiction, warning us that we are slowly turning into **tech-zombies**, we should at least consider that it's not only us young 'uns any more.</u>

3   There's the rise of the Instagram mums, who like to post **an abundance of** cute baby pictures, **showcasing** their seemingly (and oddly) put-together lifestyles and sharing their many momfeelings along the way, or the surge of over-55-year-olds who are beginning to occupy

and curate Facebook. ③They are the so-called "Facebook mum generation", a growing group of parents that like to overshare and, in the process, are slowly pushing out young people who can't bear to see another one of mum's embarrassing **gin**-and-**tonic**-on-a-holiday **selfies**. ④While many millennials are slowly leaving Facebook because our **timeline** seems to only **clog up** with fake news, dog videos and repetitive memes these days, our parents might see the platform as a way of keeping up with the social lives of their old schoolmates or, paradoxically, in my mother's case, "to see what my children are up to since phone calls have been running a bit dry". They're a little late to the party, but are still arriving in their droves, with Facebook expecting its largest growth of new members joining the platform in the UK to be among the over-55s users this year (a predicted 500,000, in fact).

4   And while all of this might be fine, and even a little **humorous,** new research suggests that parents' technology addiction is negatively affecting their children's behaviour. According to the study, 40% of mothers and 32% of fathers have admitted to having some sort of phone addiction. This has led to a significant fall in **verbal interactions** within families and even a decline in mothers encouraging their children. ⑤"Technoference" is the term used here to describe the increasing trend that sees people switching their attention away from those around them to check their phones instead—one that seems to be **infiltrating** far beyond friendship circles and now also into family life. And by family life, I mean not only young teens and children who are glued to their phones or tablets, but also their parents, who are now joining in on the antisocial fun. What are the consequences if we don't deal with this? And why don't we recognise it in the first place, when all the signs are there?

5   There is no denying that I get annoyed when I receive the "I'll be with you shortly line" from a parent, when all I want to do is ask one question. But, at the same time, leaving the room to wait until my father is finished with his "serious business" (ie Farmville), has now become the norm. Whether you want to escape your **pestering** children for a bit, or want to stay up late **flicking through** Twitter, know that wanting to do all of this is normal. We—your children—know how addictive it can be and how difficult it is to switch off. ⑥But before calling us out and telling us to "put our phones away at the table" or even worse, pulling up statistics of how damaging social media can be for us, maybe **lead by example** and consider how much time you spend on the phone as well as how this is impacting your children and your relationship with them. Maybe in this way we can work on our addiction together.

◆ 课文小助手

一、生词和词块释义

meme /miːm/ *n.* 表情包

demographic /ˌdeməˈɡræfɪk/ *n.* 特定年龄段的人口

antisocial /ˌæntɪˈsəʊʃ(ə)l/ *adj.* 不爱交际的

digital natives 数字原住民

fancy /ˈfænsɪ/ *v.* 喜爱

tech-zombie 科技僵尸

showcase /ˈʃəʊkeɪs/ *v.* 展现

gin /dʒɪn/ *n.* 杜松子酒

tonic /ˈtɒnɪk/ *n.* 汤力水

selfie /ˈsɛlfɪ/ *n.* 自拍照

timeline /ˈtaɪmlaɪn/ *n.* 时间轴，时间线

humorous /ˈhjuːm(ə)rəs/ *adj.* 诙谐的，幽默的

infiltrate /ˈɪnfɪlˌtreɪt/ *v.* 渗入

pester /ˈpestə/ *v.* 纠缠，烦扰

an abundance of 大量的

clog up 堵塞

verbal interaction 语言交流

flick through 浏览，（快速）翻阅

lead by example 以身作则

二、话题概要

大意:

Para. 1: 离开房间等父亲完成他的"重要事务"（比如开心农场），现在已经成为了一种常态。

Para. 2: 在成长的过程中，我们被不断提醒着：年轻人是受科技影响最大的群体。

Para. 3: Instagram 上出现了一个"妈妈群体"，她们喜欢上传大量的可爱宝宝的照片，展示她们看似光鲜亮丽的生活方式，并分享她们一路走来的众多做母亲的感想。她们就是所谓的"Facebook 妈妈一代"。

Para. 4: 虽然这一切可能都没什么问题，甚至还有一点幽默，但新的研究表明，父母的科技成瘾对孩子的行为产生了负面影响。

Para. 5: 不可否认的是，当我从父母那里收到"我一会儿和你线上聊"的消息时会感到恼怒，因为我只是想问一个问题而已。但与此同时，离开房间等父亲完成他的"重要事务"（比如开心农场），现在已经成为了一种常态。

◆ 同步练习

一、长难句翻译（见文章划线处）

二、词块填空

1. The area has _____wildlife.

2. 22,000 tourists were _____ the pavements.

3. The present paper concentrates its attention on metapragmatic phenomena and their

functions in _____of both Chinese and English.

4. I'll just _____ the pages until I find the right section.

5. I've learned to trust and depend on others, to work hard and _____.

三、佳句模仿

原文佳句	And while all of this might be fine, and even a little humorous, new research suggests that parents' technology addiction is negatively affecting their children's behaviour.
亮点评析	while 引导让步状语从句，含义为"虽然"，作者旨在强调另外半句，即"父母的过分依赖手机成瘾的趋势正在消极地影响孩子们使用手机不当甚至成瘾"。
写作应用	While Achal explained that this process is highly accurate, it is not perfect. 虽然 Achal 解释说这个过程高度精确，但是并不完美。

原文佳句	And by family life, I mean not only young teens and children who are glued to their phones or tablets, but also their parents, who are now joining in on the antisocial fun.
亮点评析	not only...but also... 意思是"不仅……而且……"强调 but also 引导的部分。突出本文主旨：家里的老人沉溺手机不亚于年轻人。
写作应用	In production, we demand not only quantity but also quality. 我们的产品不但要求数量多，而且要求质量高。

◆ 答案

一、长难句翻译

1. 我们是毁灭了英语的"数字原住民"，因为我们喜欢用心形眼睛表情符号告诉某人我们喜欢他们，而不是直接说出来。

2. 尽管有无穷无尽的研究向我们揭示了我们对社交媒体的上瘾程度，警示我们正在逐渐变成"科技僵尸"，但我们至少应该想到，这不再仅仅是年轻人的问题了。

3. 她们就是所谓的"Facebook 妈妈一代"，这是一个不断壮大的家长群体，她们喜欢过度分享，并在这个过程中，将不愿再看到妈妈们"在假期喝杜松子酒和汤力水"尴尬自拍的年轻人排挤出 Facebook。

4. 许多千禧一代正在逐渐退出 Facebook，因为近来我们的时间线上似乎只充斥着虚假新闻、小狗视频和千篇一律的表情包，但我们的父母可能把这个平台看作跟老同学保持社交往来的一种途径，或者很矛盾的是，就我的母亲而言，想看看孩子们到底忙什么，电话的次数一直有点少。

5. "技术干扰"一词在这里被用来描述这种增长的趋势，即人们将注意力从周围的人身上转移到手机上——它似乎已经渗透出友谊圈外，现在也渗透进了家庭生活中。

6. 但在叫我们"把手机放在桌上"或更糟糕的，拿出统计数据告诉我们社交媒体可以对我们造成多大伤害前，或许你们可以以身作则，想一想你们在手机上花了多少时间，以及它是如何影响你的孩子以及你与孩子的关系的。

二、词块填空

1. an abundance of

2. clogging up

3. verbal interaction

4. flick through

5. lead by example

30　New Materials Could Usher in Faster-Charging, Higher-Power Batteries[M]

新材料将助力造出更快速充电、更高功率的电池

1　Lithium-ion batteries（锂离子电池）could have much higher power and recharge far more rapidly using a new class of complex oxide electrodes（氧化电极）, a new study finds. <u>①Such research could lead to batteries that can store large amounts of energy in minutes rather than hours, helping speed the adoption of technologies such as electric cars and grid-level storage of renewable energy, researchers say.</u>

2　In their simplest form, batteries **consist of** three components—a positive electrode called a cathode（阴极）, a negative electrode called an anode（阳极）, and an electrolyte（电解质）connecting both electrodes. When a lithium-ion battery is discharging（放电）, lithium ions flow from the anode to the cathode; when recharging, from the cathode to the anode. The faster lithium ions can move, the faster the battery can charge and the greater its power (that is, the more energy it can deliver during a given time). The most commonly used approach to improve lithium-ion flow speeds is to make electrode particles nanometers in size to shorten the amount of distance that lithium ions have to travel. However, there are many challenges to this approach. Nanoparticles（纳米粒子）can prove difficult to pack tightly together, limiting the amount of energy they can store per unit volume（每单位体积）. They can also **result in** more unwanted chemical reactions with electrolytes **compared with** regular electrode materials, so such batteries do not last as long. Moreover, nanoparticles can also prove complex and expensive to make.

3　Instead, senior author Clare Grey, a materials chemist at the University of Cambridge, in England, and her colleagues investigated niobium tungsten oxides（铌钨氧化物）. <u>②They noted these materials have rigid（刚性）open crystalline structures（晶体结构）that they reasoned lithium ions（锂离子）could quickly flow within, even when comparatively large micron-sized（微米）particles of the oxides were used instead of nanoparticles.</u> The researchers analyzed the performance of two different kinds of niobium tungsten oxide anodes—$Nb_{16}W_5O_{55}$ and $Nb_{18}W_{16}O_{93}$. They used pulsed-field-gradient（脉冲场梯度）nuclear magnetic resonance

（核磁共振）(akin to（类似于）an MRI) to measure the movement of lithium ions through the oxides.③"Much of this research was completely new, as these atomic structures are not common and few studies exist on them in any field," says study lead author Kent Griffith, a materials chemist at the University of Cambridge.

4　The scientists found that lithium ions moved hundreds of times as fast in these oxides（氧化物）than typical anode materials. This suggests they could lead to higher-power and faster-charging batteries. "We were most surprised at just how fast the measured **diffusion** and rate performance were in these micrometer-scale particles（微米级粒子）," Griffith says. "These materials can recharge on the timescale of minutes." A great deal more work is needed to develop a commercial battery from this research, he cautions.

5　④The researchers also warned that while niobium tungsten oxides could lead to lithium-ion battery cells with higher power than **conventional** types, these new batteries would also have lower battery-cell voltages（电压）. Basically, while energy can move in and out of these niobium tungsten oxides quickly, this would involve lower amounts of energy per unit time compared to conventional anode materials. However, lower battery-cell voltages could result in safer batteries. **For instance**, most current lithium-ion batteries possess graphite（石墨）anodes. The electrical properties of graphite lead to higher battery-cell voltages but also can make them form spindly lithium-metal fibers **known as** dendrites（树突）when they charge at high rates. These dendrites can **trigger** short circuits（短路）, causing batteries to catch fire and possibly explode. "Thus, it is likely necessary to use a cell with lower voltage, like ours, for a very high-rate battery," Griffith says.

6　One potential criticism of these new materials is that niobium（铌）and tungsten（钨）are heavy atoms, leading to heavy batteries. However, Griffith notes niobium tungsten oxides can store about twice as many lithium ions per unit volume or more than conventional lithium-ion battery anodes. ⑤As such, he says niobium tungsten oxides can store a similar amount of charge per unit weight as conventional lithium-ion battery materials while potentially avoiding the complexity and cost of nanoparticles. The scientists are now trying to find the best cathode and electrolyte materials to accompany niobium tungsten oxide anodes. They also suggest there are potentially other materials with structures and properties much like those of niobium tungsten oxides. "We are optimistic that there are other promising materials yet to be discovered," Griffith says.

◆ 课文小助手

一、生词和词块释义

diffusion /dɪ'fjuːʒn/ *n.* 扩散；传播

conventional /kən'venʃənl/ *adj.* 传统的；
习用的

trigger /'trɪɡə(r)/ *v.* 引发，触发

consist of... 由……组成

result in 导致

compared with... 与……相比较

for instance 例如

known as... 以……命名

二、话题概要

大意：一项来自剑桥大学科学家的研究表明，在未来可将锂离子电池充电过程缩短至几分钟！

Para. 1: 一项新的研究发现，锂离子电池在使用一种新型的复合氧化物电极后，具有更高的功率和充电速度。

Para. 2: 在最简单的形式中，电池由三个组成部分组成：正电极称为阴极，负电极称为阳极，以及连接两个电极的电解质。

Para. 3: 英国剑桥大学的材料化学家 Clare Grey 和她的同事们研究了铌钨氧化物。

Para. 4: 科学家发现锂离子在这些氧化物中的迁移速度比典型的阳极材料快几百倍。

Para. 5: 研究人员还警告说，虽然铌钨氧化物可能导致比传统类型更高功率的锂离子电池，但这些新电池也会具有较低的电池单元电压。

Para. 6: 对这些新材料的一个潜在的批评是铌和钨是重原子，导致电池很重。然而，Griffith 指出铌钨氧化物可以存储大约两倍于单位体积的锂离子或比传统的锂离子电池阳极更多的锂离子。

◆ 同步练习

一、长难句翻译（见文章划线处）

二、词块填空

1. A healthy diet should _____ wholefood.

2. Fatigue and stress quickly_____ a dull complexion and a furrowed brow.

3. _____ her achievements, her shortcomings are, after all, only secondary.

4. They will be concerned to do the right thing—to dress properly, _____.

5. Computer systems throughout the country are being affected by a series of mysterious rogue programs, _____ viruses

三、佳句模仿

原文佳句	Basically, while energy can move in and out of these niobium tungsten oxides quickly, this would involve lower amounts of energy per unit time compared to conventional anode materials.
亮点评析	basically 的含义是"从根本上来说"。作者强调重要内容时提醒读者关注。
写作应用	This gun is designed for one purpose—it's basically to kill people. 这种枪只有一个用途——就是用来杀人。

原文佳句	It is likely necessary to use a cell with lower voltage, like ours, for a very high-rate battery.
亮点评析	It is likely necessary to do sth. 的含义是"有必要做某事"。说话人强烈推荐某事时用。
写作应用	To understand why they are doing it, it is necessary to know where they are coming from. 要弄清楚他们这样做的原因，必须要了解他们的意图。

◆ 答案

一、长难句翻译

1. 研究人员说，这样的研究可以使电池能够在几分钟内而不是几小时内储存大量的能量，有助于加快诸如电动汽车和可再生能源的电网级存储等技术的应用。

2. 他们指出，这些材料具有刚性的开放晶体结构，他们认为锂离子可以在内部快速流动，即使当使用相对较大的微米大小的氧化物颗粒代替纳米粒子。

3. "这项研究的大部分都是全新的，因为这些原子结构并不常见，在任何领域都很少有研究，"剑桥大学的材料化学家 Ken Griffith 说。

4. 研究人员还警告说，虽然铌钨氧化物可能导致比传统类型更高功率的锂离子电池，但这些新电池也会具有较低的电池单元电压。

5. 因此，他说铌钨氧化物作为常规锂离子电池材料可以储存相当量的单位电量，同时潜在地避免了纳米颗粒的复杂性和成本。

二、词块填空

1. consist of

2. result in

3. Compared with

4. for instance

5. known as

31 Probe Memory Packs[M]

探 针 存 储 器

New automated approach could help make STM probe memory commercially viable

1 ①Researchers at the University of Alberta in Canada have developed a new approach to rewritable data storage technology by using a scanning tunneling microscope (STM) to remove and replace hydrogen atoms (氢原子) from the surface of a silicon wafer (硅晶片). If this approach realizes its potential, it could lead to a data storage technology **capable of** storing 1,000 times more data than today's hard drives, up to 138 terabytes (百万兆字节) per square inch. ②As a bit of background, Gerd Binnig and Heinrich Rohrer developed the first STM in 1986 for which they later received the Nobel Prize in physics. In the over 30 years since an STM first imaged an atom by **exploiting** a phenomenon known as tunneling—which causes electrons to jump from the surface atoms of a material to the tip of an ultrasharp electrode **suspended** a few angstroms (长度单位) above—the technology has become the backbone of so-called nanotechnology.

2 In addition to imaging the world on the atomic scale for the last thirty years, STMs have been experimented with as a potential data storage device. Last year, we reported on how IBM (where Binnig and Rohrer first developed the STM) used an STM **in combination with** an iron atom to **serve as** an electron-spin resonance sensor to read the magnetic pole of holmium atoms. The north and south poles of the holmium atoms served as the 0 and 1 of digital logic. ③The Canadian researchers have taken a somewhat different approach to making an STM into a data storage device by automating a known technique that uses the ultrasharp tip of the STM to apply a voltage pulse above an atom to remove individual hydrogen atoms from the surface of a silicon wafer. Once the atom has been removed, there is a vacancy on the surface. These vacancies can be patterned on the surface to create devices and memories. "We have automated the removal procedure so that it is possible to enter a design, and have it created without user intervention," explained Roshan Achal, a Ph.D. student at the University of Alberta and lead author on the research described in the journal Nature Communications.

3 While Achal explained that this process is highly accurate, it is not perfect. Sometimes hydrogen atoms can be removed from incorrect locations. This type of error would require another attempt from scratch to create a design. "We have developed a procedure that allows us to replace individual atoms on the surface, to erase these mistakes, instead of starting from zero each time an error occurs," he explained. In order to replace an atom on the surface, a hydrogen atom must be sitting on the surface of the tip. By bringing the tip closer and closer to the surface, it is possible for it to jump from the tip to the surface. "We discovered that there are two unique signatures when a transfer occurs, that can be used to help automate this procedure as well," he added.

4 ④While these techniques could fall into the broad categories of nanoscale fabrication, the major difference with this technique, according to Achal, is the level of accuracy and degree of automation that has been achieved in fabricating structures on this silicon surface. In addition, no other nanofabrication technique had managed to replace in a controlled way several hydrogen atoms on the surface in succession. Perhaps one of the biggest restrictions of STMs in data storage has been the need for cryogenic (低温的) temperatures. However, with this latest approach, the hydrogen-terminated (氢端基) silicon system, **by its nature**, enables the fabrication of structures that are stable well above room temperature. "This stability comes **at the cost of** increased **difficulty in** fabricating structures," said Achal. "However, with these new techniques we have overcome many of the associated problems, making this system a very interesting candidate for new technological applications."

5 This approach certainly addresses the issue of cryogenic temperatures being needed to allow such a device to work, but does it scale? Achal argues that there are no physical limitations preventing the speeds of these processes from reaching practical levels. ⑤Achal and his colleagues are looking into new schemes to improve speeds, but there are also currently available ways to scale these processes that don't involve changing the procedures significantly. The most accessible solution would be the parallelization (平行化) of many tips inside an STM, according to Achal. He also noted that there are some tip materials that are known to hold up to a thousand hydrogen atoms simultaneously (同时地). If these materials **turn out to be viable** options for a tip, then they would allow for even faster erasing/rewriting speeds.

In the meantime, the specter of IBM's Millipede project looms over proposals of massive parallelization. The IBM Millipede essentially used an array of thousands of miniaturized（小型化的）Atomic Force Microscopes (AFMs) as a memory device. Paul Seidler, a researcher at IBM Research in Zurich, said seven years ago that IBM had abandoned the Millipede project as an alternative data storage technology and instead had found its most likely role as probes（探针探头）for lithography. [6]If this STM approach is to experience a more successful fate than the Millipede project in data storage, Achal and his colleagues will need to take the huge step of parallelization of tips inside a STM.

◆ **课文小助手**

一、生词和词块释义

exploit /ɪkˈsplɔɪt/ *v.* 利用

suspend /səˈspend/ *v.* 暂停；悬挂

capable of... 有……能力

viable /ˈvaɪəbl/ *adj.* 切实可行的

in combination with 与……联合，与……结合

serve as 充当

by its nature 从本质上来讲

at the cost of 以……为代价

difficulty in 有困难于

turn out to be 事实证明结果是

二、话题概要

大意: 研究人员利用扫描隧道显微镜(STM)删除和替换硅晶片的表面的氢原子，对可重写数据存储技术产生了一种新方法。

Para. 1: 加拿大艾伯塔大学的研究人员利用扫描隧道显微镜(STM)删除和替换硅晶片的表面的氢原子，对可重写数据存储技术产生了一种新方法。

Para. 2: 除了对物体进行极高分辨率的成像，研究人员还试图开发扫描隧道显微镜作为数据存储设备的潜力。

Para. 3: Achal 解释说，这个过程是非常准确的，它是不完美的。

Para. 4: 虽然这些技术可能落入纳米制造的大类，根据 Achal 的说法，这种技术的主要区别，是精度与自动化程度已在硅表面制备结构上所达到的水平。

Para. 5: 这种方法当然解决了允许这种装置工作的低温需求问题，但是它是否具有规模呢？

◆ **同步练习**

一、长难句翻译（见文章划线处）

二、词块填空

1.In the wake of developments in science and technology, man has become more _____ conquering nature.

2. The new treatment can be used either alone or _____the traditional one.

3. Several painters were working on a huge piece of canvas which would _____the scenery.

4. The higher education, _____ , is concerned with abstractions& both in the sciences and in

humane studies.

5. The lessons learned _____ blood helped to sober us.

6. Most people have very little _____ seeing why a Van Gogh is a work of genius.

7. Everyone is hoping that these hi-tech companies will _____ the Microsofts of the future.

At the moment, they look more like the focus of a speculative bubble.

三、佳句模仿

原文佳句	In addition to imaging the world on the atomic scale for the last thirty years, STMs have been experimented with as a potential data storage device.
亮点评析	in addition to 是 "除此之外还有……" 的意思。强调还有的部分。
写作应用	In addition to my weekly wage, I got a lot of tips. 除了每周的薪水外，我还能得到不少小费。

原文佳句	Once the atom has been removed, there is a vacancy on the surface.
亮点评析	once 引导条件状语从句，强调在某种条件下会实现对应的结果。
写作应用	We didn't know how we would cope once the money had gone. 钱一旦花光，我们就不知所措。

◆ 答案

一、长难句翻译

1. 加拿大艾伯塔大学的研究人员利用扫描隧道显微镜 (STM) 删除和替换硅晶片的表面的氢原子，对可重写数据存储技术产生了一种新方法。

2. 1986 年，基德·比林 (Gerd Binnig) 和海因里希·罗赫 (Heinrich Rohrer) 在 IBM 公司发明了世界上第一台扫描隧道显微镜，后来被授予诺贝尔物理学奖。该显微镜利用了一种被称为隧道效应的物理原理，即电子从被观测物体表面的原子中跳出，到达在观测材料上方不到 1 纳米处的接收电极，通过处理形成图像，这一事件已经过去 30 年了。扫描隧道显微镜是今天纳米技术的基础。

3. 加拿大研究人员采用了另外一种基于扫描隧道显微镜构建存储器的方式。他们用电极对材料发射电脉冲，移除硅片表面的单个氢原子。

4. 虽然这些技术可能落入纳米制造的大类，根据 Achal 的说法，这种技术的主要区别，是精度与自动化程度已在硅表面制备结构上所达到的水平。

5. Achal 和他的同事正在研究新的改进速度的方案，但是目前也有一些有效可行的方法来扩大这些过程，这些过程不需要显著改变程序。

6. 如果这个 STM 方法在数据存储上比千足虫项目更加成功，Achal 和同事将有必要在对 STM 的探针平行化技术上迈出一大步。

二、词块填空

1. capable of

2. in combination with

3. serve as

4. by its nature

5. at the cost of

6. difficulty in

7. turn out to be

Chapter 6

社会 / Society

32 Mini-grids May Be the Best Way to Illuminate the "Bottom Billion"[E]

照亮底层民众的最佳方式——小型电网

1 Electricity powers growth, **boosts** education and improves lives. Yet about 1.1bn mostly rural dwellers (居民) in Asia and Africa remain stuck **in the dark**. They have no electric light, rely on kerosene (煤油) and diesel (柴油) for power, and struggle to irrigate their crops. The good news is that people can be connected to clean, reliable power faster than ever before. But to realize the potential, governments need to rethink the role of utilities (公共事业).

2 Typically, countries connect citizens with vast **grid-extension** programs. Big grids make perfect sense for populous (人口稠密的) places. ①They can cheaply supply power **generated** far away to millions and, as they incorporate (结合) more wind and solar energy, they are becoming greener. But in remote places, the economic case for grids becomes hard to make.

3 Many utilities **are short of** cash, if not bankrupt (破产的). The cost of taking power to those least able to afford it **adds to** their debts. China and Thailand took 20 years to improve electrification (电气化) rates from about 30-40% to 85-90%. Reaching the remaining sliver (小片) took a further 20 years; China managed it only in 2015. ②And universal electrification, a slogan beloved of politicians, is frequently less than it seems. In April India celebrated the electrification of its last village, yet about 240m people remain without power and connections are often **unreliable**.

4 ③Enter mini-grids, which can operate independently of national grids, and are a way for private companies to offer services more quickly and reliably than frequently state-owned incumbents (企业). Mini-grids are banks of batteries often charged by solar arrays (太阳能电池板). ④Unlike "rooftop" solar systems, which are increasingly common in parts of Africa but provide little juice, mini-grids provide round-the-clock electricity capable of powering machinery(机械), irrigation systems and freezers, as well as lighting. Although they are expensive, mini-grids are likely to become cheaper as they grow more common. In the interim (过渡时期), providers are using specialists in rural development and microfinance (小额信贷) to teach people how to set up businesses that benefit from a lot of power. They find that if people learn how to make money from electricity, they willingly pay for it.

5   ⑤The International Energy Agency, a forecaster, **reckons** mini-grids could **account for** $300bn of investment by 2030, making them the most important means of achieving universal access. Yet for that to happen, governments must embrace (欣然接受) them. Officials are often unwilling to decentralise (分权) the power supply **for fear of** losing political control. For their part, mini-grid providers fear being left in the lurch (挫折) if the main grid suddenly arrives in one of their markets.

6   Both problems can be solved if governments see mini-grids not as autarkic (自给自足的) outposts (边远村落), but as part of a master plan. Mini-grids and rooftop solar systems can one day **be hooked up to** the main grid; they should not compete as paths to rural electrification. The more **strategic** planning of this sort there is, the less risk that mini-grids will **end up as** "stranded assets (资产搁置)". Governments could reallocate the subsidies (补贴) available for extending grids to lower the cost of expanding mini-grids. They would be able to promote mini-grids across neighbouring villages, improving the economies of scale for developers. Countries like Nigeria are already pioneering such initiatives (主动权). Call it enlightened (进步的) thinking.

◆ 课文小助手

一、生词和词块释义

boost /buːst/ *v.* 推动

grid /grɪd/ *n.* 输电网

extension /ɪk'stenʃən/ *n.* 延伸

generate /'dʒenəreɪt/ *v.* 产生（热、电等能量）

unreliable /ˌʌnrɪ'laɪəbl/ *adj.* 不可靠的

reckon /'rekən/ *v.* 估计

strategic /strə'tiːdʒɪk/ *adj.* 战略（性）的

in the dark 在黑暗中

be short of 缺少

add to 增加

account for （数量或比例上）占

for fear of 唯恐

be hooked up to 连接

end up as 最终成为

二、话题概要

大意：亚洲和非洲，约 11 亿偏远农村居民尚未通电。政府积极地将发展小型电网纳入规划，这是照亮这些尚在黑暗中的芸芸众生的有效方法。

Para. 1–3: 发展小型电网的背景：虽然电力惠及我们生活的方方面面，亚洲和非洲的约 11 亿农村居民仍然处在无电可用的黑暗之中。所幸，人们比以往任何时候都能更快地连接到清洁、可靠的电力。

Para. 4: 小型电网的工作原理：小型电网可以独立运作，可以让私营企业更快、更可靠地提供（电力）服务。

Para. 5–6: 小型电网的发展前景、面临的问题及其解决方法：国际能源机构估计，到 2030 年，小型电网可以占到 3,000 亿美元的投资，成为实现普遍联网的最重要手段。

◆ 同步练习

一、长难句翻译（见文章划线处）

二、词块填空

1. Added together, the factors _____ about 50% of the risk.

2. You were created to _____ life on earth, not just take from it.

3. If you are knowledgeable, then you will never _____ conversational topics.

4. These displays could _____ any kind of electronic device, also inside the body.

5. Instead of having beautiful even uninterrupted cheeks, our faces _____ a series of hills and valleys.

三、佳句模仿

原文佳句	The good news is that people can be connected to clean, reliable power faster than ever before.
亮点评析	这是一个复合句，that 引导表语从句。
写作应用	The good news is that more and more people choose the bicycle as the means of transportation in China because there is too much traffic in the busy streets. 好消息是，中国越来越多的人选择自行车作为交通工具，因为在繁忙的街道上交通太拥挤了。

原文佳句	The more strategic planning of this sort there is, the less risk that mini-grids will end up as "stranded assets".
亮点评析	"the more...the more..." 句型表示"越……越……"。该句型为复合句，前面的句子是状语从句，后面的句子是主句。此句型中的 more 代表形容词或副词的比较级。
写作应用	His research indicates that the more the children use both Spanish and English, the greater their intellectual advantage in skills underlying reading ability and nonverbal logic. 他的研究表明，孩子们使用西班牙语和英语越多，他们在阅读能力和非语言逻辑方面的智力优势就越大。

◆ 答案

一、长难句翻译

1. 他们可以廉价地向数百万人供应远方生产的电力。随着他们综合运用更多的风能和太阳能，他们变得更环保。

2. "全民通电"是政客们钟爱的口号，往往比表面上看起来要少。

3. 推荐运用小型电网。小型电网可以不依赖国家电网，独立运作。对私营企业而言，小型电网是比国有运营商更快、更可靠地提供（电力）服务的方法。

4. 屋顶太阳能系统在非洲的部分地区越来越普遍，但提供的电力有限。与屋顶太阳能系统不同，小型电网提供 24 小时的电力，能够驱动机械、灌溉系统、冷冻设备以及提供照明。

5. 一家预测机构——国际能源机构——估计，到 2030 年，小型电网能够占到 3,000 亿美元的投资，使它们成为实现普遍联网的最重要手段。

二、词块填空

1. account for

2. add to

3. be short of

4. be hooked up to

5. end up as

33 Job-Skills Gap May Curb Growth, Report Warns[E]

工作与技能差距抑制经济增长

1 White House economists have identified a potential stumbling block (绊脚石) to maintaining the U.S. economy's momentum (动力): a lack of well-trained workers. The economy appears poised (平稳的) to expand this year **at the fastest clip** since the recession (经济衰退) ended in 2009. ①That has allowed employers to extend their streak (时期) of consistent hiring, which began in 2010, and push the unemployment rate to nearly its lowest level in 50 years.

2 But there also is **a growing gap** between the rising number of job openings (职位空缺) and the number of workers equipped to fill them, and this could limit growth **in the long run**, according to a paper from President Donald Trump's Council of Economic Advisers released Tuesday. ②"There simply aren't enough unemployed workers in the current **pool** of those looking for work to match the growth **in demand for** new workers," the paper said.

3 One problem is the overall size of the pool. ③A smaller share of adults between 25 and 54 years old are working or looking for jobs than before the recession began in 2007, even though the unemployment rate is lower, at 4% in June.

4 Another problem, the economists wrote, is many Americans on the sidelines (兼职) of the labor market need more education or other skills to fill the types of jobs that are being created. ④The paper found a dis-proportionate (不均衡的) share of those not seeking or holding jobs don't have college degrees, an indication they don't have the advanced skills needed to fill many job openings.

5 A lack of skills, however, is only one reason many Americans are out of the workforce. Other economists have pointed to other reasons, including the rising cost of child care, the need to care for elderly parents and the opioid (鸦片类药物) crisis.

6 The White House paper suggests that helping some of those adults who are out of the workforce improve their skills would enable them to seek and get jobs.

7 Spending on education and training in the U.S. is focused almost entirely on people younger than 25 years old and in school, the paper said. ⑤<u>Relatively little is spent during a person's working life by employers or the government, potentially leaving them without the ideal skill set for modern jobs, according to the paper.</u>

8   Many employers **are reluctant to** provide that training, fearing they will bear the cost, only to see their competitors **reap** the benefits by hiring away their skilled workers, White House economists said. To address the **reluctance**, Mr. Trump will host an event at the White House on Thursday with large employers and have them sign "a pledge (誓言) to the American worker" to make significant new investments in training their current and future workers.

◆ 课文小助手

一、生词和词块释义

pool /puːl/ *n.* 人力资源

reap /riːp/ *v.* 收获

reluctance /rɪˈlʌktəns/ *n.* 不情愿

at the fast clip 快速地

a growing gap 日益扩大的差距

in the long run 长远看来

in demand for 对……有需求

be reluctant to 不愿意做

二、话题概要

大意: 美国国内缺乏训练有素的工人。本文分析这一社会现象、存在的问题和政府推出的举措。

Para. 1–2: 引出话题: 白宫经济学家发现,缺乏训练有素的工人将是维持美国经济发展势头的潜在障碍。增加的职位空缺数量和训练有素的可以填补这些空缺的工人数量之间的差距日益扩大。从长远来看,这可能会限制经济增长。

Para. 3–5: 分析存在的问题: 存在的问题主要有: 25 至 54 岁之间的就业主力军在整体人力资源中的比例较小;劳动力市场上兼职的许多美国人需要更多的教育和技能;育儿成本增加、照顾年迈双亲的需要和鸦片类药物危机也是导致失业的原因。

Para. 6–8: 陈述政府的解决措施: 白宫建议帮助一些失业的成年人改进技能,这可以让他们找到工作。雇主或政府还要适当增加针对在就业人员的培训投入。特朗普还将在白宫主持活动,督促大公司老板签署《对美国工人誓言》,对培训工人加大投资。

◆ 同步练习

一、长难句翻译(见文章划线处)

二、词块填空

1. The Food and Drug Administration has been approving new drugs _____.

2. So unless we all work very hard, there will be _____ between rich and poor.

3. It has been rather costly to install the machinery, but it should pay off _____.

4. Through my own work I have seen the growth _____ a variety of portal applications.

5. But international pharmaceutical companies say they would _____ develop a drug only for the Chinese market.

三、佳句模仿

原文佳句	The White House paper suggests that helping some of those adults who are out of the workforce improve their skills would enable them to seek and get jobs.

亮点评析	这是一个复合句。其中，that 引导宾语从句；该宾语从句的主语是动名词短语。
写作应用	The specialist suggested that helping children who eat too much sugar kick the habit would enable them to form a good life style. 专家建议，帮助那些吃太多糖的孩子改掉这一习惯将使得他们能够养成良好的生活方式。

◆ 答案

一、长难句翻译

1. 这允许雇主延长始于 2010 年的持续雇佣期，还可推动失业率达到 50 年来的最低水平。

2. 报告称，"在目前的那些寻找工作的人力资源当中，没有足够的失业工人来满足新工人的需求增长"。

3. 尽管失业率较低，6 月份为 4%。但是，在 25 岁至 54 岁的成年人中，正在就业或找工作的份额比 2007 年经济衰退开始前更小。

4. 报告发现，在那些未找工作或失业的人中，有不成比例的一部分人没有大学学位。这表明他们不具备填补许多职位空缺所需要的先进技能。

5. 在个人的职业生涯中，雇主或政府（用于提供培训的）花费相对较小。这可能会使他们不具备现代工作所要求的理想技能。

二、词块填空

1. at a fast clip

2. a growing gap

3. in the long run

4. in demand for

5. be reluctant to

34 Your Children Need a Launch Plan[M]

孩子需要离巢计划

1 Financial advisers are adding a new wrinkle (妙计) to retirement planning: a launch plan to prepare clients' children to leave the nest when they're grown adults in the not-so-distant future.

2 This can get touchy (棘手的). ①Some parents are reluctant to think about **letting go**, or give **higher priority** to supporting their children's academic success **at the expense of** their long-term financial well-being. For others, talking about money is taboo. Preparing children and teens to support themselves, however, **instills** crucial money-management skills they may not learn in other ways.

3 Financial adviser Matthew Papazian makes launch planning for clients' children a part of **mapping out** retirement. One couple he advised saw their retirement plans derailed (打乱) after they helped an adult child buy a house he couldn't afford on his own. Mr. Papazian often offers to talk with clients' children to coach them on financial skills. But persuading parents to back off "is harder than I ever imagined," says Mr. Papazian, founding partner of Cardan Capital Partners in Denver.

4 One-third of young adults ages 25 to 29 in 2016 were living in multigenerational households, typically with their parents, a recent Pew Research study shows. ②And for the first time in more than a century, more 18-to-34-year-olds in 2014 were living with their parents than in other setups, including with a spouse (配偶) or partner, an earlier Pew Research survey shows.

5 Some parents who provide financial support simply enjoy keeping their children close. And many young adults genuinely need help. The rising cost of housing, health care and other essentials (生活必需品) has been outpacing gains in entry-level salaries in recent years.

6 But other parents use handouts as a way of controlling their children, says Kate Levinson, author of "Emotional Currency". ③They may be anxious about their children's ability to **fend for** themselves, sending the message, "I don't believe you can make it, so let me help you," says Dr. Levinson, a marriage and family therapist (治疗师). Nearly half of adults in their 20s still receive some financial support from parents, says a 2015 poll (调查) of 1,000 adults ages 21 to

29 by Clark University.

7 Parents who give a child more money than they can afford risk creating what Dr. Levinson calls a toxic (有毒的) situation. Some parents don't think they know enough to coach their children on managing money. <u>④But all teens want is basic know—how that can be shared by any parent who manages household expenses, regardless of whether they can afford a financial adviser.</u> Some 96% of 128 college students in a recent study said they wished their parents had taught them practical skills, such as budgeting and saving. Parents' teaching has more impact than taking financial-skills classes in school, according to the study by researchers at Brigham Young University.

8 Becoming self-reliant "starts with the mind-set that you can do it," an attitude parents can start to instill early, says Deborah Meyer, a financial planner. Learning about saving and comparison shopping can start in childhood. let the child earn money to pay the premium (额外费用) , says Lisa Bayer, principal of Opus Financial Solutions in Boulder, Colo. Teens benefit from holding a job and learning to budget. <u>⑤Ms. Kenawell-Hoffecker, founding partner of Avantra Family Wealth in Mechanicsburg, Pa., sometimes meets with clients' teenagers and shows them their parents' budget, including their income minus housing, taxes, health insurance, clothing and groceries.</u> For many teens, this is the **aha moment** when they realize how much their parents sacrifice to pay for college, Ms. Kenawell-Hoffecker says.

9 Sharing a joint credit card account with a parent and helping make payments is good training. One student in the study told researchers that he once thought, "Oh, they're going to give me student loans? Awesome!" the study says. Looking back later, he realized he could have lived on half the amount he borrowed.

10 Parents should start talking with their children early in high school about what they can and can't provide for college, and again in junior year when they prepare to apply, says Jeffrey Arnett, a psychology professor at Clark University. Having children shoulder at least part of their college costs is a good idea so they have skin in the game, says Ms. Bayer, the financial planner.

11 When Dennis Quimby's daughter, Rachel, was 18, he persuaded her to start a Roth IRA with her earnings from a fast-food job, rather than buying the car she wanted. "I want my kids to have the good life. And the good life, in my opinion, includes financial independence," says Mr. Quimby. He also had Rachel meet with his financial adviser, Ms. Bayer, to help her invest her savings.

◆ 课文小助手

一、生词和词块释义

client /'klaɪənt/ n. 客户

instill /ɪn'stɪl/ v. 逐渐灌输

let go 放手

high priority 当务之急

at the expense of 以……为代价

map out 安排

fend for 抚养

aha moment 顿悟时刻

二、话题概要

大意：怎样帮助即将成人的孩子顺利离巢成为父母和财务顾问关心和需要解决的问题。

Para. 1–3: 引出话题：财务顾问为退休计划又增加了一个问题：为客户即将成人的孩子准备离巢计划。

Para. 4–6: 分析现象和现象产生的原因：出现这一现象的原因如下：一、一些父母想通过提供财务支持来让孩子亲近他们；二、因为用于房屋、医疗和生活必需品开支的攀升速度超过刚入职人员的收入的增长速度，许多刚成年的年轻人确实需要帮助；三、有父母用经济帮助作为控制孩子的手段。

Para. 7–11: 分析后果和提出实际可行的解决办法：专家提出的可行性办法包括：父母要早早向孩子灌输"你能做到"的理念；学习储蓄和货比三家可以从童年开始；要求孩子挣钱分担额外费用（孩子可以从工作和学习预算中受益颇多）；与父母共享一个绑定的信用卡账户并帮助付账；父母在孩子上高中时就尽早和孩子讨论能否提供大学教育费用，孩子申请大学时再讨论关于大学费用的问题，要求孩子至少分担部分大学开销。

◆ 同步练习

一、长难句翻译（见文章划线处）

二、词块填空

1.However, this comes _____ releasing all your personal information to parents should they ever want to contact you.

2. When we _____ of our hurts and forgive others, we are reflecting the grace of our heavenly Father who forgave us and continues to forgive us.

3.She had that "_____" in the summer of 2009 when an old photo of her slimmer self made her decide it was time she took charge of her weight.

4. It means that residents, most living on less than one U.S. dollar a day, must _____ themselves without any illusions that their government or the rest of the world cares.

5. As patterns begin to emerge regarding who gets infected with the H1N1 flu virus, health officials are beginning to _____ strategies for a potential wide-spread vaccination campaign.

三、佳句模仿

原文佳句	Mr. Papazian often offers to talk with clients' children to coach them on financial skills.
亮点评析	coach 在本句中是动词，意思是"指导"，可用于 coach sb in/on sth。
写作应用	Acting as coaches for one or more teams during the term, we try to coach them on developing collaborative skills, and we observe the individual students' interactions with their teammates. 在一个学期里作为一个或者更多团队的导师，我们尽力训练他们的开发协作技能，注意观察学生个体和团队成员之间的相互影响。

原文佳句	Having children shoulder at least part of their college costs is a good idea so they have skin in the game, says Ms. Bayer, the financial planner.
亮点评析	have skin in the game 意思是"参与其中 / 共担风险 / 换位思考"。
写作应用	Not only does it ensure you understand what the most effective solution will be, but it will make the users feel they have "skin in the game". 它不仅确保你能理解什么将是最有效的解决方法，它还让用户感觉他们也参与其中了。

◆ 答案

一、长难句翻译

1. 一些父母亲不愿意考虑放手，或者不愿意以自己的长期经济利益为代价优先支持孩子学业有成。

2. 这是一个多世纪以来第一次（出现这种现象）。 皮尤研究中心之前的调查显示， 2014 年， 在十八到三十四岁之间的人中，跟其他的包括与伴侣或伙伴同住的形式比，更多的人与父母同住。

3. 婚姻和家庭治疗师莱文森博士说，他们可能会担心他们的孩子自己照顾自己的能力，但这种做法释放的信息是，"我不相信你能做到，那么让我帮助你吧。"

4. 但是青少年想要的是基本的（理财）知识。不管父母能否负担得起财务顾问，这些知识都可以由任何一位管理家庭开支的家长分享（给孩子）。

5. 宾夕法尼亚州梅卡尼克斯堡的阿凡特拉家族财富机构的创始合伙人 Kenawell-Hoffecker 女士有时候会见客户的青少年孩子，向他们展示他们父母的预算，包括他们的收入减去住房、税收、医保、服装和食品杂货（的预算）。

二、词块填空

1. at the expense of

2. let go

3. aha moment

4. fend for

5. map out

35 Why Do Women Shun STEM?[A]

女性为何会回避科学、技术、工程和数学行业

1   Why do relatively few women work in science, technology, engineering and mathematics? <u>[1]University of Washington lecturer Stuart Reges—in a provocative (引起争论的) essay, "Why Women Don't Code"—suggests that women's verbal (语言的) and analytical (分析的) skills lead to career choices outside STEM.</u> I'm a female engineering professor with decades of experience as well as a background in the humanities (人文科学) and social sciences, so perhaps I can lend some **perspective** to the controversy (争论).

2   I've observed that women tend to choose disciplines (科目) other than STEM, often for the reasons Mr. Reges mentions. Yet his argument is incomplete. An important but often neglected factor is the attitudes of undergraduate professors. Not STEM professors, but professors in the humanities and social sciences.

3   Professors **have a profound influence over** students' career choices. I'm sometimes extremely surprised at the level of bias (偏见) and antagonism (敌意) toward STEM from professors outside scientific fields. I've heard it all: STEM is only for those who enjoy "rote" work. Engineering is not creative. There's only one right answer. And, of course, it's sexist. [2]<u>All this from professors whose only substantive experience with STEM is a forced march through a single statistics course in college.</u>

4   My colleagues in the humanities unthinkingly speak ill of STEM in front of me. Their bias has become so deeply **ingrained** that they don't **think twice**. Even a few untoward (不当的) remarks like this to students can have profound effects. It's too bad, because science, technology, engineering and math can be among the most creative and satisfying disciplines.

5   [3]<u>Many studies, including a critical review by Elizabeth Spelke in American Psychologist, have shown that on average men and women have the same abilities in math and science.</u> But as Mr. Reges notes, women tend to do better than men verbally—a consequence of early developmental advantages.

6   How does this **alter** career choice? A student named Bob might get a C in Physics 101 but a D in English composition. His English professor probably won't try to recruit (录取) him into the field. Bob's choice to become an engineer **makes sense** because he's less likely to be good at

the social sciences or humanities.

7　Women who are average in physics classes, on the other hand, are often better at other subjects. When Sara has a C in physics 101, she's more likely to have a B or even an A in English composition. Her English professor is more likely to recruit her. ④And, crucially, the "STEM is only for uncreative nerds（书呆子）" **characterization** can play well here, which can provide a mental boost for Sara to hear a powerful figure like her professor denigrate（贬低）the subject she's struggling with.

8　Even when a professor isn't working to recruit Sara to the social sciences or humanities, she might be recruiting herself. Grades mean something; if Sara's working hard to get a C in calculus（微积分）, but she earns an A in English with less effort, she's going to experience a powerful pull toward the humanities.

9　Consider a student who gets an A in every subject. Let's call her Nadine. She's the type of student who could **excel in** whatever she chooses. Her engineering professors might be telling her that an electrical engineering degree is a great career choice that will open doors and pay well. But her non-STEM professors may be telling her something completely different: "You won't use your fantastic writing skills. And besides, you'll just sit in a cubicle（格子间） crunching（大量运算）numbers." Nadine can begin to feel she's untrue to her full set of talents if she picks engineering. So Nadine jumps the STEM ship.

10　What about the women who go into STEM and discover bias in the workplace? Jerks（混蛋） exist in every work-place. Bullying is so common in nursing, for example, that it's the subject of dozens of studies. ⑤"Bullying behaviors fall on a continuum（统一体）ranging from eye-rolling and exclusion to humiliation, withholding information, scapegoating（替罪）, intimidation（恐吓）, and backstabbing（陷害），" a 2016 article in American Nurse Today notes. "The bully sets out to destroy the victim's confidence as a way to gain power and control."

11　It can be easy for a woman who has landed in a **toxic** software-development environment to say, "There's horrible bias here!" And she'd be right. But there are toxic pockets in every discipline or field. STEM is **no different**. I have experienced bias in my career, but I also would not be where I am today without the strong support of many wonderful men. Women are vitally important to STEM, so professors outside these disciplines should stop mischaracterizing（曲解） to poach（挖走）the best students, who are often women.

◆ 课文小助手

一、生词和词块释义

perspective /pə'spektɪv/ *n.* 看法

ingrained /ˌɪn'greɪnd/ *adj.* 根深蒂固的

alter /'ɔːltə(r)/ *v.* 改变

characterization /ˌkærəktəraɪ'zeɪʃn/ *n.* 特性描述

toxic /'tɒksɪk/ *adj.* 有害的

have a profound influence over 对……有深远影响

think twice 再三考虑

make sense 有道理

excel in 在……方面很擅长

no different 不例外

二、话题概要

大意 作者通过举例子来分析在科学、技术、工程和数学领域工作的女性相对较少的原因。

Para. 1: 引出话题：由华盛顿大学的讲师斯图尔特·雷克斯的文章——《为何缺少女码农》——中的观点引出本文话题：为什么在科学、技术、工程和数学领域工作的女性相对较少？

Para. 2–5: 作者对 STEM 领域女性较少这一现象的个人见解：作者认为斯图尔特·雷克斯的论点有道理，但是不完整。她认为，一个重要但经常被忽视的因素是：本科教授的态度——不是 STEM 领域的教授，而是人文和社会科学的教授的态度对学生的职业选择有着深远的影响。

Para. 6–9: 举例说明非 STEM 教授的偏见是如何改变女性职业选择的：一个叫鲍勃的学生在物理课上得了 C，但在英语作文中得了 D。鲍勃会选择成为一名工程师，因为他不太可能擅长社会科学或人文学科。

Para. 10–11: 分析已经进入 STEM 领域的女性的遭遇：已经进入 STEM 领域的女性会遭遇职场欺凌和对女性的偏见。作者在职业生涯中也经历过偏见，但如果没有许多优秀男士的大力支持，她不会成就今天的事业。

◆ 同步练习

一、长难句翻译（见文章划线处）

二、词块填空

1. As a result, likability can _____ who gets a job.

2. In other words, there might be a range of other reasons why people in disease-ridden countries don't _____ IQ tests.

3. You wouldn't _____ about taking a quick coffee break at work, so allow yourself similar breaks at home so you don't get burnt out.

4. People who buy homes and the banks who give them loans are _____, in principle, than investors in the stock market, or shop owners.

5. If you have different classes of tasks with radically different characteristics, it may _____

to have multiple work queues for different types of tasks.

三、佳句模仿

原文佳句	Perhaps I can lend some perspective to the controversy.
亮点评析	lend some perspective to 意思是"为……提供视角 / 看法"。
写作应用	Her attitude lends a fresh perspective to the subject. 她的态度提供了看待这一问题的一个新视角。

原文佳句	Women are vitally important to STEM, so professors outside these disciplines should stop mischaracterizing to poach the best students, who are often women.
亮点评析	be vitally important to/ for 意思是"对……来讲极其重要 / 性命攸关"。
写作应用	In families affected by divorce, non-resident fathers continue to be vitally important for the general development of their children. 受离婚影响的单亲家庭，非同住的父亲仍然对孩子的成长扮演了极其重要的角色。

◆ 答案

一、长难句翻译

1. 华盛顿大学的讲师斯图尔特·雷克斯在他的一篇引发争论的文章——《为何缺少女码农》——中表明，女性在语言和分析方面的技能导致她们选择科学、技术、工程和数学领域外的事业。

2. 所有这一切（偏见）都来自于教授。他们唯一的关于 STEM 的实质性经验就是在大学里急行军似地通过单一的统计学课程。

3. 许多研究，包括发表于《美国心理学家》的伊丽莎白·斯波克的一篇评论文章，都表明：通常，男性和女性在数学和科学上的能力是一样的。

4. 而且，最重要的是，"STEM 只适用于那些缺乏创造力的书呆子"的特性描述在此处发挥了充分作用，这为萨拉提供了精神动力，（欣然）听取诸如教授这样的有影响力的人物贬低她学起来吃力的科目。

5. 2016 年，发表于《今日美国护士》上的文章提到，欺凌行为是一个统一体，从翻白眼、排挤到羞辱、隐瞒信息、甩锅、恐吓和陷害不一而足。

二、词块填空

1. have a profound influence over
2. excel in
3. think twice
4. no different
5. make sense

36 How Much Screen Time Is too Much for Kids?[M]

对孩子来说接触网络时间多长算太长？

1   Parents have been advised to limit media consumption, but research suggests it's the nature of it that matters.

2   For many parents in the digital age, **battles over** screen time and devices have become a depressing part of family life, and knowing how much is too much has become a moving target.

3   ①Whether it's three-year-olds throwing **tantrums** when the iPad is taken away, seven-year-olds watching YouTube all night, nine-year-olds demanding their own phones, 11-year-olds **nagging** to play 18-rated video games that "all their friends" are, or 14-year-olds who are never off Instagram, every stage of childhood and adolescence is now accompanied by its own delightful new parenting challenges.

4   ②Up until a few years ago parenting advice **centred around** the concept of "screen time" **quotas** with a Goldilocks-style sweet spot of two or so hours of screens a day, beyond which media use could become harmful.

5   The American Academy of Pediatrics (AAP) still recommends a maximum of one hour of "high-quality programming" for children under 6, but **thereafter** simply encourages parents to "place consistent limits on the time spent using media" and **designate** screen-free time as a family.

6   **It's unclear whether** that means four hours playing a video game on a Sunday is okay, **or** whether it is better to have three 20-minute sessions with the iPad than one hour-long session. Is it really that bad if my 18-month-old watches a couple of **episodes** of the Twirlywoos（趣趣知知鸟）before dinner?

7   Many parents will **be relieved to** hear that recent research suggests that it's not so much the length, but the nature of the screen time that matters. Whether it's passive TV or social media monitoring, active video game playing, socialising with WhatsApp, or getting creative in iMovie.

8 Jocelyn Brewer, a psychologist who specialises in the concept of "digital nutrition", likens media diets to what's on our plates: rather than counting calories (or screen time), think about what you're eating.

9 ③"It's not just about whether you consume any potential digital junk foods, but also your relationship to technology and the role it plays in your family life," says Brewer. "We know that using screens to **soothe** or pacify kids sets up some concerning patterns of relying on devices to calm or distract a child (or teen, or adult) from their experience of unpleasant or uncomfortable emotions—so we want to avoid using screens to **placate** tantrums, just like we want to avoid eating 'treats' to calm emotional storms."

10 For young children, the most important thing is whether parents and kids are playing, watching or browsing together.

11 A study of 20,000 parents published late last year by the Oxford Internet Institute and Cardiff University determined that there was no **correlation** between limiting device use and children's wellbeing. The study's lead author Dr Andrew Pryzbylski said: "Our findings suggest the broader family context, how parents set rules about digital screen time, and if they're actively engaged in exploring the digital world together, are more important than the raw screen time."

12 Another study from December by the University of Michigan on people aged four to 11 similarly found that "how children use the devices, not how much time they spend on them, is the strongest predictor of emotional or social problems connected with screen addiction". But the authors said that concern over a child's screen use is **warranted** when it leads to poor behaviour, loss of interest in other activities, family or social life, withdrawal, or **deception**.

13 Most research agrees that although specific screen time limits are dated, there does come a point where **excessive** device use has negative impacts, affecting sleep, health and mood. One study from January found that "adolescents spending a small amount of time on electronic communication were the happiest", though its suggestion of one hour of daily screen time for teenagers is laughable to anyone trying to parent one.

14 Talk about kids and technology usually tends towards the negative, but it doesn't have to be so. The internet and video games can be fun, social and provide a new creative outlet for children.

"Evidence-based benefits identified from the use of digital and social media include early learning, exposure to new ideas and knowledge, increased opportunities for social contact and support," says the AAP.

15 The consensus is that screen time, in and of itself, is not harmful—and reasonable restrictions vary greatly, depending on a child's behaviour and personality. ^④**There is little point in obsessing over** how many minutes a day your kids are spending with screens. Instead, parents should be doing what they can to ensure that what they're watching, playing and reading is high-quality, age-appropriate and safe—and joining in wherever possible.

16 ^⑤"It's important there is balance in the online and offline worlds and in leisure and learning, but what that looks like for different kids at different ages and in different families is hard to 'prescribe'," says Brewer. "Research shows that not having access to the digital world has a negative impact on kids—so it's about finding the right amount with a **holistic** approach."

◆ 课文小助手

一、生词和词块释义

tantrum /ˈtæntrəm/ n. 耍孩子脾气

nag /næg/ v. 跟……纠缠不休

quota /ˈkwəʊtə/ n. 定额

thereafter /ˌðeərˈɑːftə/ adv. 以后

designate /ˈdezɪɡneɪt/ v. 指定

episode /ˈepɪsəʊd/ n. (尤指电视或广播节目的) 一集

soothe /suːð/ v. 使平静

pacify /ˈpæsɪfaɪ/ v. 平息

placate /pləˈkeɪt/ v. 安抚

correlation /ˌkɒrəˈleɪʃən/ n. 相互关系

warrant /ˈwɒr(ə)nt/ v. 使有必要

deception /dɪˈsepʃən/ n. 欺诈

excessive /ɪkˈsesɪv/ adj. 过度的

holistic /həʊˈlɪstɪk/ adj. 整体的

the battle over 因……而战斗

centre around 以……为中心

It's unclear whether...or... 目前尚不清楚

be relieved to do 很欣慰地……

There is little point in doing 这样做没有什么意义

obsess over 为……而着迷，痴迷

二、话题概要

大意: 父母总是被建议要限制孩子使用各种电子媒介的时间，但研究表明实际上电子媒介上所呈现的内容的本质才是关键。文章给我们的建议是，屏幕时间本身并不是有害的，家长应该尽其所能确保孩子们所观看、玩耍和阅读的内容是高质量的、适合年龄的和安全的，并尽可能地加入进来和孩子一起看和玩。

Para. 1: 父母总是被建议要限制孩子使用各种电子媒介的时间，但研究表明实际上电子媒介上所呈现的内容的本质才是关键。

Para. 2–6: 孩子们（无论哪个年龄阶段）总是着迷于屏幕所能呈现给他们的数字世界。因此，童年和青春期的每一个阶段现在都伴随着新的对父母养育的挑战。

Para. 7–12: 使许多家长感到欣慰的是，最近的研究表明，不是时间长度，而是电子媒介呈现的内容的本质才是关键。

Para. 13–14: 大多数研究都同意，虽然限定屏幕时间的做法是过时的，但确实过度的设备使用会产生负面影响，影响睡眠、健康和情绪。

Para. 15–16: 共识是，屏幕时间本身并不是有害的，对屏幕时间的合理的限制很大程度上取决于孩子的行为和个性。

◆ 同步练习

一、长难句翻译（见文章划线处）

二、词块填空

1. Apple will sell millions of these devices, and many people will love and _____ them.

2. To this day, _____ he shot himself _____ was murdered.

3. The less daring among us will _____ know that medical workers are also interested in the technology—to improve patient care.

4. The Great Barrier Reef is attracting urgent concern. There's a huge _____ mining and port development.

5. And the improvement of the course and teaching should _____ students' ability of teaching, vocation and linguistic competence.

◆ 答案

一、长难句翻译

1. 无论是 3 岁的孩子因 iPad 被拿走而发脾气，7 岁的孩子整夜看 YouTube，9 岁的孩子要求拥有自己的手机，11 岁的孩子纠缠不休非要玩 18 岁限制级视频游戏（"他们所有的朋友"都在玩），或者是 14 岁的孩子从未关闭过 Instagram——童年和青春期的每一个阶段现在都伴随着新的父母养育的挑战。

2. 直到几年前，对父母养育的建议还集中在"屏幕时间"配额的概念上，即每天屏幕前两个小时左右的黄金分割点，超过此限则媒体的使用可能变得有害。

3. Brewer 说：这不仅仅是你是否消费了任何潜在的数字垃圾食品，还包括你与技术的关系以及它在家庭生活中的所扮演的角色。我们知道，使用屏幕来安抚孩子们，会建立一些依赖于设备的模式，来镇静或分散孩子（或青少年或成人）的不愉快或不舒服的情绪体验——所以我们希望避免使用屏幕来安抚脾气，正如我们避免用吃的"治疗方式"以平息情绪风暴。

4. 困扰于你孩子每天在屏幕前花费多少分钟是没有什么意义的。相反，家长应该尽其所能确保他们所观看、所玩和所读的内容是高质量的、适合年龄的和安全的——而且家长随时随地都能加入进来。

5. Brewer 说："休闲和学习方面，在线和离线世界间的平衡是很重要的，但是对于不同年龄和不同家庭的孩子来说，这似乎很难'规定'。研究表明，不接触数字世界对孩子是有负面影响的——所以这实际是用一个整体的方法找到正确的数量的问题。"

二、词块填空

1. obsess over

2. it's unclear whether…or…

3. be relieved to

4. battle over

5. centre around

37 The Relationship Between Time, Money, and Happiness[M]

时间、金钱和幸福之间的关系

1　The older I get, the more I'm convinced that time is money (and money is time). We're commonly taught that money is a "store of value". But what does "store of value" actually mean? It's a **repository** of past effort that can be applied to future purchases. Really, money is a store of time. (Well, a store of productive time, anyhow.)

2　Now, having made this argument, I'll admit that time and money aren't exactly the same thing. Money is a store of time, sure, but the two concepts have some differences too.

3　For instance, time is **linear**. After one minute or one day has passed, it's **irretrievable**. You cannot reclaim it. If you waste an hour, it's gone forever. If you waste (or lose) a dollar, however, it's always possible to earn another dollar. Time **marches forward** but money has no "direction".

4　More importantly, time is **finite**. Money is not. Theoretically, your income and wealth have no upper bound. On the other hand, each of us has about seventy (maybe eighty) years on this earth. If you're lucky, you'll live for 1000 months. Only a very few of us will live 5000 weeks. Most of us will live between 25,000 and 30,000 days.

5　I've always loved this representation of a "life in weeks" of a typical American from the blog Wait But Why.

6　<u>①If you allow yourself to conduct a thought experiment in which time and money are interchangeable, you can reach some **startling** conclusions.</u>

Wealth and Work

7　When I began to fully grasp the relationship between money and time, my first big insight was that wealth isn't necessarily an abundance of money—it's an abundance of time. Or potential time. When you accumulate a lot of money, you actually accumulate a large store of time to use however you please.

8　<u>②And, in fact, this seems to be one of the primary reasons the Financial Independence</u>

movement is gaining popularity. Financial Independence—having saved enough that you're no longer required to work for money—provides the promise that you can use your time in whichever way you choose. When I attend FI gatherings, I ask folks what motivates them. Almost everyone offers some **variation** on the theme: "I want to be able to do what I want, when I want."

9   To me, one of the huge **ironies** of modern society is that so many people spend so much time to accumulate so much stuff—yet never manage to set aside anything for the future. Why is this?

10   In an article on Wealth and Work, Thomas J. Elpel explores the complicated relationship between our ever-increasing standard of living and the effort required to achieve that level of comfort.

11   ③**Ultimately** you are significantly wealthier than before, but you are also working harder too. Nobody said you had to pay for oil lamps and oil or books and freshly laundered clothes, but you would feel **deprived** if you didn't, so you work a little harder to give your family all the good things that life has to offer.

12   It's a catch-22. You work more to have more money to buy more stuff…but because you have so much stuff, you need more money, which means you have to work more. It's almost as if the more physical things you possess, the less time you have.

13   How do you escape this vicious cycle? There are two ways, actually.

Spend Less, Live More

14   The first (most obvious) way to remove yourself from this hedonic treadmill is to deliberately reduce your spending so that it's below the level needed to maintain your lifestyle. As I've argued before at Get Rich Slowly, **frugality** buys freedom.

15   When you reduce your lifestyle, it takes less time to fund it. If you're earning $50,000 per year take-home and spending all $50,000, you leave no margin for error. If something goes wrong— you lose your job, **inflation** skyrockets—you're **in a bind**. Plus, you don't give yourself a chance to seize unexpected opportunities!

16   But if you reduce your spending to $40,000 per year, you give yourself options. You can choose

to continue earning $50,000 and bank the difference (building a store of time) or you can choose to work less today (taking the advantage of the time savings immediately).

17 Spending less also helps fund your future. Learning to live with a "lesser" lifestyle means you don't need to save as much for retirement. If you spend $50,000 per year, for example, then you need roughly $1.25 million saved before you can retire. But if you decrease spending to $40,000 per year, your target drops to around $1 million.

18 <u>④It takes much less work to fund an ongoing lifestyle of $40,000 per year than it does to maintain a lifestyle that costs $50,000 per year. And if you're in the fortunate position where you can slash your lifestyle from, say, $120,000 per year to $30,000 per year, you can really reduce the time you spend working.</u>

Buying Time Promotes Happiness

19 But what if you like your lifestyle and don't want to cut back? Or what if you're not able to cut back? There's still a way to use the relationship between time and money to increase your sense of well-being.

20 Last year, the Proceedings of the National Academy of Sciences journal published an interesting article that declared buying time promotes happiness. The authors conducted a series of experimental studies to look at the link between time, money, and happiness. Their conclusion?

22 Around the world, increases in wealth have produced an unintended consequence: a rising sense of time scarcity. We provide evidence that using money to buy time can provide a buffer against this time famine, thereby promoting happiness.

22 Using large, diverse samples…we show that individuals who spend money on time-saving services report greater life satisfaction. A field experiment provides causal evidence that working adults report greater happiness after spending money on a timesaving purchase than on a material purchase.

23 Together, these results suggest that using money to buy time can protect people from the detrimental effects of time pressure on life satisfaction.

24 If you want to improve your quality of life, don't use your money to buy stuff, use it to relieve "time pressure". Instead of buying a fancy car, purchase time-saving devices. Hire a housekeeper or a yard-**maintenance** company. Maybe consider a meal-delivery service.

25 ⑥Interestingly, the effects of "buying time" have the greatest impact on folks who have less money: "We observed a stronger relationship between buying time and life satisfaction among less-**affluent** individuals," the authors write.

Finding Balance

26 My biggest takeaway from thinking about the relationship between time and money is this: When you spend less, you can work less. In a very real way, frugality buys time. But on a deeper level, frugality buys freedom—financial freedom, freedom from worry, freedom to spend your time however you choose.

27 When you treat time as money (and money as time), you can better evaluate how to allocate your dollars and your hours. When you know how much your time is worth, you can decide when it makes sense to "outsource" specific jobs.

28 Ultimately, there's a balance to be had, and that balance is different for each of us. You have to decide how much time you're willing to spend on present comfort and how much time you want to bank for the future. I believe there's no single right answer to this dilemma.

29 What about you? How do you view the relationship between time, money, and happiness? Do you have some examples from your own life of buying time in order to improve your happiness? What balance have you arrived at—and how did you get there?

◆ 课文小助手

一、生词和词块释义

repository /rɪˈpɒzɪt(ə)rɪ/　*n.* 智囊

linear /ˈlɪnɪə/　*adj.* 连续的

irretrievable /ɪrɪˈtriːvəb(ə)l/　*adj.* 无法纠正的

finite /ˈfaɪnaɪt/　*adj.* 有限的

startling /ˈstɑːtlɪŋ/　*adj.* 惊人的

variation /veərɪˈeɪʃ(ə)n/　*n.* 变化

irony /ˈaɪrənɪ/　*n.* 反效果

ultimately /ˈʌltɪmətlɪ/　*adv.* 最终

deprived /dɪˈpraɪvd/　*adj.* 短缺的

frugality /fruːˈgælɪtɪ/　*n.* 节约

inflation /ɪnˈfleɪʃ(ə)n/　*n.* 通货膨胀

maintenance /ˈmeɪnt(ə)nəns/　*n.* 维持

affluent /ˈæfluənt/　*adj.* 富裕的

march forward 前进

in a bind 处于困境

二、话题概要

大意：作者就人们普遍相信的观点时间就是金钱，展开进一步讨论，发现时间和金钱之间存在辩证的关系。你工作更多是为了有更多的钱去买更多的东西。但是因为你有这么多东西，你需要更多的钱，这意味着你必须工作更多。打破这种恶性循环的方法，一是减少开支，仅维持最低生活水平即可，这样就可以减少工作的时间。二是用钱来缓解"时间压力"。

Para. 1–6: 人们普遍相信，时间就是金钱（金钱就是时间）。但作者认为时间和金钱不是完全一样的东西。金钱是时间的储存。

Para. 7–13: 财富和工作：财富不一定是一大笔钱 —— 而是充足的或潜在的时间。当你积累了很多钱时，你实际上积累了大量的时间来使用。

Para. 14–18: 花得少，活得多：第一种方法是特意减少你的开支，使其低于维持生活方式所需的水平。

Para. 19–25: 花钱买时间以促幸福：如果你不想或不能削减开支，那第二种方法是可以利用时间和金钱之间的关系来增加你的幸福感。

Para. 26–28: 找到平衡点：最终，我们都要找到一个平衡点。我们每个人的平衡点是不同的，你必须决定你愿意花多少时间在现在的舒适度上，以及你想为未来准备多少时间。这个困境没有一个正确的答案。

Para. 29: 最后抛给读者一系列问题去思考：你如何看待时间、金钱和幸福之间的关系？

◆ 同步练习

一、长难句翻译（见文章划线处）

二、词块填空

1. This leaves Labour _____ over whether to position itself to the SNP's right or left.

2. This seems urgent, as artificial intelligence (AI) and computing power rapidly _____ to create autonomous robots, that is, machines capable of making decisions on their own.

◆ 答案

一、长难句翻译

1. 如果你允许自己进行一个时间和金钱互换的思想实验，你可以得出一些令人吃惊的结论。

2. 事实上，这似乎是财政独立运动日益流行的主要原因之一。财政独立——储蓄足够了，你不再需要为钱而工作——这就保证了你可以以你选择的任何方式使用你的时间。

3. 最终你比以前更富有，但你也更努力工作。没有人说你必须为油灯、油、书和刚洗过的衣服付钱，但是如果你不付钱，你会觉得自己少了些什么，所以你要更加努力地工作，让你的家人得到生活所能提供的一切美好事物。

4. 为维持一种每年四万美元的生活方式，要比维持每年五万美元的生活方式花费更少的工作量。如果你处在一个幸运的境地，你可以把你的生活方式从每年十二万美元削减到每年三万美元，这样你就可以减少工作的时间。

5. 有趣的是，"购买时间"的影响对那些拥有较少金钱的人来说是最大的："我们观察到在不那么富裕的个体中购买时间和生活满意度之间的关系更强，"作者写道。

二、词块填空

1. in a bind 　　　　　　　　　　2. march forward

38　The Best Way to Make a Decision Under Pressure[M]

顶着压力做决定的最好办法

When temperatures run hot, we make decisions differently.

1　Some of the most important decisions you will make in your lifetime will occur while you feel stressed and anxious. From medical decisions to financial and professional ones, we are often required to **weigh up** information under stressful conditions.

2　Take for example **expectant** parents who need to make a series of important choices during pregnancy and labor, when many feel stressed. Do we become better or worse at processing and using information under such circumstances?

3　My colleague Neil Garrett, now at the Princeton Neuroscience Institute in New Jersey, and I ventured from the safety of our lab to fire stations in the state of Colorado to investigate how the mind operates under high stress. Firefighters' workdays vary quite a bit. Some days are pretty relaxed: They'll spend part of their time washing the truck, cleaning equipment, cooking meals and reading. Other days can be **hectic**, with numerous life-threatening incidents to **attend to**. They'll enter burning homes to rescue trapped residents, and assist with medical emergencies. These **ups and downs** presented the perfect setting for an experiment on how people's ability to use information changes when they feel under pressure.

4　We found that **perceived** threat **triggered** a stress reaction that made the firefighters better at processing information—but only as long as it conveyed bad news.

5　This is how we arrived at these results. We asked the firefighters to estimate their likelihood of experiencing 40 different **aversive** events in their life, such as being involved in a car accident or becoming a victim of card fraud. We then gave them either good news (we told them that their likelihood of experiencing these events was lower than they'd thought) or bad news (that it was higher) and asked them to provide new estimates.

6　Research has shown that people are normally quite optimistic—they will ignore the bad news and embrace the good. This is what happened when the firefighters were relaxed. But when they were under stress, a different pattern emerged. <u>①Under these conditions, they became **hyper-vigilant** to any bad news we gave them, even when it had nothing to do with their job (such as learning that the likelihood of card fraud was higher than they'd thought), and altered their beliefs in response. In contrast, stress didn't change how they responded to good news (such as learning that the likelihood of card fraud was lower than they'd thought).</u>

7 Back in our lab, we observed the same pattern in undergraduates who were told they had to give a surprise public speech, which would be judged by a panel, recorded, and posted online. Sure enough, their cortisol (皮质醇) levels **spiked**, their heart rates went up and they suddenly became better at processing unrelated, yet alarming, information about rates of disease and violence.

8 <u>②When you experience stressful events, whether personal (waiting for a medical diagnosis) or public (political **turmoil**), a **physiological** change is triggered that can cause you to **take in** any sort of warning and become **fixated** on what might go wrong.</u> A study using brain imaging to look at the **neural** activity of people under stress revealed that this "switch" was related to a sudden boost in a neural signal important for learning (known as a prediction error), specifically in response to unexpected signs of danger (such as faces expressing fear). This signal relies on dopamine (多巴胺) —a neurotransmitter found in the brain—and, under stress, dopamine function is altered by another **molecule** called corticotropin-releasing factor (促肾上腺皮质素释放素).

9 Such neural engineering could have helped early humans to survive. When our ancestors found themselves in a habitat filled with hungry animals, they **benefited from** an increased ability to learn about hazards so as to avoid **predators**. In a safe environment, however, it would be wasteful to be on high alert constantly. A certain amount of ignorance can help to keep your mind at ease. So a "neural switch" that automatically increases or decreases your ability to process warnings in response to changes in your environment might be useful. In fact, people with clinical depression and anxiety seem unable to switch away from a state in which they absorb all the negative messages around them.

10 It is important to realise that stress travels rapidly from one person to the next. If your co-worker is stressed, you are more likely to tense up and feel stressed yourself. Our brains are designed to transmit emotions quickly to one another, because they often convey important information. Wendy Berry Mendes, a professor of emotion at the University of California, San Francisco, and her colleagues found that when **infants** were held by their mothers who had

just experienced a socially stressful event, the infants' heart rates went up, too. The message transferred via the mother's pounding heart to the baby was of danger—and as a result, the baby avoided interacting with strangers.

11 You don't even need to be in the same room with someone for their emotions to influence your behavior. Studies show that if you observe positive feeds on social media, such as images of a pink sunset, you are more likely to post uplifting messages yourself. If you observe negative posts, such as complaints about a long queue at the coffee shop, you will in turn create more negative posts.

12 In some ways, many of us live as if we are in real danger, like firefighters on call, constantly ready to put out the flames of demanding emails and text messages, and respond to news alerts and social media feeds. Repeatedly checking your phone, according to a survey conducted by the American Psychological Association, is related to stress. In other words, a preprogrammed physiological reaction, which evolution has equipped us with to help us avoid **famished** predators, is now being triggered by a tweet. Tweeting, according to one study, raises your pulse, makes you sweat, and enlarges your pupils more than most daily activities.

13 The fact that stress increases the likelihood that we will focus more on alarming messages, together with the fact that it spreads like a tsunami, can create collective fear that is not always justified. ③This is because after a stressful public event, such as a terrorist attack or political turmoil, there is often a wave of alarming information in traditional and social media, which individuals absorb well, but that can exaggerate existing danger. ④And so a reliable pattern emerges following terrorist attacks and financial market downturns: stress is triggered, spreading from one person to the next, which temporarily enhances the likelihood that people will take in negative reports, which increases stress further. As a result, trips are cancelled, even if the terrorist attack took place across the globe; stocks are sold, even when holding on is the best thing to do; and fearmongering (散布恐惧) political campaigns attract followers, even if they **are** not **anchored in** reality.

14 The good news, however, is that positive emotions, such as hope, are contagious too, and are powerful in inducing people to act to find solutions. ⑤Being aware of the close relationship between people's emotional state and how they process information can help us frame our messages more effectively and become conscientious agents of change.

◆ 课文小助手

一、生词和词块释义

expectant /ɪkˈspekt(ə)nt/ adj. 期待的

hectic /ˈhektɪk/ adj. 繁忙的

perceived /pəˈsiːvd/ adj. 察觉到了的

trigger /ˈtrɪɡə/ v. 引发（坏事）

aversive /əˈvəːsiv/ adj. 令人嫌恶的

hyper-vigilant adj. 高度警觉的

spike /spaɪk/ v. 使更浓烈

turmoil /ˈtɜːmɔɪl/ v. 混乱

physiological /ˌfɪzɪəˈlɒdʒɪkəl/ adj. 生理的

fixated /fikˈseitid/ adj. 异常依恋的

neural /ˈnjʊər(ə)l/ adj. 神经的

molecule /ˈmɒlɪkjuːl/ n. 分子

predator /ˈpredətə/ n. 掠夺者

infant /ˈɪnf(ə)nt/ n. 婴儿

famished /ˈfæmɪʃt/ adj. 极饥饿的

weigh up 衡量

attend to 处理

ups and downs 盛衰

take in 对……加以考虑

benefit from 受益于

be anchored in 扎根于

二、话题概要

大意: 本文主要讲如何在高压下保持乐观。

Para. 1–2: 生活中总有这样的情况发生：越是感到紧张和焦虑时，越要做出一生中最重要的一些决定。从医疗决策到财务和专业决策，我们常常需要在有压力的情况下权衡信息。在这种情况下，我们在处理和使用信息方面会变得更好还是更差？

Para. 3–9: 研究表明，当人们放松的时候通常很乐观，他们会忽略坏消息，接受好消息。

Para. 10–13: 重要的是要意识到压力是会迅速传播的。如果你的同事有压力，你更容易紧张和感到压力。

Para. 14: 然而，好消息是，积极的情绪也具有传染性，能强有力地诱导人们采取行动来寻找解决方案。

◆ 同步练习

一、长难句翻译（见文章划线处）

二、词块填空

1. To reverse these trends, I think Americans will need to _____ the nation's basic investments and industries, including manufacturing, energy and agriculture.

2. Larger companies are likely to _____ the downturn, in the sense that consolidation is

inevitable.

3. While economists probe the relationship between economic and political liberalisation, experts on international relations _____ the relationship between economic and military power.

4. Like most married couples we've had our_____, but life's like that.

5. Their eyes and ears _____ all sights and sounds hazily, without concentration and with little appreciation.

6. From a long-term perspective, economic globalization must move forward in the direction of balanced development, shared benefits and win-win progress and must _____ order, rules and ethics.

◆ 答案

一、长难句翻译

1. 在这些情况下，他们对我们给他们的任何坏消息都非常警惕，即使这与他们的工作无关（比如了解信用卡诈骗的可能性高于他们所想的），并改变了他们的信念。相反，压力并没有改变他们对好消息的反应方式（比如了解信用卡欺诈的可能性比他们想象得要低）。

2. 当你经历压力事件，无论是个人（等待医疗诊断）或公众（政治动荡），触发你的生理变化，这可能会导致你采取任何形式的警告，并固执地认为有事可能出错了。

3. 这是因为在一场充满压力的公共事件，如恐怖袭击或政治动荡之后，在传统媒体和社交媒体中经常会出现一系列令人震惊的民众密切关注的信息，但这也会夸大存在的危险。

4. 因此，一个固定模式会紧跟在恐怖袭击和金融市场低迷之后：压力被触发，从一个人蔓延到另一个人，这暂时增强了人们接受负面报道的可能性，这也进一步增加了压力。结果，旅程被取消，即使恐怖袭击发生在地球的另一边；股票被抛售，即使最好是坚持保有；而散布恐惧的政治运动吸引着追随者，即使他们没有扎根于现实。

5. 意识到人们的情绪状态和他们如何处理信息之间的密切关系可以帮助我们更有效地构架我们的信息，并成为改变的良方。

二、词块填空

1. attend to

2. benefit from

3. weigh up

4. ups and downs

5. take in

6. be anchored in

39 The Only Real Way to Acquire Wisdom[M]

获得智慧的唯一真正道路

Wisdom not only knows, but it also understands.

1   It's often been said that wisdom is the art of knowing that you are not wise.

2   The great philosopher Socrates famously denied being wise more than two thousand years ago, and since then, we have **taken him at his word**.

3   There is a truth there, but that definition isn't very helpful. I mean, I'm all for respecting uncertainty, doubting oneself, and realizing the limitations of my mind, but I think we can do better. Maybe even take a few steps forward.

4   [1]More importantly, I think we can create our own definition that separates it from just mere intelligence and then use that definition to illustrate why the distinction matters and how we can practically engage it in everyday life.

5   Intelligence is commonly associated with knowing something. Often, it also means that we can confidently apply what we know in a particular context.

6   Wisdom, to me, is different. It's different because it has more dimensions. Wisdom not only knows, but it also understands. And the distinction between knowing and understanding is what makes things interesting.

7   Knowing is generally factual. You have learned a particular kind of knowledge and you know its truth as it applies to a particular problem.

8   Understanding, however, is more **fluid**. [2]You have learned a particular kind of knowledge, but you don't see it as a fact or a truth applied rigidly to one thing. **Rather**, you understand that knowledge's **essence** and you can see how it relates to everything else, with **nuances** and contradictions included.

9   The difference is **subtle** but **potent**. While intelligence gives you specific **utility**, wisdom

inspires flexible **versatility**. It provides a more textured lens（变形镜头）for interacting with reality, very much changing how you think.

Building Relational Knowledge

10　Every time you have a perspective shift, big or small, you gain knowledge.

11　You learn something new that you maybe didn't know before, and as a result, your mind then changes itself regarding whatever that knowledge pertains to in the future. Next time, there is an added clarity.

12　If the acquired knowledge is understood, rather than just known, however, there is another step that occurs every time your mind shifts.

13　If you're a student, for example, and you're writing an exam, and it's a difficult one, let's say you decide to cheat. Now, unfortunately, when you cheat, you get caught. It leads to a failing grade in the course.

14　The thing to learn from this experience that would add to your intelligence would be the fact that cheating on an exam has consequences, and those consequences, while improbable, have a **disproportionately** negative impact on your life. It's simply not worth it in the future.

15　③The extra step that would translate the intelligence in that particular **scenario** into broadly applicable wisdom would be to realize that not only is not worth cheating on an exam due to the harsh consequences, but that most things in the world that carry disproportionately costly risks should be approached cautiously, whether they be financial decisions or personal life choices.

16　This is, of course, a very simplified scenario, but the point is that knowledge is relational and the understanding of wisdom recognizes that rather than treating it simply as an isolated information point.

17　Instead of the lesson being that cheating is bad, you combine the essence of the knowledge learned from that experience with your existing latticework of previous knowledge to really hammer home the underlying principle.

18　This way, you understand how taking shortcuts may harm your personal relationships, how your new understanding of risk may inform your business practices, and how what you say matters beyond why you say it.

19 Knowledge is always best **leveraged** when it's connected to other knowledge.

Creating an Information Network

20 In network science, there is a now-famous effect called Metcalfe's law.

21 It was first used to describe the growth of telecommunication networks, but over time, the application has been extended beyond that. It essentially states that the value of a network rises with the number of connected users.

22 In any network, each thing of interest is a node and the connection between such things is a link. The number of nodes themselves don't necessarily reflect the value of a network, but the number of links between those nodes do.

23 For example, ten independent phones by themselves aren't really all that useful. What makes them useful is the connection that they have to other phones. And the more they are connected to other phones, the more useful they are because the more access they have to each other.

Metcalfe's Law

24 Well, the relationship between different kinds of knowledge in our mind works the same way. The more connected they are to each other, the more valuable the information network that we have in our brain is.

25 ④Every time you gain knowledge, you are either isolating it within a narrow context where it's addressing a particular problem, or you are breaking it down a little further so that you can connect that knowledge to the already existing information you've accumulated so far.

26 In this scenario, intelligence is found within a pocket of information by itself. Wisdom, however, is accumulated in the process of creating new links.

27 ⑤Each node of knowledge in your mind is a mental model of some aspect of reality, but that mental model isn't fully complete until it's been stripped down and re-**contextualized in light**

of the information contained in the other mental models of knowledge around it.

28 The only way to acquire wisdom is to think in terms of the whole information network rather than the individual nodes that it contains.

29 That's where nuance is considered; that's where the respect for complexity comes in; and that's how specialized information finds it flexibility.

30 The strength of your mind depends on the value of your information network.

The Takeaway

31 The quest for wisdom is an age-old effort. It's one many have recommended.

32 It's been said to be as useful for finding inner contentment as it for fueling external successes. It's a more **prudent** way of interacting with reality.

33 While not everyone's definition of wisdom is the same, it doesn't seem too far-fetched to distinguish it by a mode of deeper understanding. One that goes beyond just the knowing we commonly associate with intelligence.

34 When we think of the acquisition of intelligence, we think of new information inspired by a perspective-shift that tells us a truth about one aspect of reality.

35 Wisdom goes further than that. It strips that same information down to its essence so that it can relate the underlying principle of that knowledge to the existing information network that exists in the mind.

36 It's the connectedness of this network that separates it from mere intelligence.

37 The more links between each pocket of information, the more valuable the whole network will be when **tackling** any other problem. It adds an extra dimension to each mental model contained in the mind.

38 Simply knowing this doesn't make a person more equipped to **soak** in wisdom, but with awareness and practice, new thinking patterns can be created.

39 The way you do this shapes everything else. It's worth working on.

◆ 课文小助手

一、生词和词块释义

fluid /ˈfluːɪd/ *adj.* (情况、想法或计划) 易变的

essence /ˈes(ə)ns/ *n.* 本质

nuance /ˈnjuːɑːns/ *n.* 细微差别

subtle /ˈsʌt(ə)l/ *adj.* 不易察觉的

potent /ˈpəʊt(ə)nt/ *adj.* 强有力的

utility /juːˈtɪlɪtɪ/ *n.* 实用性

versatility /ˌvɜːsəˈtɪlɪtɪ/ *n.* 反复无常

disproportionately /ˌdɪsprəˈpɔːʃənətli/ *adv.* 不成比例地

scenario /sɪˈnɑːrɪəʊ/ *n.* 可能发生的事态

leverage /ˈliːv(ə)rɪdʒ/ *vt.* 促使……改变

contextualize /kənˈtekstjʊəlaɪz/ *v.* 将(音素、单词等)置于上下文中研究

prudent /ˈpruːd(ə)nt/ *adj.* 慎重的

tackle /ˈtækəl/ *v.* 对付

soak /səʊk/ *v.* 吸取

taken him at his word 选择相信他的话(尽管它不一定是真话)

rather/or rather 确切地说

in light of 鉴于

二、话题概要

大意: 智慧不仅仅是知道而已，还需要真正理解。

Para. 1–9: 人们常说，智慧是知道自己不聪明的艺术。自从两千多年前伟大的哲学家苏格拉底认为自己是不明智的时候起，人们就意识到自己内心的局限性。但作者认为我们可以做得更好。

Para. 10–19: 建造相关知识：如果获得的知识被理解，而不是仅仅知道，你会学到一些以前可能不知道的新事物，你的头脑会进一步理解未来知识所涉及的事物，因而会增加你的智力。

Para. 20–23: 创建信息网络。

Para. 24–30: 梅特卡夫定律：我们头脑中的各种知识之间的关系也是一样的。它们之间的联系越紧密，我们大脑中的信息网络就越有价值。

Para. 31–39: 教训：人们一直以来总在努力追求智慧。每个人对智慧的定义并不都是一样的，我们可以将其解释为更深刻的理解模式，超越了与智力相关的知识。

◆ 同步练习

一、长难句翻译（见文章划线处）

二、词块填空

1. He read until very late last night, _____, early this morning.

2. Geoff said we could call him any time, so let's _____.

3. In general, the mentor influences what he or she can _____ personal experience, passion, and the constraints of the workplace.

◆ 答案

一、长难句翻译

1. 更重要的是，我认为我们可以创建我们自己的定义，将它与单纯的智力分开，然后用这个定义来说明为什么区别是重要的，以及我们如何在日常生活中实际地参与它。

2. 你已经学会了一种特殊的知识，但你不认为它是一个事实或一个可严格地应用于一件事的真理。确切地说，你了解了那个知识的本质，你可以看到它是如何与其他事物相关联的，包括细微差别和矛盾之处。

3. 将这一特定情景中的智力转化为广泛适用的智慧的额外步骤，是要认识到，不仅由于严重的后果而不值得在考试中作弊，而且对于在世界上大多数风险高昂的东西，无论它们是关乎财务决策还是个人生活选择，都应该是要谨慎行事的。

4. 每一次你获得知识，你要么把它孤立在一个解决一个特定的问题的狭隘的环境中，要么你进一步打破它，以便你可以把这些知识连接到你目前已经积累的已存在的信息上。

5. 你头脑中的每一个知识节点都是现实的某个方面的心智模型，但是心智模型并没有完全完成，直到它周围的知识模型中的其他信息模型所包含的信息被剥离和重新语境化。

二、词块填空

1. or rather

2. take him at his word

3. in light of

Chapter 7

教育 ／ Education

40 College for Life and Virtual Advisers May Be Key in Higher Education's Future[M]

为了生活上大学，虚拟顾问是高等教育未来的关键

1   Predictions about higher education's future often **result in** two very different visions about what is next for colleges and universities. ①In one camp: those who paint a rosy picture of an economy that will continue to demand higher levels of education for an increasing share of the workforce. In the other: those who believe fewer people will **enroll** in college as tuition costs **spiral out of control** and alternatives to the traditional degree emerge.

2   "We are living in an incredible age for learning, when there's so much knowledge available, that one would think that this is good news for higher education," Bryan Alexander told me recently. Alexander writes often about the future of higher education and is finishing a book on the subject for Johns Hopkins University Press. "Yet we've seen enrollment in higher education drop for six consecutive (连续的) years."

3   Alexander believes that for some colleges and universities to survive, they need to shift from their historical mission of serving one type of student (usually a teenager fresh out of high school) for a specific period of time. ②"We're going to see many different pathways through higher ed in the future," Alexander said, "from closer ties between secondary and postsecondary schools to new options for adults. The question is, which institutions adopt new models and which try desperately to **hang on to** what they have."

4   "The fact is that to maintain **affordability**, **accessibility** and excellence, something needs to change," Rafael Bras, Georgia Tech's provost (院长) and executive vice (副的) president for academic affairs, told me when he **unveiled** the report at the Milken Institute Global Conference this past spring.

5   The commission's report includes many **compelling** ideas, but three point to the possibility of a very different future for colleges and universities.

6   1) **College for life, rather than just four years.** ③The primary recommendation of the Georgia

Tech report is that the university turns itself into a venue for lifelong learning that allows students to "associate rather than enroll." Such a system would provide easy entry and exit points into the university and imagines a future in which students take courses either online or face-to-face, often in shorter spurts (迸发) over the course of a lifetime.

7   "Students who we educate now are expected to have a dozen occupations," Bras said. [④]"So a system that receives students once in their lives and turns them out with the Good Housekeeping seal (印章) of approval to become alums (校友) and come back **on occasion** and give money is not the right model for the future."

8   2) **A network of advisers and coaches for a career.** If education never ends, Georgia Tech predicts, neither should the critical advising function that colleges provide to students.

9   The commission outlines a scenario (方案) in which artificial intelligence and virtual tutors help advise students about selecting courses, **navigating** difficult classes and finding the best career options. The university has already successfully **experimented with** a new kind of teaching assistant in one course. In 2016, a computerized assistant named Jill Watson was used to guide students, who weren't told until the end of the semester that some of them had been seeking advice from a computer.

10 But even for a university focused on science and technology, Georgia Tech doesn't suggest in its report that computers will replace humans for all advising. [⑤]One recommendation is that the university help students establish a "personal board of directors," which includes an evolving network of peers and **mentors,** both in-person and virtual, who will help graduates throughout a lifetime of educational and professional opportunities.

11 3) **A distributed presence around the world.** Colleges and universities operate campuses and require students to come to them. In the past couple of decades, online education has grown **substantially,** but for the most part, higher education is still about face-to-face interactions.

12 [⑥]Georgia Tech imagines a future in which the two worlds are **blended** in what it calls the "atrium (中庭)"—essentially storefronts (店面) that share space with entrepreneurs and become

gathering places for students and alumni (校友). In these spaces, visiting **faculty** might conduct master classes, online students could gather to complete project work or alumni might work on an invention.

13　In some ways, as the report noted, the atrium idea is a nod to the past, when universities had agricultural and engineering experiment stations with services closer to where people in the state needed them.

14　Whether Georgia Tech's ideas will **materialize** is, of course, unclear. But as Alexander told me after reading it, "There is a strong emphasis on agility (灵活) and transformation so they can meet emergent trends." This is clear: After remaining relatively stagnant (停滞的) for decades as enrollment grew, colleges and universities are about to undergo a period of **profound** change—whether they want to or not—as the needs of students and the economy shift.

◆ 课文小助手

一、生词和词块释义

enroll /ɪn'rəʊl/ *v.* 招生

spiral /'spaɪrəl/ *v.* 逐渐加速上升

affordability /əˌfɔːdə'bɪlətɪ/ *n.* 可购性

accessibility /accessibility/ *n.* 便利性

unveil /ʌn'veɪl/ *v.* 使公之于众

compelling /kəm'pelɪŋ/ *adj.* 引人入胜的

navigate /'nævɪgeɪt/ *v.* 找到正确方法（对付困难、复杂的情况）

mentor /'mentɔː(r)/ *n.* 有经验，可信赖的顾问

substantially /səb'stænʃəli/ *adv.* 相当多地

blend /blend/ *v.* 融合

faculty /'fæklti/ *n.* 全体教职员

materialize /mə'tɪəriəlaɪz/ *v.* 具体化

profound /prə'faʊnd/ *adj.* 意义深远的

result in 导致

out of control 失控

hang on to 紧紧握住

on occasion 有时

experiment with 以……做试验

二、话题概要

大意：随着经济的发展和学生需求的转变，高等教育必须进行改革，否则将无法生存。

Para. 1: 未来高等教育的两种预测：经济发展需要更高层次的教育；学费上涨、传统学位被替代，上大学的人会更少。

Para. 2–3: Bryan Alexander 说这是前所未有的学习好时代，但连续六年大学招收人数减少。他认为一些大学为了生存，既要服务于高中生，也要选择招收成年学生。

Para. 4: Rafael Bras 院长和分管学术的副院长认为为了保持学费的可支付性、大学的卓越性和有大学可上，需要改变一些做法。

Para. 5–11: 委员会的报告包括许多引人入胜的观点，但其中三种指向迥然不同的大学未来的可能性：一、大学即生活，而不仅仅是大学四年的时光；二、职业生涯导师团队；三、大学分布在世界各地。

Para. 12–13: 佐治亚理工大学设想未来的大学能融合面对面教学和网络教学，在某些方面，"中庭"观点是对传统大学的认可。

Para. 14: 虽然佐治亚理工大学的想法是否会具体化还不清楚，但灵活、转变能满足紧急需求。总之，不论是否愿意，大学即将进入到深入改革时期。

◆ 同步练习

一、长难句翻译（见文章划线处）

二、词块填空

1. This was demonstrated in a laboratory _____ rats.

2. Competition can be healthy, but if it is pushed too far it can _____ bullying.

3. Even if you or your spouse lose your job, _____ your house.

4. Fires were burning _____ in the center of the city.

5. He translated not only from the French but also, _____, from the Polish.

三、佳句模仿

原文佳句	We are living in an incredible age for learning, when there's so much knowledge available, that one would think that this is good news for higher education.
亮点评析	incredible 在这里的意思是"惊人的",副词 incredibly 可以用来修饰形容词,起加强语气的作用;when 引导的定语从句修饰 age,从句中还有 so...that 句型。
写作应用	1. We import an incredible amount of oil from Arabia. 我们从阿拉伯进口数量惊人的石油。 2. Their father was incredibly good-looking. 他们的父亲十分英俊。 3. We are living in an incredible age for learning, when there's so much knowledge available, that we would fall behind if we refuse to study. 我们生活在有很多知识可以获取的惊人的学习时代,如果拒绝学习的话,我们就会落后。

原文佳句	The question is, which institutions adopt new models and which try desperately to hang on to what they have.
亮点评析	adopt 在这里的意思是"采用",desperately 意为"不顾一切地"。
写作应用	1. All three teams adopted different approaches to the problem. 三个队处理这个问题的方法各不相同。 2. Thousands are desperately trying to leave their battered homes. 成千上万的人不顾一切地想要离开他们千疮百孔的家园。

◆ 答案

一、长难句翻译

1. 一方观点:看好经济发展的人认为良好的经济继续需要更高层次的教育以应对劳动力需求的增长;另一方观点:有人认为学费上涨无法控制、传统学位被替代,大学招收的人更少。

2. 亚历山大说:"未来我们将看到许多不同的途径完成高等教育:从中学直接进入高等院

校或选择成年人（接受高等教育）。"

3. 佐治亚理工大学报告的主要建议是：大学变成终生学习的场所，允许学生"交往而不是招收"。

4. 因此，学生的一生只有一次被接待，然后拿着批准他们为校友的文凭回家，偶尔回校捐点钱，这样的体制不适合未来的发展。

5. 一项建议是：大学帮助学生建立"个人董事会"，其中包括一个不断发展、面对面和虚拟的同伴和导师网络，这些人将帮助毕业生终身获得教育和就业机会。

6. 佐治亚理工大学设想未来的大学能融合两个世界（面对面教学和网络教学）并称之为"中庭"——本质上是与企业家共享空间并成为学生和校友聚集的场所。

二、词块填空

1. experiment with

2. result in

3. hang on to

4. out of control

5. on occasion

41 Children Are Being Turned into Mini Robots[E]

孩子们正在被变为微型机器人

The new educational obsession with seeing the arts as inferior to science means that Britain won't be fit for the future.

1   Tyrone Musngi has been playing the **cello** for less than two years, but aged 11 he is already grade eight standard and practising for three hours a day. [①]In a speech this week in front of the Mayor of London he explained how the London Music Fund charity has transformed his life, paying for lessons to enable him to become a musician from, as he calls it, "a modest background" and win a place at the Royal College of Music's junior department. His school couldn't give him the opportunity to pick up a bow.

2   As millions of children begin GCSEs and A levels this week it has become clear that the number of pupils studying music, art, design, media and drama has plummeted (骤然跌落). State schools **in particular** are dropping arts subjects when they do the new English baccalaureate(中学毕业会考) (Ebacc) at GCSE. The number of arts entries has fallen 28 per cent between 2010 and 2016, the number of hours arts subjects are taught has gone down by 17 per cent and the number of arts teachers has dropped by 16 per cent, according to the Cultural Learning Alliance and statistics published by Ofqual. Local authorities have also **cut extracurricular** provision of arts education **in half** in some areas.

3   Hooray, you may say, children are finally focusing on maths and science, and they are. [②]Nearly a quarter of pupils take only seven GCSEs, which means they **are** probably now **limited** to the compulsory English language and literature, maths, sciences, a language and history or geography, as schools will be ranked on these exams.

4   At A level, girls are being pushed to do Stem (science, technology, engineering and mathematics) subjects so they can emulate (竞争) the boys. In fact in some areas they have overtaken them, with more sitting chemistry A level this year. But there has been no suggestion that perhaps boys should be doing more arts subjects or that pupils should focus on what they enjoy rather than what ministers think might one day be useful. They have become **obsessed** with the idea that Britain should emulate Singapore without pausing to wonder if this is a model from the past rather than one for the future.

5 Universities have also cut many arts courses and are planning to **downgrade** them further by making them cheaper, to the **dismay** of writers including Alan Bennett and Andrew Motion. The government message is clear: the humanities (人文学科) are second rate and of "less economic benefit". More than 100 artists, musicians and actors, Tracey Emin, Anish Kapoor and Antony Gormley among them, have warned of a potential disaster if pupils are **deprived** by the Ebacc of the chance to use their self-expression, imagination and creativity at school.

6 Most of the Ebacc curriculum involves training children to process and regurgitate (反刍) information. ③But increasingly, many jobs that **rely on** rote learning, formulae and basic questions will be done by artificial intelligence. What makes humans different is the ability to perform **intuitive** leaps, to **collaborate** and to create. Art, music, drama and "soft" subjects such as English teach this.

7 Britain is the global leader in the arts world after the United States. The creative industries are worth £92 billion to this country, more than the oil, gas, life sciences, automotive (汽车) and aeronautics (航空学) industries combined.

8 ④In the future, if you want an interesting job you will need to become as unlike a machine as possible, proving you can be innovative, emotionally intuitive, flexible and collegiate. But we are busy turning children into mini robots **competing against** each other for increasingly menial (卑贱的) work rather than collaborating. ⑤Any child whose mind doesn't operate along conventional, mechanical lines is being marginalized (边缘化) or even excluded, unable to cope with the sometimes stultifyingly (令人费解地) conventional routes our education system is trying to force them down.

9 It will take a decade to prove that **giving up on** the arts has been a terrible mistake. Ministers should make the intuitive leap and enable children to choose one arts subject as part of their core GCSEs. If these pursuits become the preserve of the rich, the cello an instrument only for those with wealthy parents, Britain will shrivel (枯萎). Music, dancing, acting, drawing, painting, sculpture, writing and design provide not only career opportunities but enjoyment for life and a way for Britain to distinguish itself in the 21st century.

◆ 课文小助手

一、生词和词块释义

cello /'tʃeləʊ/ *n.* 大提琴

extracurricular /ˌekstrəkə'rɪkjʊlə/ *adj.* 课外的

obsess /əb'ses/ *v.* 使……着迷

downgrade /ˌdaʊn'greɪd/ *v.* 贬低

dismay /dɪs'meɪ/ *n.* 惊愕

deprive /dɪ'praɪv/ *v.* 剥夺

intuitive /ɪn'tjuːɪtɪv/ *adj.* 直观的

collaborate /kə'læbəreɪt/ *v.* 合作

in particular 尤其

cut...in half 把……切成两半

be limited to 限于

rely on 依靠

compete against 与……竞争

give up on 放弃

二、话题概要

大意: 尽管音乐、舞蹈、设计、雕刻、写作等能创造更多就业机会、给人们的生活带来快乐,但艺术课程越来越少,学生只学习会考科目,机械记忆,缺乏创造性。

Para. 1: 出身贫寒的十一岁孩子 Tyrone Musngi 在伦敦市长前演讲时说要不是伦敦音乐基金慈善组织赞助他的话,他不可能成为音乐家。

Para. 2: 学习音乐、美术、设计、媒体、戏剧的学生数量骤降,花在艺术作品和艺术课程上的时间大大减少。

Para. 3: 学生们只专心学习数学、科学、英语、文学、语言、历史和地理等考试中要排名的科目。

Para. 4: 在高级证书考试中(A level: 英国 GCE 考试甲级标准),女生被迫学习 Stem 课程,并在某些领域超过男生,而没有人建议男生学艺术,或学生学自己感兴趣的科目。

Para. 5: 大学也砍掉许多艺术课程,并计划贬低这些课程。政府认为人文学科处于次要地位,经济效益也相对较差。许多画家、音乐家、演员认为这会剥夺学生的自我表现力、想象力和创造力。

Para. 6: 中学毕业会考的大多数课程只涉及训练孩子加工和反刍信息,缺乏合作、创新,而美术、音乐、戏剧、英语等科目能弥补这些。

Para. 7: 英国是继美国之后全球艺术界的领军人物,创意产业价值 920 亿英镑,超过石油、天然气、生命科学、汽车和航空工业的总和。

Para. 8: 我们正把孩子们变成微型机器人,为卑贱的工作相互竞争而不是合作,不守传统的孩子就会被边缘化甚至被排斥。

Para. 9: 放弃艺术是可怕的错误,意识到这一点恐怕需要十年,部长们应该转变思想,让孩子们选择一门艺术课程作为中学毕业会考的一部分，创造就业机会，享受人生，让 21 世纪的英国更加杰出。

◆ 同步练习

一、长难句翻译（见文章划线处）

二、词块填空

1. We got lost in the forest and had to _____ a compass and a lot of luck to get here.

2. The president urged them not to _____ peace efforts.

3. You can't _____ him, for he is a top player in this game.

4. The whole meal was good but the wine _____ was excellent.

5. The expenses should _____ what you can really afford.

6. Officials believe the number of deaths caused by the deadly disease could be _____ by 2030.

三、佳句模仿

原文佳句	In fact in some areas they have overtaken them, with more sitting chemistry A level this year.
亮点评析	sit 在这里的意思是"参加考试；应试"。
写作应用	Most of the students sit at least 5 GCSEs. 大多数学生至少参加 5 门普通中等教育证书考试。 Candidates will sit the examinations in June. 考生将在六月参加考试。

原文佳句	But we are busy turning children into mini robots competing against each other for increasingly menial work rather than collaborating.
亮点评析	并列非谓语动词短语 competing…rather than collaborating 作定语，修饰 robots。
写作应用	By doing so, we are turning children into those asking what our country can do for them rather than asking what they can do for the country. 这样做，我们培养的孩子不是问自己能为国家做什么，而是问国家能为他们做什么。

◆ 答案

一、长难句翻译

1. 本周在面对伦敦市长进行的演讲中，他解释了伦敦音乐基金慈善组织怎样改变了他的生活：他自称"出身贫寒"，但慈善组织支付了他的学费，让他成为音乐家，并在皇家音乐学院的初级系获得了一席之地。

2. 近四分之一的学生只学习普通中等教育证书中的七门功课，这意味着他们现在可能只限于必修英语语言、文学、数学、科学、语言、历史或地理，因为学校将在这些考试中排名。

3. 但是越来越多的依靠机械学习、死记硬背公式和基本问题的工作将由人工智能来完成。

4. 未来，如果你需要一份有趣的工作，你得尽量不像一台机器，证明你可以创新、情感上有直觉、灵活、合群。

5. 思想不跟着传统的、机械路线运作的任何孩子都会被边缘化，甚至被排除在外，（他们）无法应对我们的教育体制强迫他们走的传统路线，这些路线有时令人费解。

二、词块填空

1. rely on	4. in particular
2. give up on	5. be limited to
3. compete against	6. cut in half

42 It's Time for Universities to Make Race Equality a Priority[E]

大学该把种族平等放在首位了

1　Black people have also interacted with our island nation more recently through slavery, colonialism (殖民主义) and the Commonwealth (联邦). Yet there seems to be collective amnesia (健忘) in the UK about the contributions of people of sub-Saharan African (撒哈拉沙漠以南的非洲) origin. ①So much so that, when prominent black figures criticise our government for their inaction or complain about the racism they have experienced, they are often told they should be "grateful" to be here in the first place.

2　②Luckily, in many institutions, there is a burgeoning (迅速发展的) movement of higher learning that seeks to change our widespread ignorance, and to value the experiences and contributions of black people in Britain. Many UK universities offer degree programmes centred on Africa and black people. For more than 50 years, Soas and Cambridge University have provided excellent graduate programmes dedicated to the study of Africa, and Edinburgh, Birmingham and Oxford universities have followed suit.

3　③What's changed more recently is the emergence of the study of blackness, which looks at the cultures and politics of the African continent, as well as the lived and historical experiences of the African diaspora (移民社群). Last year, Birmingham City University launched the UK's first BA in black studies. And Bristol University is introducing an interdisciplinary MA in black humanities that will draw on the black influences in modern languages, music, feminism, literature, theatre and more.

4　Despite progress in the UK, we pale in comparison to the US. At more than 180 US universities, an undergraduate student can study the concept of blackness as well as Africa and the African diaspora. They can major in black, Africana or African-American studies, and many of these universities also offer two-year MAs and even PhDs within the field.

5　④With the success of the US in mind, I believe degrees focusing on blackness should become more of a priority for UK universities. There is growing demand: the Why is My Curriculum White campaign, founded by students at UCL, can now be found in many universities.

6 ⑤Students and academics have questioned why university <u>syllabuses</u> tend to focus on white contributions to <u>academia</u> while the significant contributions of black people and other people of colour are disregarded or added as an aside. For instance, many geography courses cover demographic (人口统计学的) changes in Africa but often fail to acknowledge studies done by people who were born and grew up there.

◆ 课文小助手

一、生词和词块释义

prominent /ˈprɒmɪnənt/ adj. 著名的

interdisciplinary /ˌɪntəˈdɪsəplɪnəri/ adj.
跨学科的

feminism /ˈfemənɪzəm/ n. 女权主义

syllabus /ˈsɪləbəs/ n. 教学大纲

academia /ˌækəˈdiːmiə/ n. 学术界

so much so that 到这种程度以致

in the first place 从一开始

centre on 围绕

follow suit 照着做

draw on 利用

in comparison to 与……相比

major in 主修

二、话题概要

大意: 英国大学的教学大纲忽视黑人对学术界的贡献，作者呼吁大学应该实现种族平等。

Para. 1: 撒哈拉沙漠以南的非洲人已经融入英国，但他们做出的贡献被遗忘，而且政府不让他们提出批评或抱怨。

Para. 2: 幸运的是很多大学如剑桥、牛津等已经提供了专门研究非洲的优秀研究生课程。

Para. 3: 最近发生的变化着眼于非洲大陆的文化和政治以及非洲侨民的生活和历史经历的研究。伯明翰城市大学和布里斯托尔大学分别提供研究黑人人文的学士、硕士学位。

Para. 4: 英国在研究黑人人文方面取得的进步与美国相比显得逊色。

Para. 5: 英国大学应该优先考虑专注于研究黑人人文的学位等事项。

Para. 6: 英国大学的教学大纲关注白人对学术界的贡献而忽视黑人做出的贡献，这点受到质疑。

◆ 同步练习

一、长难句翻译（见文章划线处）

二、词块填空

1. I'm not familiar with the process, so just watch what you do and _____.

2. Later I read a lot about American history. _____ I started to feel white guilt.

3. I will _____ arts when I study in the university.

4. Our discussion today will _____ technical innovation.

5. I am exceptionally more interested in teaching literacy and history _____ math and science.

6. I don't think we should have been there _____.

7. He _____ his experience as a pilot to make a documentary programme.

三、佳句模仿

原文佳句	Despite progress in the UK, we pale in comparison to the US.
亮点评析	句子中的 despite 相当于 in spite of, pale 作动词用，意思为：显得逊色；in comparison to 意思为：与……相比。
写作应用	When someone you love has a life-threatening illness, everything else pales in comparison. 你爱的人得了致命疾病时，其他一切事情都显得不那么重要了。

◆ 答案

一、翻译

1. 如此健忘，以致当著名的黑人批评我们政府的无为或抱怨他们所经历的种族主义时，他们常常被告知他们应该"感激"一开始就在这里。

2. 幸运的是，在很多大学有一种正在兴起的高等教育运动，旨在改变我们普遍的无知，并重视英国黑人的经验和贡献。

3. 最近发生的变化是黑人研究的出现，该研究着眼于非洲大陆的文化和政治以及非洲侨民的生活和历史经历。

4. 考虑到美国的成功，我认为专注于研究黑人人文的学位应该成为英国大学的优先考虑事项。

5. 学生和学者们质疑为什么大学教学大纲倾向于关注白人对学术界的贡献，而黑人和其他有色人种的重要贡献被忽视或捎带提一下。

二、词块填空

1. follow suit

2. So much so that

3. major in

4. centre on

5. in comparison to

6. in the first place

7. drew on

43 School Summer Holidays Should Be Shorter[E]

学校暑假应该短一些

1   You return from work on a muggy (闷热潮湿的) August evening. Your unwashed teenage son is on the sofa playing Fortnite, as he has been doing for the past eight hours. Your daughter, **scrolling** through Instagram, acknowledges your presence with a surly (粗暴无礼的) **grunt**. Not for the first time, you ask yourself: why are school summer holidays so insufferably long?

2   This is a more serious question than it sounds. Many children will return from the long break having forgotten much of what they were taught the previous year. One study from the American South found that this "summer learning loss" could be as high as a quarter of the year's education. [①]Poor children tend to be the worst affected, since rich ones typically live in homes full of books and are **packed off** to summer camp to learn robotics, Latin or the flute. A study from Baltimore found that variations in summer loss might possibly **account for** two-thirds of the achievement gap between rich and poor children by the age of 14-15. Long holidays definitely **strain** the budgets of poor families, since free school meals stop and extra child care kicks in (缴费).

3   Summer holidays vary greatly from country to country. South Korean children get only three weeks off. Children in Italy and Turkey get a whopping (异常大的) three months. [②]So do those in America, where their parents, unless they are teachers, have an average of only three weeks off a year, among the shortest holidays in the rich world. Companies should let them take a bit more, since burnt-out workers are less productive. But, for their children, six weeks out of class is plenty.

4   Youngsters will hate the idea of a longer school year. Many grown-ups will **object to** it, too. It would cost taxpayers more, since teachers would have to be paid for the extra days. Schools in hotter areas would spend a fortune on air-conditioning. Sceptics (怀疑论者) also note that, although those barely rested South Korean pupils do superbly in exams, they are often miserable. Is that really what you want for your darlings?

5   ③It would be unwise to import South Korea's pressure-cooker approach, in which a single exam determines every child's future. But plenty of Western children could usefully spend a bit longer at their books. Yes, it would cost money, but there are ways to pay for it. One is to have larger classes. ④Many parents **are obsessed with** teacher-to-pupil ratios, but there is **scant** evidence that they make much difference. The average Japanese lower-secondary class is more than 50% larger than the average British one, but Japanese children get better results.

6   More time in school need not mean repeating the same old lessons. ⑤Some extra drilling would be beneficial, particularly for those falling behind. But the summer could also be a time for different kinds of learning: critical thinking, practical skills, financial literacy, work placements with local firms—schools should be free to experiment. Space should not be a problem. Many school buildings sit idle in the summer.

7   Well-off children often already use the summer to broaden their minds and **burnish** their college applications at pricey (昂贵的) camps or doing summer jobs found through connections. Schools should help the rest catch up. Other public services do not simply **vanish** for a quarter of the year. It would be unthinkable for hospitals or the police to do so. So why do schools **get away with** it? Their responsibility to educate does not end when the **mercury** rises.

◆ 课文小助手

一、生词和词块释义

scroll /skrəʊl/　*v.* 滚动

grunt /grʌnt/　*n.* 咕哝

strain /streɪn/　*v.* 使不堪承受

scant /skænt/　*adj.* 不足的

burnish /'bɜ:nɪʃ/　*v.* 改善

vanish /'vænɪʃ/　*v.* 消失

mercury /'mɜ:kjəri/　*n.* 温度表

pack off 把……打发到

account for (在数量、比例上) 占

object to 反对

be obsessed with 困扰

get away with 不因 (某坏事) 而受惩罚

二、话题概要

大意: 学校暑假应该短一些，以缩短贫富孩子之间的差异，而且应该采用丰富多彩的学习形式。

Para. 1: 闷热的八月看到孩子们长时间玩耍，你是否觉得学校的暑假太长而令人无法忍受?

Para. 2: 暑假太长是个严峻的问题，很多孩子开学时已经忘记了前一学年所学的很多知识; 暑期贫困家庭的孩子和富裕家庭的孩子学业成就差异变得更大。

Para. 3: 不同国家暑假长短不同，短的三周，长的三个月。

Para. 4: 年轻人不喜欢更长的学年，许多成年人也反对，因为纳税者负担更多，炎热地区的学校得支付空调费用。

Para. 5: 学习韩国的方式不可取，但西方孩子看书的时间可以更长一点，可以采用大班教学以减少开支。

Para. 6: 在校时间长并不意味着重复已学功课，暑假学习方式可以多种多样。

Para. 7: 学校应该帮助贫困家庭的孩子缩短与富有家庭的孩子在教育上的差别，学校的教育责任不应该因为天气热而终止。

◆ 同步练习

一、长难句翻译 (见文章划线处)

二、词块填空

1. Computers _____ 5% of the country's commercial electricity consumption.

2. Working people everywhere _____ paying taxes.

3. He _____ his wife and children to stay in a caravan (旅行拖车) in Wales.

4. She didn't let her pupils _____ lazy thinking.

5. Your generation may seem to _____ relationships that change continually.

三、佳句模仿

原文佳句	Summer holidays vary greatly from country to country.
亮点评析	vary from…to 表示"随之变化"。
写作应用	1. The situation varies from area to area. 这种情况因地区而异。 2. Opinions vary from person to person. 各人观点不同。

原文佳句	Sceptics also note that, although those barely rested South Korean pupils do superbly in exams, they are often miserable.
亮点评析	句子中的两个副词 barely (相当于 hardly) 和 superbly (相当于 very well) 可以用到书面表达中，增添文采。
写作应用	1. Our football team played superbly. 我们的足球队踢得棒极了。 2. He was so drunk that he could barely stand. 他醉得都快站不住了。

◆ 答案

一、长难句翻译

1. 贫困家庭的孩子往往是受影响最严重的，因为富裕家庭的孩子通常生活在满是书的家里，被送去夏令营学习机器人技术、拉丁语或长笛。

2. 美国的孩子也有三个月的假期，而美国的父母(除非是教师)平均每年只有三周的假期，是假期最短的发达国家之一。

3. 在韩国，单次考试决定每个孩子的未来，引用这种"高压锅"式的方法是不明智的。

4. 许多家长担心教师与学生的比率，但很少有证据表明他们有很大的差异。日本普通的中低班额比一般的英国班级要大 50%(即学生人数多 50%)，但日本的孩子成绩更好。

5. 一些额外操练是有益的，尤其对落后学生来说。但夏季的学习时间也可以有不同形式：批判性思维、实用技能、财务素养、到当地企业实习等，学校应该自由展开实验。

二、词块填空

1. account for

2. object to

3. packed off

4. get away with

5. be obsessed with

44 Banning the Internet Is Child Abuse, Parents Told[E]

父母说：禁止网络是虐待儿童

Mark Bridge Technology Correspondent

1 [1]**Depriving** children as young as four **of** "screen time" is **tantamount** to child abuse, sociologists say in a study that **contradicts conventional** wisdom.

2 Researchers **called for** children to be allowed unrestricted access to devices. [2]They concluded that the risks from on-line interactions were often overstated and were outweighed by the social and educational advantages.

3 Researchers from Teesside University, Aston University and the University of South Australia reviewed scores of previous studies and surveyed 2,000 internet users for their **forthcoming** book Screen Society.

4 Ellis Cashmore, a co-author and **honorary** professor of sociology at Aston University, Birmingham, said that the internet gave children important opportunities for development. Parental bans were misguided and could be harmful, he said.

5 [3]"Society has been completely transformed by the combination of screens and the internet and it **opens up** a whole new world of possibilities," he said. "We know through our own day-to-day lives and through our research that many parents ban their children from using smartphones and devices because they are worried about screen addiction." But what are the consequences of this?

6 [4]"By removing screens, you are taking away an encyclopedic (百科全书) source of information, depriving young people of a vital source of communication and potentially **exposing** them **to** a form of **bullying** and **ridicule** from other young people—reducing their self-esteem and confidence. Depriving young people of screens will almost certainly have long-term negative effects for them and **is tantamount to** child abuse."

7 Professor Cashmore suggested that access to connected devices should be unrestricted for children as young as four. Once children reached eight, they would go online if they wanted to,

regardless of parental measures, he said.

8 The risks from "**trolls**" and "internet addiction" were greatly **exaggerated**, he added. Children were better at protecting themselves than most **commentators** realised.

9 The advice contradicts the **consensus** among experts who believe that parents should **exercise tight controls** over their children's screen use. ⑤The government warns that children who go on social media may see violent, extremist and pornographic (色情的) content, **fake** news and the promotion of harmful behaviour. They may also be exposed to bullying and the attention of sexual **predators**, it says.

10 The NSPCC recommends that parents should educate their children on the risks they will face and use controls to manage what they can see.

◆ 课文小助手

一、生词和词块释义

tantamount /'tæntəmaʊnt/ *adj.* 相当的

contradict /kɒntrə'dɪkt/ *v.* 与……矛盾

conventional /kən'venʃ(ə)n(ə)l/ *adj.* 传统的

forthcoming /fɔ:θ'kʌmɪŋ/ *adj.* 即将到来的

honorary /'ɒn(ə)(rə)rɪ/ *adj.* 荣誉的

bully /'bʊlɪ/ *vt.* 欺负

ridicule /'rɪdɪkju:l/ *vt.* 嘲笑

troll /trəʊl; trɒl/ *n.* 浏览

exaggerate /ɪg'zædʒəreɪt; eg-/ *vt.* 使扩大

commentator /'kɒmənteɪtə(r)/ *n.* 评论员

consensus /kən'sensəs/ *n.* 一致意见

fake /feɪk/ *adj.* 假的

predator /'predətə/ *n.* 食肉动物

deprive of 剥夺某人的……

call for 需要，提倡

open up 打开

expose...to 暴露在

be tantamount to 等同于

exercise controls over 实施控制

二、话题概要

大意: 剥夺孩子上网权利等同于虐待儿童。

Para. 1–2: 剥夺四岁孩子的屏幕时间等同于虐待儿童，社会学家在一个研究中说道。这个说法与传统的理念相矛盾。研究者希望孩子们可以被允许有无限制的上网的机会。他们得出结论：网上交流的风险经常被夸大，被社会和教育优势所压倒。

Para. 3–4: 研究者认为，网络给孩子更多重要的机会发展，父母亲的禁令会误导孩子且是有害的。

Para. 5–6: 荧屏和网络完全改变了社会，它把整个世界的可能性打开在我们眼前。通过我们自己的日常生活和研究，我们了解到许多父母亲禁止孩子使用手机和一些电子设备，因为他们担忧会引起网瘾。但是，通过取消网络，你拿走了信息的百科全书的来源，剥夺了年轻人交流的重要来源，使他们暴露在其他年轻人的欺凌和嘲笑之中，减少了他们的自尊和自信。剥夺年轻人上网的权利，对他们会有长久的消极影响，等同于虐待。

Para. 7–8: Cashmore 教授认为，不要过多地夸大网瘾，孩子比我们想象得更擅长保护自己。

Para. 9–10: 政府警告：上社会媒体的孩子们可能会看到暴力，极端分子，色情内容，虚假新闻和一些被推崇的有害行为。建议家长要教育孩子他们可能会面临的风险，控制、管理他们的所见所闻。

◆ 同步练习

一、长难句翻译（见文章划线处）

二、词块填空

1. It's a situation that _____ a blend of delicacy and force.

2. Many children are _____ good education simply because they are born in remote villages.

3. That would _____ a whole series of scientific and philosophical difficulties.

4. To stay warm in cold weather, coldblooded animals must _____ themselves _____ a source of warmth such as direct sunlight.

5. "Learning how to think" means learning how to _____ what and how you think.

6. Time is life. Gratuitous waste other people's time, it is would _____ murder.

三、佳句模仿

原文佳句	Researchers called for children to be allowed unrestricted access to devices.
亮点评析	be allowed unrestricted access to: 被允许可以无限制做某事
写作应用	Customers are allowed unrestricted access to varieties of items while shopping online. 消费者网购的时候允许无限制地购买各种产品。

原文佳句	By removing screens, you are taking away an encyclopedic (百科全书) source of information, depriving young people of a vital source of communication and potentially exposing them to a form of bullying and ridicule from other young people—reducing their self-esteem and confidence.
亮点评析	depriving young people of...and potentially exposing them to... 是并列非谓语动词做伴随状语。
写作应用	She watched the film, weeping and sighing. 看电影的时候，她且叹且泣。

◆ 答案

一、长难句翻译

1. 剥夺四岁孩子的屏幕时间，等同于虐待儿童，社会学家在一个研究中说道。这个说法与传统的理念相矛盾。

2. 他们得出结论：网上交流的风险经常被夸大，被社会和教育优势所压倒。

3. 荧屏和网络完全改变了社会，它把一整个世界的可能性打开在我们眼前。

4. 通过取消网络，你拿走了信息的百科全书的来源，剥夺了年轻人交流的重要来源，使他们暴露在其他年轻人的欺凌和嘲笑之中，减少了他们的自尊和自信。

5. 政府警告：上社会媒体的孩子们可能会看到暴力，极端分子，色情内容，虚假新闻和一些被推崇的有害行为。

二、词块填空

1. calls for

2. deprived of

3. open up

4. expose to

5. exercise controls over

6. be tantamount to

45 Their Lives Would Be Better, Even if They Did Not Learn Very Much[M]

他们的生活会变好，即使他们学得不多

1 [1]The pattern of school attendance, steadily declining with age, is not unique to Pakistan. The global share of children who do not attend primary school has fallen from 28% in 1970 to 9% in 2016. But progress is **stalling**, and is less impressive than it appears. The share of children not attending school has fallen by less than one percentage point since 2007.

2 **In principle** the world is committed to making sure every child attends school until the age of 16. In 2015 the members of the UN **pledged** that by 2030 "all girls and boys will complete free, **equitable** and quality primary and secondary education." What if that were to happen?

3 Perhaps naturally, educationists assume that it would lead to millions more children **cramming** their brains **with** knowledge. But evidence from schools in poor countries suggests otherwise. Many children learn precious little in their classes. If you want to find an uneducated child in today's world, argues Lant Pritchett, an economist at Harvard University, "you can find them in school".

4 The **extent** of the failure is **immense**. According to a survey of three east African countries (Kenya, Tanzania and Uganda) published in 2014, three-quarters of pupils in the third year of primary school could not read a sentence such as : "The name of the dog is Puppy." In rural India almost the same share could not **subtract** 17 from 46, or perform similar calculations with two-**digit** numbers. UNESCO estimates that six out of ten children worldwide (a total of more than 600m) do not meet a minimum standard of **proficiency** in reading and maths. The vast majority of these children are in school.

5 If the children not in school began attending, it is therefore unlikely that they would learn much either. To understand why, consider what happens—or does not happen—in classrooms. According to data from the World Bank, rates of teacher absenteeism in developing countries range from 11% to 30%. And teachers who do show up often cannot teach.

6 Poverty makes educating children much harder. Children who turn up tired and hungry struggle to pay attention. Teachers who do not have books, equipment or electricity cannot concentrate

on teaching arithmetic and language. But the problems in the classroom are political, not financial, in origin. ②Teachers are often appointed **on the basis of patronage**, not **merit**. Powerful teachers' unions protect **woeful** educators when they should be **sacked**. Politicians prefer cutting ribbons outside new schools to improving what happens inside them.

7   Spending more money on current education systems would probably do little to improve what happens in the classroom. A review of 30 randomised-controlled trials, published in 2013 in the journal science by Michael Kremer, Conner Brannen and Rachel Glennerster, found that "more-of-the-same" policies would have little or no effect on the quality of learning. These included **interventions** such as adding more teachers to reduce class sizes, or paying for more textbooks. ③By contrast, changes that did not cost very much but are hard to **implement,** such as changing **pedagogical** approaches or introducing short-term contracts for teachers, were associated with higher test scores for pupils.

8   ④It sounds like **a counsel of despair**. If every child went to school, millions more would sit in woeful, boring classrooms. But while this sounds awful, it would probably still be good for them, their families and broader society. For, as Justin Sandefur of CGD points out, there is plenty of evidence that even when children do not learn much at school, they still do better for having gone.

9   Some benefits are economic. ⑤Attending school for longer is associated with earning more in later life, in part because those with additional schooling are more likely to get non-agricultural jobs and move to cities. It could also be a signalling effect:a shopkeeper may prefer workers who stayed at school for at least five years.

10   ⑥Parents will send their children to school if they feel it will **give them a better shot** at life. They will keep them at home if they believe their children can make more money for the household working the fields or the marketplace, or if they worry for their children's safety in the classroom. So efforts to reform schools and improve teaching would result in more children **enrolling in** (and completing) school. But even without such reforms, the implication from the research is clear: if every child went to school, no matter how terrible, they would benefit. Even a bad school, it turns out, is better than no school at all.

◆ 课文小助手

一、生词和词块释义

stall /stɔːl/ v. 失速

pledge /pledʒ/ v. 发誓

equitable /ˈekwɪtəb(ə)l/ adj. 公正的

extent /ɪkˈstent; ek-/ n. 程度

immense /ɪˈmens/ adj. 巨大的

subtract /səbˈtrækt/ vt. 减去

digit /ˈdɪdʒɪt/ n. 数字

proficiency /prəˈfɪʃnsɪ/ n. 熟练

patronage /ˈpætrənɪdʒ/ n. 资助

merit /ˈmerɪt/ n. 功绩

woeful /ˈwəʊfl/ adj. 悲惨的

sack /sæk/ v. 解雇

intervention /ˌɪntəˈvenʃn/ n. 干预

implement /ˈɪmplɪment/ n. 实施

pedagogical /ˌpedəˈɡɒdʒɪkl/ n. 教学的

counsel /ˈkaʊnsl/ n. 建议

in principle 原则上

cram with 装满

on the basis of 以……为基础

a counsel of despair 知难而退的建议

give sb. a better shot 给某人更好的机会

enroll in 使加入

二、话题概要

大意： 学生们即使在教室里学得不多，但也能改变他们的生活。

Para. 1: 就读率随着年龄增长稳步下降的现象，不仅仅是巴基斯坦所独有的。世界范围内都存在这样的现象。

Para. 2–4: 原则上世界各地正在致力于确保每个孩子可以接受教育到 16 岁，教育者以为孩子们会学会很多知识。但是证据表明恰恰相反。教育失败的程度是巨大的，一些在读学生不会读简单的句子，不会阅读和数学。

Para. 5–6: 教育失败的原因。第一，发展中国家教师缺乏很多，教师缺乏教学能力。第二，贫穷使孩子不能专注学习，老师缺乏必备的教学材料。但是追根溯源，问题还是政治原因——教师的聘用是根据资助能力，而不是根据他们的功绩。政客们宁愿在新校建成时剪彩带也不愿意改善学校内部事务。

Para. 7: 投资更多的钱在目前的教育体制上也是杯水车薪，无济于事。比如，政府提高教师人数，缩小教室规模，或者投资更多课本。想得高分的改变现状的举措简单但很难实施，比如改进教学方法，签订短期合同等。

Para. 8–9: 学生们即使在教室里学得不多，但也能改变他们的生活。读书时间长一点与日后多挣钱是相关的。部分原因是因为你接受了一些学校教育，就更有可能得到一些脱离农业的工作，到城市生活。

Para. 10: 父母将会送他们的孩子去学校，如果他们感觉到会给他们一个更好的机会。如果他们认为孩子能够在田地里或者市场为家庭挣更多的钱，或者如果他们担忧孩子在教室里的安全，他们会把孩子留在家里。因此改革学校教育，改善教学会让更多的孩子加入到学校。

三、佳句模仿

原文佳句	Perhaps naturally, educationists assume that it would lead to millions more children cramming their brains with knowledge.
亮点评析	lead to sb. doing sth. 意思是"导致做某事"。
写作应用	People put shared-bikes wherever and whenever they like, leading to the city image being ruined. 人们可以随时随地随自己所愿地放置共享单车，这就破坏了城市形象。

原文佳句	But evidence from schools in poor countries suggests otherwise.
亮点评析	otherwise: 另一方面
写作应用	Patients are advised to turn up for appointments on Monday unless they are told otherwise. 除非另外通知，建议病人周一去赴和医生的约会。

◆ 同步练习

一、长难句翻译（见文章划线处）

二、词块填空

1. He _____ his pockets _____ as much candy as they would hold.

2. I agree with it _____ but I doubt if it will happen in practice.

3. She, too, was pro-life, just the kind of person I was trying to _____ at the American dream.

4. When asked, then, whether his perspective is _____ , he responds that there are evils in the world that one "simply has to live with for the time being."

5. It's too late to _____ that class.

6. _____ analysis to the reasons making difference, some key points and methods of health education in urban are put forward.

◆ 答案

一、长难句翻译

1. 这种就读率随着年龄增长稳步下降的现象，不仅仅是巴基斯坦所独有的。

2. 教师往往是根据他的资助被聘用，而不是根据他的教学成果。强大的教师联盟在一些教育者应该被解雇的时候保护他们。政客们宁愿在新学校外面剪彩带，也不愿意去改善学校内发生的事情。

3. 相反，那些花费不多，但是很难去实施的改变，比如说改变教学方法，引进短期教师合同，都是跟学生的较高的考试成绩相关的。

4. 听起来像一个难以实现的建议。如果每个孩子都去上学，会有很多的孩子坐在不令人愉快、令人乏味的教室里。

5. 读书时间长一点与日后多挣钱是相关的。部分原因是因为你接受了一些学校教育，就更有可能得到一些脱离农业的工作，到城市生活。

6. 父母将会送他们的孩子去学校，如果他们感觉到会给他们一个更好的机会。如果他们认为孩子能够在田地里或者市场为家庭挣更多的钱，或者如果他们担忧孩子在教室里的安全，他们会把孩子留在家里。因此改革学校教育，改善教学会让更多的孩子加入到学校。

二、词块填空

1. crammed...with	4. a counsel of despair
2. in principle	5. enroll in
3. give a better shot	6. On the basis of

46 The Miseducation of America^[M]

美国的错误教育

1   Student loan programs have vastly expanded the ranks of college graduates. Without the support of the federal government, most of this debt would never have been possible. Yet, strangely, almost no one argues that America has gotten its money's worth. Our student loan programs' main payoff is complaints.

2   Parents, students and activists **fret** that this **crushing** debt has to be repaid. ^①Student loan programs have **saddled** a generation of young people **with onerous** financial **obligations**— commitments that prevent them from starting a family or moving out of their parents' basement. Wouldn't it be better if college were affordable for everyone?

3   Yet many of these same critics also blame student loans for "sending too many kids to college." Lots of academically weak students, the thinking goes, use cheap credit to gamble on their future. ^②While this occasionally **pans out**, weaker students usually fail. And when weaker students manage to graduate, they rarely have the **prestigious** majors and high grades required to get the **lucrative** jobs they need to repay their loans. Isn't it **perverse** to **dangle** cheap credit in front of naïve young people and expect them to choose well?

4   If student loan programs are bad, what would be better? Whatever their complaints, most critics **gravitate** to the same solution: Make tuition so cheap that students no longer need to borrow. As the Wharton School's Peter Cappelli writes in Will College Pay Off, "Using loans to pay for college is an idea with great appeal to economists because the people getting the financial benefit—the graduates who get the good jobs—are the ones paying for it…If there is not a good payoff from the degree, that argument **falls apart**."

5   Suppose, however, that governments **slashed** college tuition. How would this encourage students to finish their studies or carefully choose a promising major? ^③What would this do about all the wasted time and money we already see from those who drop out or **squeak through**? Free college would plainly encourage even weaker students to **throw the dice**.

6　What's the harm of creating limitless educational opportunities? The most obvious is the massive burden on taxpayers. ④<u>The deeper problem, though, is that the more college degrees multiply, the less they mean to employers.</u> Researchers call this "**credential inflation**." Most of what you learn in college never comes up after the final exam. This is obvious for literature and history majors, but even engineers spend semesters on mathematical proofs that never come up on the job. Employers reward college degrees primarily because they **certify** graduates' intelligence, work **ethic** and **sheer conformity**. So when educational opportunities expand, employers don't respond by handing every graduate a good job. Instead, they **raise the bar**.

7　Credential inflation explains why so many of today's young people need a college degree to get the same job their parents got with a high school diploma. True, **cognitively** demanding jobs are more common than they were in the 1970s, but they remain fairly rare. Secretaries, waiters and the other classic "noncollege" jobs shouldn't require an undergraduate pedigree (血统). As an internet meme (文化基因) **quips**, "When everyone has a bachelor's degree, no one does."

8　I'm a college professor, but I still believe that the **harsh** realities of credential inflation should make us **radically** rethink the social value of college. If students' main goal is not to learn useful skills but to outshine their peers, taxpayers are fueling a zero-sum struggle. My recent book crunches (用计算机计算) the numbers and concludes that our society would be richer if half our high school grads skipped college and joined the job market. And, frankly, there's no point in making college more affordable for students who don't belong there in the first place. When the college degree was rare, there was little stigma (耻辱) against those who lacked it. Our dream should not be a world where everyone goes to college but a world where you can get a good job straight out of high school.

9　Perhaps I go too far. Some "weaker students" don't have the socioeconomic and academic advantages of those born into wealthy families. But student loans are still underrated. Even no-interest loans leave students with some skin in the game. If their educational investment **flops**, they still have to repay the principal (本金).

10　Proposals to make college cheaper, or even free—as Senator Bernie Sanders urged in the last presidential campaign—delete that vital reality check. Without tuition, the most fanciful academic experiments seem tempting. Who knows, medieval (中世纪的) studies could be the next big thing!

11　Student loan programs should be reformed. But wise reforms bolster (支持) borrowers' incentive (动机) to choose a productive path. ⑥Charging equal interest rates regardless of odds of success or intended major is a recipe for fruitless credential inflation. The **prudent** course, which is standard procedure in the private sector, is to base interest rates on expected risk and reward.

12　While there's always a chance you're a late bloomer (完全成熟的人), weaker students should know the odds are against them. Students in low-earning majors should understand the difference between a hobby and a career path. And if you're worried about class divisions and economic inequality, wouldn't both be milder if we got credential inflation under control?

13　For all their faults, student loan programs do warn students to look before they leap. The pragmatic (实用主义的) way forward is to raise interest rates for high-risk students to make these warnings loud and clear.

◆ 课文小助手

一、生词和词块释义

fret /fret/ *v.* (使)烦恼

crushing /'krʌʃɪŋ/ *adj.* 压倒的

onerous /'əʊn(ə)rəs; 'ɒn-/ *adj.* 沉重的

obligation /ɒblɪ'geɪʃ(ə)n/ *n.* 义务

prestigious /pre'stɪdʒəs/ *adj.* 有威望的

lucrative /'luːkrətɪv/ *adj.* 有利可图的

perverse /pə'vɜːs/ *adj.* 不正当的

dangle /'dæŋg(ə)l/ *v.* 追求

gravitate /'grævɪteɪt/ *v.* 受吸引

slash /slæʃ/ *vt.* 大幅削减

certify /'sɜːtɪfaɪ/ *vt.* (尤指书面)证明

ethic /'eθɪk/ *n.* 伦理

sheer /ʃɪə/ *adj.* 全然的

conformity /kən'fɔːmɪtɪ/ *n.* 一致

cognitively /'kɑːgnətɪvli/ *adv.* 认知地

quip /kwɪp/ *vt.* 嘲弄

radically /'rædɪkəlɪ/ *adv.* 根本地

harsh /hɑːʃ/ *adj.* 严酷的

flop /flɒp/ *v.* 猛落

prudent /'pruːd(ə)nt/ *adj.* 周到的

saddle sb. with sth. 使负担

pan out 成功

fall apart 崩溃

squeak through 非常勉强地通过

throw the dice 掷骰子

credential inflation 信用通胀

raise the bar 提高标杆

二、话题概要

大意：让每个学生都能够上得起大学，而有些学生本不属于这些地方，这样做是没有意义的。我们的梦想不是拥有一个所有人都能去上大学的世界，而是一个高中毕业直接可以找到好工作的世界。

Para. 1–2: 学生贷款计划很大程度上扩大了大学毕业生的数量级别。没有联邦政府的支持，大多数的贷款是不可能的。

Para. 3: 但是，这些评论家也责备学生的贷款计划送了太多的孩子去上大学。

Para. 4: 如果学生贷款项目糟糕，那么该有什么更好的选择呢？

Para. 5: 但是如果政府大幅削减大学的学费，我们该如何去鼓励学生完成他们的学业，或者选择一个有前途的专业呢？

Para. 6: 创造无限制的教育机会究竟有哪些伤害呢？最明显的就是对纳税人身上增加的大量的负担。

Para. 7: 信用膨胀解释了为什么如今很多的年轻人需要大学学历来获得当初他们的父母亲一个高中学历就能得到的工作。

Para. 8: 我们要重新思考大学的社会价值。如果学生的主要目的不是去学习有用的技能，而是想要去超越他人，比他人优越，那么纳税人的付出就是白费的。

Para. 9–10: 有一些学习能力薄弱的学生，他们没有那些出生在富有家庭的学生的社会经济的和学习的优势，但是学生贷款仍然被低估。

Para. 11: 应该要改革学生贷款项目。好的改革支持借贷者选择一个有成效的动机。收取相同利息，而不管你是否成功或选修的是何种专业，是信用膨胀的一个原因。

Para. 12–13: 挣钱少的专业的学生应该明白兴趣和职业道路之间的差别。

三、佳句模仿

原文佳句	Wouldn't it be better if college were affordable for everyone?
亮点评析	提建议时，尽量用这种委婉的说法，礼貌且易于让对方接受。
写作应用	Wouldn't it be better if the government strengthen supervision to better the environment? 如果政府加强监督来改善环境，不是更好吗？

原文佳句	If student loan programs are bad, what would be better? Whatever their complaints, most critics gravitate to the same solution: Make tuition so cheap that students no longer need to borrow.
亮点评析	提建议时，注意模仿这种表述的逻辑性。
写作应用	If introducing the ipad to the classroom is bad, what would be better? Whatever the complaints, we gravitate to the solution: take advantage of new technology in a reasonable and practical way. 如果在课堂上引入 ipad（一种平板电脑）不好，那么还有更好的吗？无论什么抱怨，我们也要引出这个措施：合理有效地充分利用科技。

◆ 同步练习

一、长难句翻译（见文章划线处）

二、词块填空

1. Things didn't _____ as he had planned.

2. Don't _____ me _____ taking care of the children.

3. I am trying to be more centred, and not _____ when I go through difficulties.

4. Election observers mostly agree that Mr Kibaki stole the decisive votes to _____ back in for a second term.

5. We decided who cleaned the room by _____.

6. Many small colleges are _____ of admission.

◆ 答案

一、长难句翻译

1. 学生贷款计划使得年轻人承担了很多经济责任，阻止他们创建自己的家庭，或者搬出父母的家庭独立生活。

2. 尽管，有的时候他们会成功，但学习成绩差的学生往往都是失败的。当学习能力薄弱的学生设法毕业，他们很少能够拥有好的专业，或者好的学习成绩去获得一些收入好的工作来偿还自己的贷款。

3. 如何去处理在那些辍学的孩子身上我们已经浪费的时间和金钱？

4. 更深的问题是，大学的学历越多，对于用人单位来说意义越少。

5. 收取相同利息，而不管你是否成功或选修的是何种专业，是信用膨胀的一个原因。

二、词块填空

1. pan out

2. saddle...with...

3. fall apart

4. squeak

5. throwing the dice

6. raising the bar

Chapter 8

文艺 / Art

47 "Mary B" Gives Sister Mary of "P&P" a Voice[M]

"Mary B" 替 "P&P" 中的 Mary 代言

1 Jane Austen had little to say in "Pride and Prejudice" about the middle Bennet daughter, Mary, and most of it was **dismissive**. She is "the only plain one in the family," who "had neither genius nor taste," with a weak voice and an affection for "threadbare (破旧的) morality."

2 Elder sister Elizabeth and Darcy got their happily ever after, while Mary **was doomed to be** the Jan Brady of Regency romance.

3 In Katherine J. Chen's ingenious (巧妙的) **debut** novel, "Mary B" (Random House), the title character gets some attitude, and a measure of **revenge**, in a story that inhabits and critiques (评判) Austen's novel. "I, too, hoped quietly for romance and also for marriage as much as any of my sisters did," she insists. She's just **disinclined** to compromise her intelligence to achieve them.

4 ①Chen is mindful, though, that a young woman among the gentry (上流社会) of early 1800s England could only act out so much, especially with parents desperate to **land** financial security (i.e., husbands) for their daughters. So Mary **abides** her sisters' **stinging** taunts (讽刺), **keeping** her **fury in check**.

5 The first third of "Mary B" roughly, somewhat ploddingly (艰难地), matches the plot of "Pride and Prejudice," with a few twists. ②The **pretentious** clergyman (牧师) Mr. Collins, who delivered a **comically** presumptuous (冒昧的) **proposal** to Elizabeth in the original novel, turns out to be a sympathetic outcast (被抛弃者) just like Mary. But his rejection of Mary in Chen's version **underscores** the culture's demand that money and looks mean more than brains.

6 Once Chen leaps past Austen's plot, "Mary B" becomes more fully inspired and free to **upend** Austen's novel. ③Darcy's storied **estate**, Pemberley, becomes a gilded (镀金的) cage for Elizabeth; Mary's impetuous (鲁莽的) sister Lydia, who eloped (私奔) to London, learns what little support society has for a woman without money or education.

7 Mary, for her part, uses a visit to Pemberley to **put** her much-**mocked** reading habits—her "silent rebellion" —**to good use**. ④She **hunkers down** with protofeminist（男女平等主义时期后的）works by Mary Wollstonecraft and writes her own novel about the "uncouth（无教养的）and **vicious** men who, despite their titles, have little learning and little breeding（教养）and absolutely no manners at all." And she finds romance as well—this is still Austen's world, after all.

8　"Pride and Prejudice" has been reimagined countless times, its characters transformed into everything from sexpots（性感的人）to zombies（无生气的人）. ⑤Rather than **remounting** the "Pride" story in **genre** dress, Chen's skillfully **roots out** blind spots in Austen's **perspective**, the way "Pride" **celebrated integrity** and honesty but **was** often **stingy with empathy** or respect for contrarian（叛逆的）women pursuing an intellectual life.

9　Chen doesn't soft-pedal（对……轻描淡写）how challenging Mary's task is—she's forced to keep much of her self-possessed spirit hidden.

10　But quietude is a powerful resource: "Only think of how much in our day-today life is lost in noise and what can be gained in its opposite—in the depths of silence," she tells Darcy. **In that regard**, "Mary B" is **a tribute** not just **to** Austen but to defiant（反抗的）women of any era.

◆ 课文小助手

一、生词和词块释义

dismissive /dɪsˈmɪsɪv/ *adj.* 轻蔑的

debut /deɪˈbju:/ *n.* 首次亮相

revenge /rɪˈvendʒ/ *n.* 报复

disincline /ˌdɪsɪnˈklaɪn/ *vt.* 使讨厌

land /lænd/ *vt.* 成功得到

abide /əˈbaɪd/ *vt.* 无法容忍

stinging /ˈstɪŋɪŋ/ *adj.* 刺人的

fury /ˈfjʊər/ *n.* 狂怒

pretentious /prɪˈtenʃəs/ *adj.* 炫耀的

comically /ˈkɒmɪkli/ *adv.* 可笑地

proposal /prəˈpəʊzl/ *n.* 求婚

underscore /ˌʌndəˈskɔ:(r)/ *vt.* 强调

upend /ʌpˈend/ *vt.* 使颠倒

estate /ɪˈsteɪt/ *n.* 房产

mock /mɒk/ *vt.* 嘲笑

vicious /ˈvɪʃəs/ *adj.* 狂暴的

remount /ˌri:ˈmaʊnt/ *vt.* 重组

genre /ˈʒɒrə/ *n.* 类型

perspective /pəˈspektɪv/ *n.* 观点

celebrate /ˈselɪbreɪt/ *vt.* 歌颂

integrity /ɪnˈtegrəti/ *n.* 正直

empathy /ˈempəθi/ *n.* 共鸣

be doomed to do sth. 注定做某事

keep...in check 控制

put...to good use 好好利用

hunker down 盘坐

root out 根除

be...stingy with 吝啬……

in that regard 从那个方面

a tribute...to 向……致敬

二、话题概要

大意： 这是一篇关于 Katherine J. Chen 的第一本小说 *Mary B* 的书评。文章介绍了小说的内容：主要人物 Mary 也希望和她的姐妹一样浪漫，也希望婚姻，只是不愿意妥协自己的智慧去实现它们。该小说不是在体裁上重组 *Pride and Prejudice*，陈巧妙地去掉了奥斯汀视角下的一些盲点，如歌颂正直和诚实，但是吝啬对追求知识生活的女性的同情和尊重。"*Mary B*" 不仅是对奥斯汀的颂扬，而且是对任何时代反抗的女性的颂扬。

Para. 1–2: 在简·奥斯汀的《傲慢与偏见》中，Mary 只是一名普通的家庭成员，没有天赋，没有品位，墨守成规。

Para. 3–4: 在 Katherine J. Chen 的小说 *Mary B* 中，Mary 有态度，甚至要复仇，也悄悄地希望和她的姐妹一样浪漫，也希望婚姻，只是不愿意妥协自己的智慧去实现它们。陈意识到 19 世纪的英国上流社会，女性也只能这样。

Para. 5–7: *Mary B* 的一些具体的故事情节介绍以及与原版简·奥斯汀的《傲慢与偏见》的区别和共同之处。

Para. 8–10: 对 *Mary B* 的写作技法和主题的评价。

◆ 同步练习

一、长难句翻译（见文章划线处）

二、词块填空

1. I strongly have the confidence that it will _____ be meaningful.

2. Finally, we should keep our emotions _____.

3. Your creative talents can also be _____, if you can work up the energy.

4. Do you think it is possible _____ crime?

5. Don't be so _____ the money!

三、佳句模仿

原文佳句	But his rejection of Mary in Chen's version underscores the culture's demand that money and looks mean more than brains.
亮点评析	underscore=underline 有"强调，突出"之意思；demand 后面跟着同位语从句，省去了 should。
写作应用	1. The report underscores/underlines the importance of pre-school education. 这份报告强调学前教育的重要性。 2. They recognized that these objectives demand that we must all practice mutual respect and accept shared responsibility. 他们认识到，若想实现这些目标，要求我们大家必须相互尊重和分担责任。

原文佳句	In that regard, "Mary B" is a tribute not just to Austen but to defiant（反抗的）women of any era.
亮点评析	in that regard 意思为"在……方面"；not...but... 意思是"不是……而是……"
写作应用	1. We've made extraordinary progress as a society in that regard. 在那个方面，我们的社会已经取得了巨大的进步。 2. He brought to the job not just considerable experience but passionate enthusiasm. 他不仅给这一工作带来了不少经验，而且倾注了极大的热情。

◆ 答案

一、长难句翻译

1. 然而，陈很清楚，19 世纪初的英国上流社会中的一个年轻女子只能做这么多的事情，尤其是在父母渴望为他们的女儿提供经济保障（如丈夫）的情况下。

2. 自命不凡的牧师 Collins 先生在原著小说中对伊丽莎白发出了可笑而傲慢的求婚，结果像玛丽一样成为一个让人同情的被抛弃者。

3. 达西的庄园，Pemberley 成了伊丽莎白的金丝笼；玛丽的浮躁的妹妹丽迪雅，私奔到伦敦，认识到社会几乎不会支持一个没有钱或受过教育的女人。

4. 她盘腿坐着，读着玛丽·沃斯通克拉夫特所写的男女平等主义时期后的作品；写她自己的关于那些粗野和恶毒的男人的小说，这些男人尽管有着头衔，但几乎没有学识，没有教养，完全没有礼貌。

5. 不是在体裁上重组 Pride and Prejudice，陈巧妙地去掉了奥斯汀视角下的一些盲点，如歌颂正直和诚实，但是吝啬对追求知识生活的女性的同情和尊重。

二、词块填空

1. be doomed to

2. in check

3. put to good use

4. root out

5. stingy with

48 On Stage, the Saga of the Lehman Brothers Is a Parable of America[M]

舞台上，雷曼兄弟的故事是一个关于美国的故事

Sam Mendes brings "The Lehman Trilogy（三部曲）" to London's National Theatre

1   Italians have long been inspired by the opening up of America. In the 1960s, for example, no year went by without a fresh serving of "spaghetti" Westerns, with their **vulpine** heroes, their **vistas** and their villains（反面人物）. ①Now, half a century after Sergio Leone brought "Once Upon a Time in the West" to the screen, the National Theatre in London is hosting a different kind of Italian Western—a grand **morality** tale about God, greed, conquest and family, featuring bankers instead of gunslingers（枪手）.

2   Part of "The Lehman Trilogy" by Stefano Massini, a Florentine **playwright**, was performed in Paris in French in 2013. By the time Sam Mendes saw a five-hour Italian version directed by his **mentor**, Luca Ronconi, in Milan two years later, it had also been translated into German and rewritten by Mr Massini as a novel. ②The challenge for Mr Mendes, a distinguished stage director who has overseen two James Bond films, and the text's **adapter**, the National's Ben Power, was to **extract** and **hone** the many themes that had **obsessed** the Italian author over the decade he spent working on the story. ③Their aim, Mr Power says, was to create a **distilled** English version that would speak to a London audience, many of whom will have an intimate knowledge of the financial crisis that is the drama's inevitable **denouement**.

3   And its beginning, the play, which opened this week, begins on September 15th 2008, the day Lehman Brothers collapsed. Immediately, though, it jumps back to September 11th 1844, when Hayum Lehmann (played by Simon Russell Beale, pictured centre), the son of a Bavarian cattle merchant, steps off the boat in New York, wearing the new shoes he has kept for the occasion.

At the **dock** he becomes Henry Lehman; he settles in Montgomery, Alabama, where he opens a modest shop. His two brothers, Emanuel (Ben Miles, right) and Mayer (Adam Godley, left), follow him. The Lehmans become cotton factors; in the late 1850s they open an office in New York and launch a bank. "Three brothers. Travellers. Immigrants. They arrived with nothing and they built an entire universe."

4　④Tracing the fortunes of the family and the firm through the civil war and the Wall Street crash, this is a saga about the making of modern America wrapped in a story of finance. But fundamentally "The Lehman Trilogy" is also about the **alchemy** of theatre. When Hayum/ Henry **disembarks** at the start of the play, he steps right into the **debris** of the ruined modern bank. Cardboard storage boxes, of the kind familiar from footage of the crisis, litter the set; in subsequent scenes they become **podiums**, desks, steps and the columns of the New York Stock Exchange. Over three hours, the three actors play many different roles. ⑤Minimalist **props**—a pair of glasses, a hat—help differentiate between them. But mostly it is **subtle** gestures that transform Mr Russell Beale from an aged rabbi（拉比，犹太教传教士）into a snivelling（哭哭啼啼的）boy, or turn Mr Godley into a rich divorcee or a **bawling toddler** in a Nebraska diner.

5　The trio（三部曲）narrate the story as they enact it. Much of the language is as rich as their performances. The Italian original was steeped in Jewish tradition (Mr Massini speaks Hebrew), a **flavour** that Mr Power **retains**. "Baruch HaShem," Henry repeatedly **intones**: "Thank God." Over time the pieties and Jewish observances **thin**. When the family first sit shiva at the death of a relative, they mourn for a week; the second time, they sit for three days. Finally, the bank is closed for three minutes.

◆ 课文小助手

一、生词和词块释义

parable /ˈpærəb(ə)l/ *n.* 寓言故事

vulpine /ˈvʌlpaɪn/ *adj.* 狐狸般的

vista /ˈvɪstə/ *n.* 景色

morality /məˈræləti/ *n.* 道德

playwright /ˈpleɪraɪt/ *n.* 剧作家

mentor /ˈmɛntɔr/ *n.* 导师

adapter /əˈdæptə/ *n.* 改编者

extract /ˈekstrækt/ *v.* 提炼

hone /həʊn/ *v.* 磨炼

obsess /əbˈses/ *v.* 使痴迷

distilled /dɪsˈtɪld/ *adj.* 净化的，提炼的

denouement /deɪnuːˈmɒŋ/ *n.* 结局

dock /dɒk/ *n.* 码头

alchemy /ˈælkɪmɪ/ *n.* 炼金术法

disembark /dɪsɪmˈbɑːk/ *v.* 下船

debris /ˈdeɪbriː/ *n.* 碎片，残骸

podium /ˈpəʊdɪəm/ *n.* 表演台

prop /prɒp/ *n.* 支柱，靠山

subtle /ˈsʌt(ə)l/ *adj.* 细微的

bawl /bɔːl/ *v.* 大喊大叫

toddler /ˈtɒdlə/ *n.* 刚学步的小孩

flavour /ˈfleɪvə/ *n.* 味道

retain /rɪˈteɪn/ *v.* 保留

intone /ɪnˈtəʊn/ *v.* 平稳清晰地说

thin /θɪn/ *v.* 变少

二、话题概要

大意: Sam Mendes 在伦敦国家剧院表演一部关于雷曼兄弟的剧，这部剧讲述了雷曼兄弟的一生。

Para. 1: 之前意大利的西部片一直深受美国的影响，带有各种美国元素。然而现在，在英国大剧院的演员们正在表演一场与众不同的意大利西部片。

Para. 2: 这部"雷曼兄弟三部曲"的编剧为 Stefano Massini。2013 年，这部用意大利语表演的 5 小时的剧第一次在法国公演，两年之后，这部片子被翻译成德文和法文。对于要将此剧引进英国的编剧和导演来说，最大的挑战是需要创制一个浓缩但完全的英语版本。

Para. 3: 这部剧以 2008 年 9 月 15 号雷曼兄弟公司破产开始。1844 年，Hayum Lehmann 第一次来到纽约，1850 年，雷曼三兄弟在纽约创办公司和银行。

Para. 4: 随着雷曼兄弟家族和公司在内战中财富的累积，故事情节也不断推进。最后，当华尔街危机爆发时，它也走到了尽头。这部剧表面是关于金融，实则是讲述现代美国的形成。同时，就舞台效果而言这部剧也堪称神剧。在 3 个小时的表演中，3 名演员表演了很多不同的角色，他们用最少的道具表演出最佳的效果。

Para. 5: 这部剧中的语言也很丰富，甚至带有犹太语。但是随着故事的发展，这些对上帝的虔诚和犹太语的出现越来越少。

◆ 同步练习

一、长难句翻译（见文章划线处）

二、词块填空

1. The crowd had _____ out and only a few people were left.

2. Oils are _____ from the plants.

3. A lot of young girls are _____ by their weight.

4. The notes I had brought back were waiting to be _____ into a book.

5. The authorities are protectors of public _____.

三、佳句模仿

原文佳句	Over time the pieties and Jewish observances thin.
亮点评析	这里的 thin, 活用为动词，意思为 "变稀少，变薄"。
写作应用	Traffic was thinning. 路上的车辆正在越来越少。

◆ 答案

一、长难句翻译

1. 半个世纪之前，Sergio Leone（意大利知名大导演）将 "曾经的西部" 搬上了大屏幕，而现在，英国国家剧院正在上演一出与众不同的意大利风格的西部片——一部主演是银行家而非枪手的片子，是一个关于上帝、贪婪、征服和家庭的道德故事。

2. Mendes，一个杰出的导演，曾监制过两部 James Bond 的电影；而本剧的编剧，是国家大剧院的 Ben Power。对他们两位来说，很大的挑战是提取和磨炼出很多的主题，而这些主题正是意大利作家花了数年想要表达和痴迷的。

3. Power 说，他们的目的是创造出一个浓缩的英语版本，这个版本能让英国的观众对金融危机有直观的认识，因为金融危机正是这剧不可避免的结局。

4. （雷曼）家族和公司从一开始的内战中积累财富到最后的华尔街危机爆发，这部剧表面是金融故事，实则讲述的是现代美国的建立。

5. 一副眼镜，一顶帽子，演员就依靠着这些最少的道具让观众区别他们表演的角色。

二、词块填空

1. thinned

2. extracted

3. obsessed

4. distilled

5. morality

49 Ottessa Moshfegh's Second Novel Is as Arresting as Her First[M]

Ottessa Moshfegh 的第二本小说和第一本一样吸引人

"My Year of Rest and Relaxation" displays her **mordant** wit and **inimitable** style

1　[1]In "EILEEN", Ottessa Moshfegh's dark and **suspenseful** first novel, the heroine reflected on how her 24-year-old self was **coaxed** into committing **foul** deeds. "This is the story of how I disappeared," she explained at the outset, before recounting her journey from **solitary misfit** to co-opted **accomplice**. Ms Moshfegh's second novel, "My Year of Rest and Relaxation", is the story of how another 24-year-old woman disappeared, this time not from a crime scene but from the world at large.

2　It is the year 2000 and the unnamed narrator has decided to go into hibernation for a year, to forget the past and "sleep myself into a new life". [2]At first glance, there is nothing wrong with her current one. She is a Columbia graduate, looks like "an off-duty model" and lives in Manhattan off a sizeable **inheritance**. But it becomes clear that she has endured some cruel blows: her parents are dead, she has lost her job and her boyfriend has ditched her. So she locks herself away and loses herself in sleep and videos, having contact only with a **credulous psychiatrist** (who prescribes a cocktail of pills), her bulimic（贪食的）best friend (who drops by to share her woes) and the Egyptian staff of her local bodega（酒店）.

3　To some readers, Ms Moshfegh's premise may seem **fey** and slight. At first the narrator's passivity can be wearing, as are the samples from her dream journal (or "book of nightmares") and her **stultifying** routine: "Sleeping, waking, it all **collided** into one grey, **monotonous** plane ride through the clouds." Eventually, though, the author injects colour and drama into her **constricted** scenario.

4　[3]When medicated **blackouts** leave the narrator with no recollection of either sleepwalking or sleep e-mailing, she is forced to **sift** receipts, photographs and call-histories to retrace her steps and account for her actions. A rare outing to attend a funeral triggers vivid memories of her father's death and her mother's decline. [4]As she sinks further into despair and self-degradation, she begins to worry less about her need to be reborn and more about

247

her chances of survival.

5 ⑤A steady supply of mordant wit and snappy dialogue help sustain momentum（动力），as does Ms Moshfegh's memorably original phrasing: "I felt myself float up and away, higher and higher into the ether（太空）until my body was just an anecdote, a symbol, a portrait hanging in another world." Even readers who anticipate the final sting will still be affected by the **poignant** end-note. A study of **alienation** and dislocation, Ms Moshfegh's compelling novel is filled with **warped** desires and **reckless** pursuits, but also with wisdom and warmth.

◆ 课文小助手

一、生词和词块释义

mordant /ˈmɔːd(ə)nt/ *adj.* 讽刺的

inimitable /ɪˈnɪmɪtəb(ə)l/ *adj.* 无与伦比的

suspenseful /səˈspɛnsfəl/ *adj.* 悬疑的

coax /kəʊks/ *v.* 哄，诱

foul /faʊl/ *adj.* 恶劣的

solitary /ˈsɒlɪt(ə)rɪ/ *adj.* 孤独的

misfit /ˈmɪsfɪt/ *n.* 格格不入

accomplice /əˈkʌmplɪs/ *n.* 共犯

inheritance /ɪnˈherɪt(ə)ns/ *n.* 遗产

credulous /ˈkredjʊləs/ *adj.* 易上当的

psychiatrist /saɪˈkaɪətrɪst/ *n.* 精神科医生

fey /feɪ/ *adj.* 古怪的

stultifying /ˈstʌltɪfaɪɪŋ/ *adj.* 令人呆滞的

collide /kəˈlaɪd/ *v.* 相撞

monotonous /məˈnɒt(ə)nəs/ *adj.* 单调的

constrict /kənˈstrɪkt/ *v.* 压紧，限制

blackout /ˈblækaʊt/ *n.* 昏厥

sift /sɪft/ *v.* 细查

poignant /ˈpɔɪnjənt/ *adj.* 令人同情的

alienation /eɪlɪəˈneɪʃ(ə)n/ *n.* 疏离

warped /wɔːpt/ *adj.* 扭曲的

reckless /ˈreklɪs/ *adj.* 轻率的

二、话题概要

大意：这篇文章主要介绍了 Ottessa Moshfegh 的第二本小说——《休息放松的一年》。

Para. 1: Ottessa Moshfegh 的第一部小说——《艾琳》主要讲述了 24 岁的女主角是如何一步一步陷入犯罪的。而她的第二本小说——《休息放松的一年》则是讲述了另一个 24 岁的女孩是如何从这个世界消失的。

Para. 2: 故事发生在 2000 年，小说的女主人刚从大学毕业，父母双亡，没有工作，男朋友也抛弃了他。她的生活也是一团糟，整天睡觉，看电视。所以她决定陷入休眠忘记过去，从而开始新生。

Para. 3: 故事的一开始似乎非常单调和乏味，只是纯粹地介绍女主角的日常生活，在书的结尾，作者注入了一些有色彩和比较紧张的片段。

Para. 4: 因为药物的作用，女主角失去了记忆。她不得不不断地浏览照片、收据等来找回她的记忆。一次偶然外出的机会勾起了女主角对她老爸死亡的回忆。因此，她陷入绝望之中。

Para. 5: Ms Moshfegh 的小说虽然充满着各种扭曲的欲求，但是同时也充满着智慧和温暖。

◆ 同步练习

一、长难句翻译（见文章划线处）

二、词块填空

1. I ran around the corner, and almost _____ with Mrs Laurence。

2. Pandas are _____ creatures.

3. He was accused of causing death by _____ driving.

4. He entertained us in his own _____ way.

5. firefighters managed to _____ the man down from the roof.

三、佳句模仿

原文佳句	A rare outing to attend a funeral triggers vivid memories of her father's death and her mother's decline.
亮点评析	这里的 "...trigger vivid memories of..." 意思为 "唤起……的生动回忆"。
写作应用	For some readers, the book will trigger vivid memories of battle-axe matrons, remarkably cultured teachers, great-aunts whose stories were never explained. 在有些读者看来，本书会让她们想起当年恶毒无比的女舍监、满腹经纶的教师，还有姑婆那辈人鲜为人知的故事。

◆ 答案

一、长难句翻译

1. Ottessa Moshfegh 的第一部小说——《艾琳》充斥着黑暗、悬疑的情节。在这本书讲述了 24 岁的女主角是如何被引诱进邪恶的事件中的。

2. 第一眼扫过，似乎女主角的现在的生活并没有什么问题。

3. 药物昏厥之后，女主角失去了记忆。她不记得有过任何梦游或者睡梦中发邮件的行为。她不得不检查收据、照片和语音留言来回忆过往以及解释她现在的行为。

4. 当女主角越来越沉浸在绝望和自弃中，她开始越来越少地担心重生的需求，而越来越多地担心存活的机会。

5. 书中大量讽刺的幽默以及轻快的对话推动故事的发展。正如作者一开始写下的令人难忘的句子："我感觉自己飘起来，飘得越来越高，飘进太空，直到我的身体变成挂在另一个世界的一个传说，一个符号，一幅肖像，"

二、词块填空

1. collided

2. solitary

3. reckless

4. inimitable

5. coax

Chapter 9

语言 / Language

50 Beyond Wakandan[H]

语言——好莱坞电影的瓦坎达

Language is the last frontier for newly **enlightened** Hollywood film-makers

1   "Red Sparrow", a new thriller featuring Jennifer Lawrence as a Russian spy, is not entirely a paint-by-numbers（追随大众的）film. Its hero is a woman. A few of its twists are genuinely surprising. But in one way, it is Hollywood **to the core**. Its Russian characters display their Russianness by speaking accented English to each other. ①And just one line of real dialogue is in Russian: another spy complains about a drunken American woman he and Ms Lawrence's character are **cultivating**, saying that if he has to spend another minute with her he will shoot her in the face. The accents might give the viewer the same feeling.

2   Hollywood's attention to the detail of foreign settings, from clothing to sets, has advanced beyond the old lazy **stereotypes** of years past. But in things linguistic, the situation is **patchy**. "Red Sparrow" hardly improves on "The Hunt for Red October", released in 1990, in which Sean Connery mumbles（咕哝）a few lines in Russian, then speaks with a modest foreign twinge to his Scottish burr（颤动小舌的 r 音）.

3   The other classic option seems to be to give a British accent to every character in a foreign clime（地域）—especially the villains（反派）—whether the locale is ancient Rome or the Seven Kingdoms of Westeros in "Game of Thrones". It is a rare movie in which an actor successfully masters not only a foreign accent, but foreign-language dialogue. The impressively multilingual Viggo Mortensen **puts** Ms Lawrence and Mr Connery **to shame** with his **fluid** Russian in "Eastern Promises" (2007).

4   A few recent films have tried to make the creative difficulty of a foreign-language setting a feature rather than a bug. One example is "Black Panther". For most of the movie, African-American actors speak English with a kind of pan-African accent, which does not, in fact, exist; Africa is home to around 2,000 languages. But the film-makers also took the unusual step of making a real language—Xhosa（科萨语）, which was Nelson Mandela's mother tongue—stand in for the fictional "Wakandan". ②Ignoring the potential charge of cultural

appropriation—borrowing a real-world culture for an American popcorn film—the use of Xhosa did at least give a suitably foreign **flair** to the setting. Sadly, it did little more than that; its **scattered** use and the random switches to English did nothing to advance the plot or **flesh out** the characters.

5   The award for most **audacious** use of language in a recent film has to go to "Arrival", in which aliens land on Earth and stay put in their ships without explanation. ③A linguist is sent to **discern** their intentions; she **deciphers** their visual language in scenes that rely on the expertise of actual working linguists, many of whom were pleased to see more of their ideas make it to the big screen.④The film's crux（关键）**draws on** a theory of language and the mind—that learning a new language "rewires" the brain and its processes—taking that premise（假定）to such an extreme that the viewer is in no doubt about being in a land of science fiction. Still, the story took the question of language seriously.

6   ⑤Why can't more film-makers simply work language into their plot in a realistic way that will let viewers recognize the world they live in? "Inglourious Basterds" (2009) is set in second-world-war Germany and France. Several multilingual characters, including the marvellous Christoph Waltz, alternate languages in the service of crucial plot points. Michael Fassbender speaks fluent German (his real-life father is German). His character, an English spy in Germany, makes a fatal mistake not with his spoken German but with a hand gesture that crucially differs between the two countries. All through the film, the viewer has to ask why the characters are choosing the language they employ at any given time. It is as though language is a character itself.

7   Many non-American films **integrate** language-switching much more naturally, as the process is a routine part of many people's daily lives. It seems that Hollywood has simply not developed the confidence that its viewers are willing to tolerate such disjunctures（分离）. The assumption is that they want foreign climes, but familiar faces and sounds. Yet successes such as "Inglourious Basterds" and "Arrival" prove that Anglophone viewers aren't necessarily **turned off** by subtitles if there is a reason for them. Hollywood is leading more films with non-white actors and women. Why not put the world's languages **in the spotlight** too?

◆ 课文小助手

一、生词和词块释义

enlightened /ɪnˈlaɪtənd/ *adj.* 开明的

cultivate /ˈkʌltɪveɪt/ *v.* 结交（朋友）

stereotype /ˈsteriətaɪp/ *n.* 老套俗见

patchy /ˈpætʃi/ *adj.* 差强人意的

fluid /ˈfluːɪd/ *adj.* 流畅的

appropriation /əˌprəʊpriˈeɪʃən/ *n.* 盗用

flair /fleə/ *n.* 资质

scattered /ˈskætəd/ *adj.* 疏疏落落的

audacious /ɔːˈdeɪʃəs/ *adj.* 大胆的

discern /dɪˈsɜːn/ *v.* 辨别出

decipher /dɪˈsaɪfər/ *v.* 解读

integrate /ˈɪntɪgreɪt/ *v.* 使成为一体

to the core 彻底地

put...to shame 使相形见绌

flesh out 以细节（或资讯）充实

draw on 利用；动用

turn off 使失去兴趣

in the spotlight 备受瞩目的

二、文化背景词汇

Wakandan：瓦坎达王国是美国漫威漫画中虚构的非洲国家，位于非洲东北部。它表面上是一个贫穷落后的农业国家，实际上是地球上科技最先进的国家，拥有独一无二的稀有资源。主要出现在电影《黑豹》《复仇者联盟3》中。

Arrival：外星人来到地球并降落在 12 个地点，由于语言无法沟通，人类无法探明他们来到地球的真实目的，美国选择与外星人谈判，而中俄决定正面动用武力，其实他们来到地球是想要寻求帮助，并送给了人类一份礼物——他们的语言，也是在他们的维度里对于他们无意义的"时间"要素。

三、话题概要

大意：好莱坞电影在语言方面的表现差强人意，即使情景设定在国外，但语言转换却令观众抓狂。但也有几部电影在这方面作出了突破，例如《降临》《无耻混蛋》。作者认为，如果电影足够精彩，英语母语的人并不一定会排斥外语影片。同时指出，好莱坞电影应该加入不同的语言。

Para. 1–3：引入话题——好莱坞电影对异域元素把握得当，唯独在语言方面差强人意：电影《红雀》并未完全随大溜（主角是女性且剧情跌宕），但该片仍是一部彻底的好莱坞片。与 1990 年上映的《猎杀红色十月》（肖恩·康纳利在其中咕哝几句俄语以及用他的不太熟的通用的苏格兰颤舌音讲话）相比，《红雀》并无长进。另一经典做法就是，让每个异域角色，尤其是大反派都带有英国口音。不管场景是在古罗马，还是《权利的游戏》中的维斯洛特，一概如此。当然也有值得肯定的，譬如 Viggo Mortensen 在《东方承诺》中显出语言天资及流利的俄语，足以让 Lawrence 和 Connery 感到羞愧。

Para. 4-6: 一些电影尝试使影片中外语的设定成为其特色而非缺陷，表现可圈可点：电影《黑豹》的制作人，在虚构的国度瓦坎达中借入了科萨语——这是曼德拉的母语，展示了合适的外语情景。《降临》也是一部在语言方面值得被赞扬的电影，它严肃讨论了语言问题，让观众置身于科幻之地。因此作者合理地推断：为什么更多的电影制作人不能将语言加入情节中，使观众感同身受呢？影片《无耻混蛋》就成功地将语言变成角色的一部分。

Para. 7: 总结并呼吁，要让语言成为瞩目的对象：似乎好莱坞对观众接受外语仍没有信心——认为观众想要异域的电影背景，却仍要熟悉的面孔和语言。然而事实证明，如果电影足够精彩，英语母语的人并不一定会排斥外语影片。既然好莱坞电影里正以更多非白人演员和女性为主人公，为什么不通过电影，让世界上的不同语言也成为关注的焦点？

◆ 同步练习

一、长难句翻译（见文章划线处）

二、词块填空

1. He beat back his enemies; he _____ them _____.

2. He was a bureaucrat _____.

3. These plans need to be _____ with some more figures.

4. What _____ teenagers _____ science and technology?

5. The senator has been _____ recently since the revelation of his tax frauds.

6. As an actor, you often _____ your own life experiences.

三、佳句模仿

原文佳句	But in things linguistic, the situation is patchy.
亮点评析	句式简短，可提炼 "…, the situation is patchy" 作为写作时的总起句。
写作应用	But in things related to environmental protection, the situations is patchy. 但在保护环境方面，情况就好坏不一了。

原文佳句	A few recent films have tried to make the creative difficulty of a foreign-language setting a feature rather than a bug.
亮点评析	"make…a feature rather than a bug"，意思为 "使……成为一种特征，而非漏洞（缺陷）"
写作应用	Measures should be taken to make the flood of information online a feature rather than a bug. 应当采取措施，让海量的网络信息成为(互联网)的特征，而非缺陷。

原文佳句	Yet successes such as "Inglourious Basterds" and "Arrival" prove that Anglophone viewers aren't necessarily turned off by subtitles if there is a reason for them.
亮点评析	此句中 "not necessarily" 意思为"并不一定"；"turn off" 意思为"使……失去兴趣"；整个句子是复合句，其中 that 引导宾语从句，if 引导条件状语从句
写作应用	Yet popularity of "Black Friday" proves that customers aren't necessarily turned off by retail shops if there is a reason for them. "黑五"备受欢迎，这证实：如果有缘由，消费者并不一定对实体店失去兴趣。

◆ 答案

一、长难句翻译

1. 整部电影只有一组对话是用俄语说的：另一名俄国间谍吐槽那个他和劳伦斯扮演的角色刚结识的喝醉了的美国女人，说要是再和她待上一分钟，就会朝她脸开上一枪！

2. 这部美国商业电影挪用了真实世界的文化，忽略其可能会受到的盗用文化的指控，该片中科萨语的使用至少增添了适当的外国风情。遗憾的是，电影做到的也仅止于此。零散的科萨语的使用以及随意转换成英语，并没有推进情节或充实人物。

3. 一位语言学家被派去解读他们的意图。她借助现实中语言学家的专业知识，在场景中解读了外星人的视觉语言。这些语言学家中的大部分人，都乐于见到自己的想法被搬上大屏幕。

4. 这部电影的关键在于语言和思维的理论，即学习一门新语言可以重塑大脑及其处理过程。影片将此运用到极致，毫无疑问，观众会感觉处于科幻之境。

5. 为什么不能有更多的电影制作人，简单地将语言以真实的方式运用到所需情节中，从而使观众产生共鸣？

二、词块填空

1. put...to shame

2. to the core

3. fleshed out

4. turns...off

5. in the spotlight

6. draw on

51 Out of the Mouths of Babes[M]

学习新的语言，宜早不宜迟

Convincing evidence that you should start early if you want to master a new language

1   Those who want to learn a foreign language, or want their children to, often feel they are racing **against the clock**. People seem to get worse at languages as they age. Children often learn their first without any instruction, and can easily become multilingual with the right exposure. But the older people get, the harder it seems to be. Witness the **rough edges** on the grammar of many immigrants even after many years in their new countries.

2   Scientists mostly agree that children are better language learners, but do not know why. Some **posit** biological factors. Is it because young brains have an extreme kind of plasticity（可塑性）? [1]Or, as Steven Pinker, a Harvard psychologist, argues, an instinct for language-learning specifically, which fades as the brain ages and (in evolutionary terms) is no longer needed? Others think children have special environments and **incentives**, not more **conducive** brains. They have a strong motivation to communicate with caregivers and imitate peers, and are not afraid of making mistakes in the way adults are.

3   Some believe any "critical period" may only **apply to** the sounds of a foreign tongue. [2]Adults struggle with accents: eight decades after immigrating to America and four after serving as secretary of state（国务卿）, Henry Kissinger still sounds fresh **off the boat** from Fürth—in what is nevertheless **elaborately** accurate English.

4   But grammar is different, and some researchers have **reckoned** that adults, with their greater reasoning powers, are not really **at a disadvantage** relative to children. One study found that when adults and children **are exposed to** the same teaching materials for a new language for several months, the adults actually do better. Most such research has had to rely on small numbers of subjects, given the difficulty of recruiting them; it is hard to know how meaningful the results are.

5   Now a large new study led by Joshua Hartshorne of Boston College (with Mr Pinker and Joshua Tenenbaum as coauthors) has **buttressed** the critical-period hypothesis. The study **ingeniously**

recruited 670,000 online test-takers by framing the exercise as a quiz that would guess the participants' native language or dialect. This made it a viral hit. <u>③The real point was to test English learners' knowledge of tricky bits of grammar, and to see how this **correlates with** the age at which their studies began.</u>

6　Do younger beginners do better because their earlier start gave them more learning time, or because they learned faster in early years? It can be hard to **tease** apart these two questions. But testing a huge amount of data against a number of possible learning curves (学习曲线) allowed Mr Hartshorne to do precisely that. Many previous researchers had posited a drop-off at around puberty (青春期). The new study found it to be rather later, just after 17.

7　Despite that later cut-off, learners must begin at around ten if they are to get to near-native fluency. If they start at, say, 14, they cannot accumulate enough **expertise** in the critical period. Unfortunately, 14 or so is precisely when many students, especially in America, are first introduced to a new language. (Even worse, this is an age when children are acutely sensitive to embarrassment in front of peers.)

8　Children who start at five don't do noticeably better than those who start at ten over their lifetimes. But there is still reason to begin in the first years of school, as in Denmark and Sweden. <u>④Because mastery takes a long time—perhaps 30 years until improvement **ceases**— those who begin at five and **are obliged to** read and write English at university will by then have made much more progress than those who **took the plunge** at ten, even if their level is roughly the same by 40.</u>

9　The existence of the critical period is not a reason for anyone 11 or older to give up. Some people remain excellent language students into adulthood. And Mr Hartshorne tested some truly subtle features of grammar that take years to master. A language learned even to a lower level can still be extraordinarily useful at work or enjoyable while travelling.

10　But for policymakers, the **implication** is clear. Earlier is better. Students outside the English-speaking world will eventually face English in the classroom or at work: they'll have a better shot if they start younger. As for the Anglophone (以英语为母语) countries, getting foreign languages into the tender years is a **hard sell**. Many bureaucrats can hardly see past reading and maths. That is a mistake for many reasons. This study demonstrates one of them.

◆ **课文小助手**

一、生词和词块释义

posit /ˈpɒzɪt/ *v.* 假定

incentive /ɪnˈsentɪv/ *n.* 刺激

conducive /kənˈdjuːsɪv/ *adj.* 有利的

elaborately /ɪˈlæbərətli/ *adv.* 精美地

reckon /ˈrekən/ *v.* 认为

buttress /ˈbʌtrəs/ *v.* 支持（想法或论点）

ingeniously /ɪnˈdʒiːnɪəsli/ *adv.* 巧妙地

tease /tiːz/ *v.* 梳理清楚

expertise /ˌekspɜːˈtiːz/ *n.* 专门技能（知识）

cease /siːs/ *v.* 停止，中止

implication /ˌɪmplɪˈkeɪʃən/ *n.* 含意

against the clock 争分夺秒

rough edges（无伤大雅的）瑕疵，小毛病

apply to（对……）适用

off the boat 初来乍到的

at a disadvantage 处于劣势，处于不利地位

be exposed to 接触

correlate with 与……相关联

be obliged to 必须做某事

take the plunge（尤指经过长时间考虑后）决心行动

hard sell 强行推销

二、话题概要

大意：有确凿证据表明：如果你想掌握一门新的语言，那么早点开始。本文通过实例，以及相关研究的介绍，对此进行论述，最后指出：学习新的语言，宜早不宜迟。

Para. 1–2: 引出话题：年龄越大，学习外语越困难。究其原因，科学家各持己见。有人假定是生理机制方面的因素；有人认为这与语言学习的本能有关；也有人认为是因为孩子有特殊的学习环境和刺激。

Para. 3–4: "关键期"理论并不能适用于语法学习：虽然在掌握外语的语音语调方面，有"关键期"一说，但是在语法学习方面，并非如此。与孩子相比，成年人有着更好的推理能力，表现更好。但由于此研究样本人数较少，很难判断其结论的意义有多大。

Para. 5–8: 一项新的研究证实了语言学习的"关键期"理论：借助大量数据及学习曲线，研究发现语言学习能力在 17 岁后大幅下降。同时指出：一、如果想有接近母语的流利程度，学习者在 10 岁左右就要开始语言学习。二、因为"语言的掌握"需要长期的累积，语言学习宜早不宜迟。

Para. 9–10: 该研究的启示：对于任何 11 岁及以上的人而言，错过"关键期"并不是放弃学习外语的理由。毕竟，哪怕只是较低水平地掌握一门语言，不论是在工作还是在旅途都是有用的。对于政策制定者而言，该研究的启示则毫无疑问：让孩子学外语，越早越好。作者还指出，在以英语为母语的国家，不让孩子在较小的时候开始学习外语，则是个错误。

◆ **同步练习**

一、长难句翻译（见文章划线处）

二、词块填空

1. Poverty and poor housing _____ a shorter life expectancy.

2. They're finally _____ and getting married.

3. Everyone is racing _____ to get things ready in time.

4. Some children _____ never _____ classical music.

5. This new law places poorer families _____.

6. The show, despite some _____, was an instant success.

7. Doctors _____ legally _____ take certain precaution.

8. The offer only _____ flights from London and Manchester.

三、佳句模仿

原文佳句	People seem to get worse at languages as they age.
亮点评析	"as…"，意思为"随着……"；"age"此处为动词，意思为"变老"
写作应用	People seem to attach more importance to self-improvement as they age. 随着年龄增长，人们似乎更关注自我提升。

原文佳句	They have a strong motivation to communicate with caregivers and imitate peers, and are not afraid of making mistakes in the way adults are.
亮点评析	"in the way adults are"，此处为避免重复，有省略，可还原为"adults are afraid of making mistakes"，且此句是定语从句。
写作应用	The youth have a strong motivation for new things, and are not afraid of failure and loss in the way adults are. 年轻人强烈渴望尝试新鲜事物，而且不会像成年人般害怕失败和失去。

原文佳句	But testing a huge amount of data against a number of possible learning curves allowed Mr Hartshorne to do precisely that.
亮点评析	此句中动名词做主语，与常见短语"allow sb. to do…"搭配，可提炼为"sth./doing sth./ 句子 + allow sb. to do…"
写作应用	Being exposed to a large amount of reading materials allows language learners to have a better knowledge of vocabulary and even culture. 接触大量阅读材料，使语言学习者对词汇和文化都有更好的理解。

◆ 答案

一、长难句翻译

1. 又或者，如哈佛大学心理学家 Steven Pinker 所言，随着大脑的成熟，语言学习的特定本能会逐渐消失，直至从进化角度来看不再被需要吗？

2. 成年人遭受着口音的困扰。即使移民至美国已有八十年，并任美国国务卿四年，基辛格说起英语来，依然像刚从菲尔特市到这儿。尽管如此，他所说的又确实是精准的英语。

3. 该研究真正的目的是测试英语学习者对复杂语法知识的掌握，并分析语法掌握与他们开始学习英语的年龄的相关性。

4. 因为掌握一门语言需要很长时间，大概 30 年后语言水平的提升才会停止。与从 10 岁开始学习英语的孩子相比，5 岁就开始学的孩子们，到了大学面对英语读写时，将表现出更大的进步，尽管他们的英语水平到 40 岁也大致相同了。

二、词块填空

1. correlate with	5. at a disadvantage
2. taking the plunge	6. rough edges
3. against the clock	7. are obliged to
4. are exposed to	8. applies to

52 Alexa's Biscuits[M]

语音助手，识别"标准"口音？

In the world of voice-recognition, as in life, not all accents are equal

1   In a spoof (滑稽模仿) advertisement on a humorous website, a woman asks her Echo, Amazon's voice controlled speaker system and assistant, to play "the country music station". The device, mishearing her southern American accent, instead offers advice on "extreme constipation (便秘)". Soon she has acquired a southern model, which understands her accent better. <u>①But before long, the machine has gone **rogue**, **chiding** her like a southern mother-in-law for putting canned biscuits on the shopping list. (A proper southern lady makes the doughy southern delicacy (美食) herself.)</u> On the bright side, it corrects her children's manners.

2   The outcome may be **far-fetched**. But the problem is not. More and more smart phones and computers (including countertop (平板) ones such as the Echo) can be operated by voice commands. These systems are getting ever better at knowing what users tell them to do—but not all users equally. They struggle with accents that differ from standard British or American. Jessi Grieser, a linguist at the University of Tennessee, Knoxville, speaks the "Northern Cities shift", a set of vowels around America's Great Lakes that differ from the standard set. Her smart phone hears her "rest in peace" as "rust (生锈) in peace".

3   To train a machine to recognize what people say requires a large body of recorded speech, and then human-made **transcriptions** of it. A speech-recognition system looks at the audio and text files, and learns to match one to the other, so that it can make the best guess at **a new stream of** words it has never heard before.

4   America and Britain, **to say nothing of** the world's other English-speaking countries, are home to a wide variety of dialects. But the speech-recognizers are largely trained on just one per country: "General American" and Britain's "Received Pronunciation". Speakers with other accents can throw them off.

5   Some might consider that an unlucky but avoidable consequence of "having an accent". But everyone has an accent, even if some are more common or respected. <u>②The rise of voice-</u>

activated technologies threatens to split the world further into accents with privileges—in this case, the ability to command the Echo, Apple's Siri, Google Assistant and other such gadgets (小装置) —and their poor relations.

6   As part of her PhD in linguistics at the University of Washington, Rachael Tatman studied automatic speech-recognition of various regional accents. In one study, she looked at the automatic subtitling (字幕) on YouTube, which uses Google's speech-recognition system. Ms Tatman focused on speakers of five different accents, reading a list of isolated words chosen for their susceptibility (敏感度) to differing pronunciation. The automatic captioning (字幕) did worst with the Scottish speakers, **transcribing** more than half of the words incorrectly, followed closely by American southerners (from Georgia). It also did worse with women: higher-pitched voices are more difficult for speech-recognition systems, one reason they tend to struggle with children. In a follow-up experiment, Ms Tatman used both YouTube and Bing Speech, made by Microsoft, to test only American accents. Both found black and mixed-race speakers harder to comprehend than white ones.

7   The makers of these systems are aware of the problem. They are trying to offer more options: you can set Apple's Siri or the Echo to Australian English. But they can still reach only so many accents, with a bias (偏好) towards standard rather than regional ones. India, with its wide variety of English accents, presents the firms with both a **tempting** market and a huge technical challenge.

8   ③One solution is for people to train their own phones and gadgets to recognize them, a fairly straightforward task, which lets users take control rather than waiting for the tech companies to deliver a solution. The Echo already allows this. ④And a new function, called Cleo, works like a game, to **tempt** users **into** sending Amazon new data, whether on new languages Echo has not yet **assimilated** or accents for a language it **in theory** already knows.

9   Janet Slifka of Amazon describes the **chicken-and-egg** nature of such adaptive systems (自适应系统) : they get better as customers use them. An app lets users tell Echo whether they have been understood properly, for example, supplying further training data. But if they don't work well immediately, people will not use them and thus will not improve them. Those with non-standard accents may have to persevere if they are not to **be left behind**.

◆ **课文小助手**

一、生词和词块释义

rogue /rəʊg/ *adj.* 异常的

chide /tʃaɪd/ *v.* 责骂

far-fetched /ˌfɑːˈfetʃt/ *adj.* 难以置信的

transcription /trænˈskrɪpʃən/ *n.* 录音文本

transcribe /trænˈskraɪb/ *v.* 记录下

tempting /ˈtemptɪŋ/ *adj.* 吸引人的

assimilate /əˈsɪmɪleɪt/ *v.* 融入

a stream of 一连串

to say nothing of sth. 更不用说……；而且还

tempt sb. into doing... 诱惑某人做……

in theory 理论上

a chicken and egg (situation / problem...)
先有鸡还是先有蛋的状况 / 问题等

leave sb./sth. behind 把……抛在后面

二、文化背景词汇

Alexa：亚马逊开发的家庭语音助理（前身是 Amazon Echo），支持闹铃、音乐播放控制、天气查询、网络搜索以及新闻查询等多种功能，而所有操作都通过语音控制完成。除此之外，它还能让你的房子更加智能：你可以用它通过语音控制照明开关、房门锁和恒温器；用语音直接在亚马逊上购物；或者让软件播报当前时间、天气状况，甚至像人一样讲笑话。

三、话题概要

大意： 语音控制系统正在崛起，各大公司也开发了声控操作程序。在某种程度上，这又在分化人类。因为并不是所有的口音都能被很好地识别，某些口音成为"标准"，其他的就相形见绌。不想要"非标准"的口音被系统抛弃，使用者就得锲而不舍。

Para. 1–2: 引入话题： 由一则关于亚马逊 Echo（语音控制扬声系统和助手）的搞笑广告，引出本文话题，语音识别系统无法辨别带口音的指令。广告中的结局令人瞠目，但现实中确实也存在这样的问题。譬如所举例子中，智能手机未能辨别不同于标准设定的元音发音。

Para. 3–4: 介绍语言识别系统的原理及局限性： 此类识别系统通过匹配音频和录音文本，达到辨别大量新词的程度。但一般来说，系统只能辨别标准化的语音，譬如"通用美国英语（GA）""（英式）标准发音（RP）"。

Para. 5–6: 语言识别系统并没有平等地对待每位用户： 某种程度上说，能够声控操作 Echo、Siri 等装置，表明你有标准口音。但同时这会分化不同口音，让其他一些口音、方言逊色。语言学博士 Rachael Tatman 就此做了对比研究，发现遇到苏格兰口音时，自动转译字幕几乎要错一半，紧随其后的是美国南方人的口音；另外，在女性身上，情况也不容乐观——因为语音系统更难识别高音调，那么也就不容易识别孩子的语音；最后，与白人相比，黑人或混血儿的口音也更难懂。

Para. 7–8: 开发者已意识到该问题，并提出应对策略： 用户可以设置语言，但是该系统依然对标准英语有所偏好。以印度为例，由于多种英语口音，它既是一个诱人的市场，又带来了巨大的技术挑战。解决方案之一就是用户训练自己的手机和装置"辨识"他们的语言——

Echo 已经这么做了。同时增加了一项新功能 Cleo，让用户把新的语言数据自动发送回亚马逊公司。

Para. 9: 总结：亚马逊公司的 Janet Slifka 则认为，该自适应系统陷入了"先有小鸡还是先有蛋"的境地。程序让用户反馈信息，一旦问题未能得到及时修正，用户就会停止使用该应用程序。并指出，带有"非标准"口音的人，如果不想被抛下，就还得要锲而不舍。

◆ 同步练习

一、长难句翻译（见文章划线处）

二、词块填空

1. The offer of a free car stereo _____ her _____ buying a new car.

2. _____, everyone will have to pay the new tax.

3. _____ steady visitors came to the house.

4. Britain is being _____ in the race for new markets.

5. It was too expensive, _____ the time it wasted.

三、佳句模仿

原文佳句	In the world of voice-recognition, as in life, not all accents are equal.
亮点评析	"not all..."是部分否定句式，意思为"并不是所有口音都是平等的"。
写作应用	In the world of online relationships, as in real life, not all friends deserve cherishing. 网络交往，正如真实生活中一样，并非所有的朋友都值得珍惜。

原文佳句	On the bright side, it corrects her children's manners.
亮点评析	句中"on the bright side"意思为"从好的方面来看"，可用于引出对比类观点。
写作应用	The Internet is flooded with information, some unreliable. On the bright side, it offers people a convenient way of searching information indeed. 网络上有海量信息，一些并不可靠。从好的方面来看，它又确实给人们提供了一种便捷的信息搜索方式。

原文佳句	America and Britain, to say nothing of the world's other English-speaking countries, are home to a wide variety of dialects.
亮点评析	句中"to say nothing of"意思为"更不必说……"，类似"not to mention"；"be home to"意思为"是……的家园"。

| 写作应用 | Unemployment leads to a sense of uselessness, to say nothing of financial problems.
失业会让人觉得自己一无是处，更何况还会带来经济问题。 |

◆ 答案

一、长难句翻译

1. 但没多久，该装置就表现异常，就像南部的婆婆那样，会因为她把罐装饼干列入了购物清单而呵斥她。（因为，真正的南方女士会自己动手做这些食物。）

2. 声控技术的崛起造成了威胁，进一步地分化世界：带有某些口音就享有特权，而别的口音则相形见绌。这种情况下，"特权"就是我们能够声控操作亚马逊 Echo、苹果语音助手 Siri、谷歌助手，以及其他类似装置。

3. 一种方案就是让人们训练自己的手机和装置，进而能"辨识"他们的语音。这是相当明确的任务，用户能有主动权，而不是坐等科技公司的解决方案。

4. 此外，还有一项叫做 Cleo 的新功能。类似游戏操作，Cleo 诱使用户不断给公司发回新的语言数据——不管是 Echo 尚未掌握的语言，还是理论上已经知道的口音。

二、词块填空

1. tempted into

2. In theory

3. A stream of

4. left behind

5. left behind

53 Build It and They Will Come[M]

法语复兴——发展经济为先

Motivation must come before means in getting people to learn your language.

1 Remarkably, a French president had never addressed the Académie Française before. ①The French **have a soft spot for** authority, and the **mighty** presidency (atypical（非典型的）for Europe) and the academy (founded to guarantee the purity of the French language) are both symbols of that. So when Emmanuel Macron told the academicians of his ambitions to **revitalize** French around the world, it was a very French affair indeed.

2 In some ways Mr Macron **constitutes** a break with Gallic（法国的）tradition. ②He speaks English not only well but gladly, **in contrast to** his **predecessors**, François Hollande (whose ropy（糟糕的）English **was the butt of jokes**) and Jacques Chirac (who often **pointedly** refused to talk in English, though he could). But in the best French tradition, Mr Macron spoke with passion about French and confidence in its future. He announced more money for the Alliance Française, for example, to teach the language, and more support for teaching French to refugees who have arrived in France. His aim is to see French go from being the world's fifth-most-spoken language to its third.

3 It is very French to think that this can be accomplished by determined state action. Yet people don't learn a language because somebody has built a fancy new school nearby. These days there are plenty of language-learning options, especially online. The cost of learning a language is mainly measured not in money but in time. You have to give someone a reason to do the work, before even bothering with the means and opportunity.

4 Think about the rivals to French. One is English. Americans and Britons might think foreigners learn English because their culture is appealing. But if that was ever true, it no longer is. Foreigners learn English simply because there are already a lot of people to speak it with— a majority of them, today, outside the chief Anglophone countries. A Swede learns English to do business in Brazil. This is why, despite the **irony**, English will probably still dominate the European Union after Brexit（英国脱欧）.

5 Or consider Chinese, a language of booming interest to foreign learners. It is in a way the opposite of English: the vast majority of its speakers live in just one country. But what a country. China's economy will soon be the world's largest, and its people still do not speak very good English. Learning Chinese is an obvious way to exploit an **unrivalled** economic opportunity.

6 Finally, take German. In the 19th century it was a posh (上流社会的) language of science and scholarship, expected of all educated Europeans. But two wars, horrific atrocities (暴行) and four decades of division **wrecked** its image.

7 However, it has recovered. As Germany's economy **roared back** from a long post-reunification (重新统一) **slump**, German-learning increased by 4% between 2010 and 2015 (a lot, **in historical terms**). Perhaps more surprisingly, a country once considered **stolid** and conservative has developed a reputation for cool. Berlin is seen as the hippest (时尚的) capital in Europe. German is both useful and attractive.

8 French could combine all these **attributes**. Like English, it is found around the world. Like Chinese, it is economically important: French-speaking countries **account for** 8.4% of global GDP. And like Germany recently, France has long had cultural cachet (声誉). How, then, to **revive** the optimism for the language itself?

9 Much of the work will be done outside France, and by growth in Africa in particular. ③<u>Mr Macron knows this; after an initial announcement, in Burkina Faso, that he wanted to give new **vigour** to the French-speaking world, he was seen as neocolonialist (新殖民主义者). His speech at the Academy was better, **conceding** that French had "emancipated (解放) itself from France".</u> He told the Academy that it was high time French schools began teaching literature written in French outside France.

10 By one **projection**, in 2050 there will be 700m French-speakers—80% of them in Africa. ④<u>To keep that forecast **on track** and keep Africans speaking French—not switching to English, as Rwanda (卢旺达) did—France would be wise to continue this approach of fraternité rather than autorité with its African friends, by helping those countries develop economically.</u> And the best thing Mr Macron could do at home is release the talents of the French people. ⑤<u>Reforms that get the French economy growing as Germany's has done would do more than all the shiny new French-teaching schools in the world.</u>

◆ 课文小助手

一、生词和词块释义

mighty /'maɪti/ *adj.* 强有力的

revitalize /ˌriː'vaɪtəlaɪz/ *v.* 使复兴

constitute /'kɒnstɪtjuːt/ *v.* 被看作

predecessor /'priːdɪsesə(r)/ *n.* 前任

pointedly /'pɔɪntɪdli/ *adv.* 明确地

irony /'aɪrəni/ *n.* 讽刺

unrivalled /ʌn'raɪvld/ *adj.* 无可匹敌的

wreck /rek/ *v.* 毁掉

slump /slʌmp/ *n.* 萧条（期）

stolid /'stɒlɪd/ *adj.* 淡漠的

attribute /ə'trɪbjuːt/ *n.* 特质

revive /rɪ'vaɪv/ *v.* (使) 复兴

vigour /'vɪgə(r)/ *n.* 活力

concede /kən'siːd/ *v.* 承认

projection /prə'dʒekʃən/ *n.* 预测

have a soft spot for 偏爱

in contrast to 与……对比鲜明

be the butt of sb's joke 成为 (某人的) 笑柄

roar back 重新恢复

in...terms 在……方面

account for (在数量上) 占

on track 有可能获得 (想要的结果)

二、话题概要

大意：法国总统马克龙希望复兴法语，这是非常"法国"的行为。与英语、汉语和德语对比，法语具备复兴的要素。作者指出，要想实现法语的复兴，除了重视非洲国家、与他们保持友爱和善的朋友关系，更重要的是刺激人才、推动法国经济发展。

Para. 1–2: 重振法语是一件非常"法国"的事：法国人对权威十分看重，当马克龙总统提出重振法语时，这是非常"法国"的行为。某种程度上说，马克龙打破了法国传统。与前几任不同，他会愉快地讲英语。但他又非常遵循传统，对法语的未来充满热情与信心，并宣布了拨款等一系列举措，旨在让法语跃居世界第三大语言。

Para. 3–7: 在提供语言学习的机会之前，先要让人们有学习的动机：首先在第三段指出，学习语言的机会很多，人们不再是以金钱而是以时间去计算成本。因此，要给他们学习一门语言的理由。接着在第四至七段，作者列举英语、汉语和德语来论证此观点：一、英语依然占主导地位，并非是英美文化的吸引力，而是已经有许多人 (英语非其母语) 说英语 —— 瑞士人学英语，能与巴西人进行贸易往来。二、中国即将成为世界最大的经济体，而中国人英语说得并不好，因此学习汉语是为了能抓住经济机遇。三、德语在经历战争与分裂之后，曾经的上层语言形象受损。但随着德国经济恢复，德语也逐渐恢复了活力。

Para. 8–10: 复兴法语，发展国家经济比开设法语学校更有效：法语有以上语言的特性，像英语一样在全世界可见；像汉语一样有其经济重要性；像德语一样，法语有着文化底蕴。就此，作者对如何复兴提出自己的看法：一、重视法语在非洲国家的传播；二、更重要的是作为经济体，法国要发展自身。

◆ 同步练习

一、长难句翻译（见文章划线处）

二、词块填空

1. The decision was disastrous _____ political _____.

2. I've always _____ my old maths teacher.

3. They're _____ to make record profits.

4. Students _____ the vast majority of our customers.

5. _____ his predecessor, Bush has little appetite for foreign travel.

6. He was fed up with _____ of their jokes.

三、佳句模仿

原文佳句	Motivation must come before means in getting people to learn your language.
亮点评析	"come before" 意思为"比……重要，先于……"；此处可提炼为"A come(s) before B in…"
写作应用	To some degree, creativity must come before accuracy in encouraging people to come up with ways to solve problems. 某种程度来说，在鼓励人们提出解决问题的方法时，创造力要先于精准度。

原文佳句	This is why, despite the irony, English will probably still dominate the European Union after Brexit.
亮点评析	此句中 "despite the irony" 是插入语，意思为"讽刺的是……"；why 引导表语从句，句式 "this is why…"，意思为"这就是为何……"
写作应用	This is why, despite the high cost, people in remote area still choose to sacrifice the environment to develop the economy. 尽管代价昂贵，但这就是为何偏远地区的人们依然选择牺牲环境来发展经济。

原文佳句	He told the Academy that it was high time French schools began teaching literature written in French outside France.
亮点评析	此句中 "it was/is high time that…"，为虚拟语气，从句中用 did 或 should do，意思为"是该做……的时候了"。
写作应用	It's high time that measures should be taken to prevent teenagers from being addicted to social media like WeChat. 是该采取措施来阻止青少年沉溺于诸如微信等社交媒介了。

◆ 答案

一、长难句翻译

1. 法国人偏爱权威。法国总统位高权重——这在欧洲国家中并不典型，为确保法语的纯正而设立了研究院，由此可窥见一斑。

2. 马克龙总统不仅英语说得好，他还乐意说。这与之前几任形成了鲜明对比：奥朗德糟糕的英语通常是笑柄；希拉克虽然会说，但他明确表示拒绝讲英语。

3. 马克龙深谙其道。在布吉纳法索，他首次宣告，希望给法语世界注入新活力，这让他被视为是新殖民主义者。他在学会上的演讲则更妥当，承认法语已经"不再束缚于法国"。

4. 为了确保此推测按预期发展，让非洲国家的人说法语(而不是像卢旺达一样转向英语)，法国继续走"亲善"而非"权威"之道，帮助这些国家发展经济，此举是明智的。

5. 进行改革，让法国的经济像德国那样增长，这远比各处建立的崭新的法语学校都要有效。

二、词块填空

1. in…terms

2. had a soft spot for

3. on track

4. account for

5. in contrast to

6. being the butt

图书在版编目（CIP）数据

三味外刊精华：汉英对照 / 孙三五，徐志坚，吴则磊编著. —北京：中国人民大学出版社，2019.7

ISBN 978-7-300-26759-3

Ⅰ．①三… Ⅱ．①孙…②徐…③吴… Ⅲ．①英语-汉语-对照读物②散文集-世界 Ⅳ．①H319.4：I

中国版本图书馆CIP数据核字（2019）第028175号

三味外刊精华

孙三五 徐志坚 吴则磊 编著

Sanwei Waikan Jinghua

出版发行	中国人民大学出版社
社　址	北京中关村大街31号　　　　　邮政编码　100080
电　话	010-62511242（总编室）　　　010-62511770（质管部）
	010-82501766（邮购部）　　　010-62514148（门市部）
	010-62515195（发行公司）　　010-62515275（盗版举报）
网　址	http://www.crup.com.cn
	http://www.1kao.com.cn（中国1考网）
经　销	新华书店
印　刷	北京昌联印刷有限公司
规　格	185mm×260mm　16开本　　　**版　次**　2019年7月第1版
印　张	17.75　　　　　　　　　　　　**印　次**　2019年7月第1次印刷
字　数	357 000　　　　　　　　　　　**定　价**　48.00元